K

Flora Tristan

Flora Tristan

Feminism in the Age of George Sand

Sandra Dijkstra

PLUTO  PRESS

First published in 1992 by Pluto Press
345 Archway Road, London, N6 5AA

British Library Cataloguing-in-Publication Data
Dijkstra, Sandra
    Flora Tristan: feminism in the age of George Sand.
    1. France. Feminism Tristan, Flora. 1803
    I. Title II. Centre for socialist History
    305.4'2'0924

    ISBN 0-7453-0316-1
    ISBN 0-7453-0450-8 pbk

Library of Congress Cataloging-in-Publication Data
Dijkstra, Sandra, 1942-
    Flora Tristan : feminism in the age of George Sand / Sandra
Dijkstra.
        p. cm.
    Rev. ed. of author's thesis (Ph. D.)–University of California,
San Diego, 1976.
    Includes bibliographical references and index.
    ISBN 0-7453-0316-1
    1. Tristan, Flora, 1803–1844. 2. Feminists–France–Biography.
3. Feminism–France–History–19th century. I. Title.
HQ1613.T75D55 1992
305.42'0944'092–dc20   89-26663
                                                                CIP

Typeset by Stanford Desktop Publishing Services, Milton Keynes
Printed and bound in the UK by Billing and Sons Ltd, Worcester

Contents

Preface

Flora Tristan began as a dissertation for the PhD *Feminism in the Age of George Sand* and has to be seen in the context of the women's movement of the early 1970s. It stimulated my interest in Flora Tristan as a subject. She was after all an astonishing woman, and despite my findings of the contradictions in the motives that mark her literary and political *oeuvre*, she made a very significant contribution to feminist and socialist thought and activity.

Giselle Pincetl generously offered to translate the numerous French passages. She has written on Flora Tristan from quite a different perspective and deserves praise for her good work, and for participating in a project whose thesis diverged so from her own. Gratitude is owed Sarah Lumpkin who undertook the arduous task of reviewing and checking footnotes of the revised manuscript.

Bram Dijkstra enthusiastically supported me and my intellectual pursuits, encouraged me at low points, and celebrated the high ones.

The woman who gave birth to me, née Helen Rosen, deserves perhaps the greatest gratitude. Her constant and solid support of a project with which she had little sympathy, and of a daughter whose opinion frequently rankled her, is a testimony to her maternal and humane qualities. She, my grandmother Ida Rosen, my aunt Betty Feldman, and my sister Barbara Hernandez, provided me with encouragement and faith in woman power humanely used.

Adri Hasselbach provided invaluable assistance by copying Flora's difficult script, thus making accessible to me Tristan's letters housed at the Institute for Social History in Amsterdam.

Fredric Jameson, who as dissertation director presided over the early stages of this work, introduced me to new ways of looking at the nineteenth century and at literature.

Herbert Marcuse's utopian vision and sense of humour offered me alternative futures and presents, and I only fear that he would find Flora taken much too seriously here ... though he would have undoubtedly adored her, had she been able to dance off the page.

All work is in some sense collective, a fragment of the spirit of an age. I only hope that I have imbibed some of its essence, and been able to transmit the vision of a better society which so inspired Flora Tristan.

August 1991
Del Mar, California

vi

Introduction

During the July Monarchy in France, the search to define the social categories of woman and of artist was intense and complex. With regard
to the role of woman, two contradictory tendencies stand out: the
attempt to delineate a concept of woman that would further consol-
idate and bolster the ascendant bourgeois social and economic order,
and the attempt to create a nearly mythological 'new woman', through
whose extraordinary qualities the injustices and inequities of that
same bourgeois nexus might be broken.

Both tendencies took many forms. One of the bizarre features of the
age was that the spectrum of duties assigned to woman as a force for
integration and cohesion of the new capitalist power structure joined,
at certain points, the role ascribed to woman as an agent of social
change.

But this paradox was also central to the definition of the role of the
artist during the 1830s and 1840s. Inspired (according to legend) by
female muses, the artist seemed to confront alternatives similar to those
offered to women of the time: should the artist serve private happiness
or the public good? Somehow, these two impulses seemed to be
increasingly irreconcilable, the first implying an acceptance of the
new social order, and a consecration of its ideology, and the second
allied to the forces for change.

Not surprisingly, women artists faced similar demands during this
period from the diverse groups which sought to control the present and
shape the future of France. The 1830s saw a crucial moment in the
transfer of power to the class known as the 'grande bourgeoisie
montante'. Both groups offered redemption from materialism: in their
ideal form they had no 'exchange value' in the marketplace.

According to the Romantic conception promulgated by Fourier
and the Saint Simonians, the artist exhibited his resistance to the new
money system, and thus his superiority, through his poverty, his suffering and his exclusion; woman incarnated the mystique of a deity,
a goddess whose extraordinary attributes were designed to lift her out
of the murky marriage market and recuperate her lost splendour and
status, at least on the level of the imagination.

1

This mythicization of the character and mission of women and artists was originally designed to accomplish too much: to imbue these groups with a sense of power and purpose, to recuperate for them the status they were losing as capitalist values and structures changed France's ideological and industrial landscape, and to make them saviours of the new society. Thus, it failed miserably in all areas, and provided only a temporary illusion of attaining personal power and social change with women and artists in the vanguard.

During the July Monarchy, many artists and women succumbed to the temptation to view themselves through the filter of the new secularized religion that was Romanticism; they believed in the illusion of power it attributed to them, yet they were unable, despite all their attempts, to persuade a third group, the workers, to share in their deformation of reality. But their mythicization of the role of the working class certainly added fire to the very real and explosive content of the workers' plight.

Like women and artists, the worker did not profit from the new capitalist society, although he seemed to be a more integral part of it. Like them, he was defined as the Other, now that the bourgeois had moved to the centre of society. In this role of outsider, he shared their sense of powerlessness and found himself alternately exalted and denigrated by his contemporaries. He, too, experienced exploitation and felt himself being used by a system from which he was not allowed to benefit. But his complaint was based on more legitimate grounds in terms of the values of the capitalist system, whose wealth was enhanced by his labour. He was not *outside* production, as both women and artists seemed to be.

Women were, of course, either workers, wives or artists in this period, and often filled two of these roles. However, in each instance, they were first of all defined by their gender, and certain demands were made of them on that basis. As workers, they were also expected to carry on the domestic and reproductive functions primarily associated with their sex. For this 'home-work', so critical to the smooth functioning of the capitalist system, they received no material remuneration. For their work in the atelier or factory, they received lower wages than their male counterparts. The more fortunate bourgeois women found themselves assigned the complete responsibility for the socialization of their children, as the new society sought greater control of its offspring. It therefore fell to the daring (and often upper-class) woman to become an artist, and manifest the conscience of her sex. But, as artist, she, like her male colleagues, was viewed as marginal, a non-essential member of the new society, since the work of artists was hardly considered necessary to its survival.

In a society in which work was valued in terms of earning power, the worker was powerless because he earned so little. Since neither artists nor women were yet viewed primarily in terms of the exchange of labour for money, these two groups could acquire a certain symbolic power during this period of redefinition of values. However, the ideologues of the July Monarchy, whether they strove to strengthen and entrench the bourgeois hegemony or to undermine it, soon realized that, wielded together, all three categories of the (materially) powerless members of society – women, workers and artists – could exert a powerful force in either direction. Thus new schemes had to be designed to make better use of these potentially disorderly elements which comprised the 'powerless'.

In the early 1830s, the rebellious voices and deeds of these groups were still imbued with the energy and idealism of the July Revolution. Stiff government reaction soon led to a general repression of all revolutionary and reformist manifestations of discontent. By the mid-1830s, the silkworkers of the Croix-Rousse in Lyon, who had led one of the first strikes in modern France, were back at work in their ateliers; the Saint-Simonian meeting halls were empty and silent; and the press was under strict censorship. Fearing imprisonment, some artists would choose to escape from the suffocating social order into the realms of private fantasy and precious craftsmanship, producing objects which could resist bourgeois comprehension and consumption. Thus was born the 'art for art's sake' theory and school of painting and writing.

As the chiefs of the Republican and Saint-Simonian movements filed into jail, a great void was left. Their audiences, the masses of workers and women, had begun to articulate their own history in the spaces between the slogans of these leaders. Was this chapter of France's revolutionary history to be closed so ignominiously by the autocratic Louis Philippe? Hardly. The struggle for social change passed into the hands of artists and writers whose access to the printed (albeit censored) word allowed them to carry on the quest for social change under the guise of art. But increasingly their efforts would be limited by the tastes and demands of the literate, largely bourgeois audience as well as by the burgeoning mass press designed for it. In many cases, the dispute over politics was continued under the cover of a dispute over the purpose of art.

Indeed, we can look for the origins of the realistic novel in this transference of the class and sex struggle to the safer literary arena, and to the aesthetic articulations that it engendered. For as the remnants of the French social conscience struggled, within the limits set by the government, to carry on a battle for which they were insufficiently equipped, as they tried to elaborate a workable theory of social art and social change from the marginal position that they occupied in French society, the realistic novel developed almost in counterpoint to their efforts to describe the Ideal.

In representing the status quo, the realistic novel helped to establish the new social order by providing a mirror in which bourgeois society could contemplate itself, and perpetuate its preoccupation with individual self-interest and success. The less studied, less popular novels of those who refused to fill this function, who instead sought to transform the society, offer a valuable index to what the July Monarchy would accept and what it would reject in art and ideology.

To study the way in which a new social order establishes its hegemony, it is useful to turn to the writings of those who have been excluded from that order. Who the powerless are, and how their powerlessness is transformed into the stuff of literature, and sometimes anti-literature, is an important gauge of the ideological space available to the artist in a specific historic period. If writing is a manifestation of power or of the will to power, then aesthetic choices, when they are expressed by the powerless, can be seen as commitments to social change. However, the conscious artistic decision to seek change can be undermined by prevailing codes of expression and modes of representation.

The July Monarchy fostered the illusion of the connection between art and progress. But this progress was deceptive, because its benefits would not be available to all, and the possibility that progress could be achieved through art was illusory. In fact, often it was only by breaking with the generally accepted definition of art that the hoped-for connection between art and social change could be realized. In part, the July Monarchy presided over the conversion of the revolutionary potential of early Romanticism into a form which minimally disturbed the new economic arrangements. But other artists and writers – marginalised by their class, sex, and allegiances – chose to formulate a programme for social change, and in the process to trace the outlines for a new, more political kind of art.

Some, influenced by Saint-Simonian doctrines of the social role of art, rejected the increasingly conservative 'aesthetic' position being adopted by more popular writers and chose to believe that the artist had a specific mission to accomplish, that of saving mankind. Unfortunately this concept, like the rest of the Saint-Simonian ideology conceived under the sweeping aegis of 'progress', would aid and ultimately facilitate the development of capitalism. But at first it seemed to offer a real potential for social change.

Flora Tristan y Moscoso: Rebel with a Cause

The notion that people can shape their destinies according to values and ideals emerged from the Enlightenment and the French Revolution – freeing individuals, so the promise seemed to be, to order their own lives. A half-century later, the rulers of the July Monarchy encouraged the rampant individualism of its supporters, and the new industrialists and bankers grew rich. Not ironically, those who found themselves excluded from this prosperity chose an increasingly social, communitarian option. This tendency on the part of a minority of articulate women, artists and workers was looked upon with great fear by the bourgeois establishment, which espoused self-expression for itself only: It preferred to keep the woman in the family, the artist in the realm of pure art, and the worker within the confines of a quest for survival.

One of those who came to believe she represented the powerless, the outcasts of the new economic system – namely women, artists and workers – was Flora Tristan y Moscoso. Sometimes called 'Femme Chazal' even after she had fled from her husband André Chazal, and often remembered because she was grandmother of the painter Paul Gauguin (although she never lived to know him), Tristan united in her life and work all the problems and possibilities that the July Monarchy in particular and capitalism in general posed for women, artists and workers.

Tristan provided the link between revolution and art: inspired by the example of her father's friend Simon Bolívar, who became famous as the liberator of South America, she herself would later inspire her grandson, Gauguin, to become a liberator of art. But first she would seek to fuse the two. Tristan also provided the link between feminism and socialism: influenced by Mary Wollstonecraft's *Vindication of the Rights of Woman*, Tristan's feminism incorporated men as well, for she understood the connection between the plight of women and that of workers, and her practice and theory of socialism led directly to Marx, whom she may not have known but whose ideas she anticipated and probably influenced.

Born in Paris in 1803, Flora Tristan came of age during that anticlimactic post-Revolutionary period known as the Restoration. As a child, her imagination was fired by her mother's reminiscences of her dashing Peruvian aristocrat lover, Don Mariano de Tristan y Moscoso (who died leaving Flora fatherless at age four), and of her father's friend, Simon Bolívar, who passed through Flora's life when she was only a child. Like others of her generation, Tristan grew up in the presence of the legendary Napoleon.

She realized very early on the limits society placed on her. A beautiful woman, she was considered a bastard because her parents had never legally married; nearly assassinated by her husband, from whom divorce was impossible because of the laws of the day, she was disinherited by her father's rich Peruvian family after the publication of her forthright memoirs of her visit to Peru, *Les Pérégrinations d'une paria* (1833–4), a book her uncle burned publicly in Lima. Tristan came with good reason to think of herself as a pariah.

1
'Womanhood' in Nineteenth-century France

The *Code Napoléon* or the Legal and Economic Incarceration of Women

To assess what it meant to be a woman writer in 1830, we must first recognize that few other arenas for self-expression were available to intelligent women of the time. Excluded from government, and increasingly restricted from all public life, any efforts by women to move beyond the family sphere were satirized. One aspect of a woman's being influenced all others: her gender. The 'womanhood' of the female sex received increasing attention and manipulation (as a concept) after the French Revolution, and especially with the coming to power of the bourgeoisie during the July Monarchy.

To harness and fully exploit the productive capacities of workers, capitalism demanded the increasing regulation of sexuality, as Max Weber has shown.[1] In the transition from the *ancien régime* to the July Monarchy, women's sexuality was strenuously subjected to this process of 'rationalization', so that their role as mothers could become primary. Thus, the anarchic and pansexual tendencies associated with their participation in the libertine aristocracy of pre-Revolutionary days or the radical sisterhood of the French Revolution had to be repressed.

Indeed, the liberties allowed women during the *ancien régime* were dangerous. Together with economic rights, they fostered too much autonomy and audacity. For nearly a century, women had run the intellectual life of the country through the salons, and now they wanted to run the country itself.[2] Sick of being imprisoned in the hothouse atmosphere of libertine sexuality exemplified by *Les Liaisons dangereuses* and the paintings of Boucher, women were also refusing to accept the stereotype of the tame milkmaid so often drawn by Greuze. Instead, as Laclos had predicted in the *Discours sur l'éducation des femmes*,[3] they were demanding to be treated as full human beings, calling for a *Déclaration des droits de la femme et de la citoyenne*,[4] equal

7

to the one proposed by men. For her efforts to extend rights and liberties to women, one of their leaders, Olympe de Gouges, was guillotined. Minutes before she was beheaded, she protested: 'Woman has the right to be beheaded, she must also have the right to participate in government.'[5]

During the French Revolution, women had begun to seek the amelioration of their situation: to attain the right to work, the right to education, the reform of marriage, and sexual freedom. These and other rights were demanded by women, who were encouraged by the strength their sex had exhibited during the Revolution and by the boldness of the demands issued by men. 'The time has come for women to emerge from their degrading nothingness.' One of the more militant among them, Théroigne de Méricourt, shouted, 'Let us arm ourselves.'[6]

If the Revolution marked the culmination of a period dominated by feminist energies, so the period that followed marked their repression. Before too long the few rights that women had managed to acquire were to be excised by Napoleon in his famous *Code Napoléon*. Their political clubs were ordered closed, the schools for girls were abolished, and soon the ideology professed decades earlier by Rousseau in *Émile* was to be incarnated in the legal code of the nation. The famous orator Chaumette explained its justification:

> Nature tells woman: Be a woman. The tender care of children, the sweet concerns of motherhood, those are your duties. But your diligence deserves a reward? Well! you will have one! You will be the divinity of the domestic sanctuary, you will rule over your household through the powerful charm of your graciousness and virtue. Foolish women who wish to become like men, don't you already have great advantages? What more do you want? You rule over our senses! You have the legislators at your feet.[7]

With sentiments like those expressed in this passage, the new role of woman was to be ushered in and the complete legal incapacity of woman to be justified. Several articles from the *Code Napoléon* sanctified and bolstered this essentially bourgeois view of woman's role in maintaining the 'integrity of the family':[8]

- A married woman has no other domicile but that of her husband [Article 108].
- A husband owes protection to his wife, a wife owes obedience to her husband [Article 213].
- A wife is bound to live with her husband, and to follow him wheresoever he deems it proper to reside [Article 214].
- The husband will administer all the personal property of his wife [Article 1428].[9]

If the Revolution marked the culmination of a period dominated by feminist energies, so the period which followed marked their repression. In effect, with the institution of the *Code Napoléon*, a married woman had no civil or economic rights at all. Her person, her children, her fortune were all in her husband's control. The long tradition of French women's involvement in commerce dating back to medieval times was broken: women were no longer masters of their own salaries.[10] Women's working organizations were forbidden, and illegitimate children and their mothers were left to fend for themselves. The double standard for crimes of adultery was instituted, permitting men the right to murder their unfaithful wives. The effect of this new system of laws was that 'woman appeared powerless but was protected precisely because of her powerlessness.'[11] The prohibition of divorce in 1816 sealed woman's fate for much of the nineteenth century in France. Only a 'séparation des corps' was legal: a wife could live apart from her husband, but she had to seek his permission for any economic venture. Thus she was still in his power. This legal subjugation of woman was to be bolstered by evidence from the medical sphere, where under the guise of 'science', the incapacitation of woman was institutionalized as a physical necessity.

As the power of the Catholic Church was eclipsed, medicine was recruited by the scientifically-oriented nineteenth-century positivists to take its place. One historian has described the 'rise of "moral medicine"'[12] whose function it was to assure the integration of female sexuality into the new scheme of things. In essence the function of medicine in this period was to reinforce sexual stereotypes with 'scientific evidence', to assert the view that, as Michelet later put it, 'woman is sick',[13] and that she needs a husband to take care of her. Indeed, moral medicine allowed husbands and fathers of the new order to retain better control over the sexuality and the thinking of women.

'Moral medicine' reinforced the July Monarchy's condemnation of excessive sexual indulgence and independence in women. In the early nineteenth century, it was geared primarily toward middle-class women. The promiscuity of lower-class women, although increasingly bemoaned, had to be permitted to provide the necessary population of workers, and to provide an outlet for the repressed sexuality of middle- and upper-class males.

The focus on middle-class women's sexual functions and dysfunctions was a way of harnessing their energies to the new social order, and reinforcing men's power in that order. If women only fully expressed themselves in marriage and motherhood – that is, relative to men – then indeed one could believe with Hugo that 'Man has received from Nature a key with which he rewinds his wife every 24 hours.'[14] The woman who was self-sufficient, who could do without a husband and his 'key', was considered abnormal. Based in part on Rousseau's injunction to women in *Émile* that they breastfeed,[15] this scientific ideology served to chain women to their bodily functions just at the very moment they were beginning to discover and propound their right to be full human beings. Indeed:

> A Frenchman who perused any popular medical text produced in the first half of the nineteenth century would put down the volume with his belief in male superiority agreeably reinvigorated. The woman's procreative function, he was informed, doomed her to a half-healthy existence that began at puberty and required the constant control and guidance of a male.[16]

But legal and medical opinion were only the nails which helped to hammer the planks of economic realities in place. Increasingly, men were taking over professions which had previously been dominated by women. (This of course included medicine, a field in which women had been prominent for centuries.) The following passage, written by Jules Janin, columnist for the powerful *Journal des Débats*, the organ of the bourgeoisie, records the transition that was taking place in the area of women's work:

> Poor women! One should feel sorry for them. ... The trades that had traditionally been theirs have been taken over by enterprising men. Open your eyes, what do you see everywhere? Men as milliners, as dressmakers, even as shirtmakers; the needle, woman's natural tool, has been taken away from her frail hands.[17]

In spite of the not-too-subtle sexism implied in the last sentence, this passage clearly marks an enormous economic change in the lives of women.

There is evidence, especially in the period preceding 1848, however, that some of the effects of these changes were not being felt fully. Bourgeois men were trying to retain the best of the system of aristocratic libertinism for themselves, while making sure they would never be embarrassed by the excesses of their wives.

In his *Physiologie du mariage*, Balzac – one of the chief architects of the new edifice of bourgeois morality – invoked Metternich and Napoleon, comparing 'a husband to a government' and 'the family to a little state in which the husband must learn to govern properly if he is to retain his dominance'. His aim was to 'make your wife a captive in the home by combining various ways of subjugating her'.[18] For keeping wives at home was the best means of assuring their fidelity, according to Balzac, who chronicled the fear and misery of cuckolded men of the 1820s. This book, whose publication coincided with the beginning of the July Monarchy, was an instant bestseller. In describing the tactics of the 'politique maritale', Balzac explained that the best of all was to learn how to 'exhaust all of your wife's energy'.[19] It was above all important to 'discourage her passing interest in science', and to involve her either in art or motherhood:

> If your wife is not musical, which would be surprising, you must relentlessly flatter her vanity so as to get her interested in painting or some artistic activity or other, but let it be something essentially sedentary, something that brings pleasure within the home, so as, in short, to suppress her freedom.[20]

This advice, revealing the obvious disdain with which men regarded women's artistic achievement, was only partially effective. Only total incapacitation could put the worried husband's mind at rest. The more permanent means of keeping women at home was of course childbirth and motherhood:

> Get her immersed in the troubles and cares of pregnancy and breast-feeding, you will thus postpone the danger for at least a year or two. A woman giving birth to and nursing a baby has really no time to think about taking a lover; moreover, she is in no shape before and after confinement to go out in society.[21]

But sometimes, mere physical incapacity was insufficient; ideological reinforcement was needed. In that case: 'You read Jean-Jacques' l'*Émile* to her, you fire her imagination with duties of a mother.'[22]

So it was that an elaborate system of defence of the virtue of young wives was to be worked out.

Truly Annoyed to be a Woman

If we consider Tristan, raised in this ambiance of economic restriction, legal incapacity and ideological injunction, we can see that nineteenth-century society offered her (and all women) essentially three options: to be mother – a victim of her body, its periodic flow, its procreative capacities, and thus to be eternally incapacitated, allowing herself to be harnessed in this manner to the new rigid moral code that preserved and strengthened the bourgeois family; to be that 'other woman' – the prostitute or courtesan, the woman who broke the taboos, giving free rein to her sexuality, and thus incarnating all that men feared and worshipped in woman, the voracious woman whose desires they could never satisfy, whose needs simultaneously disrupted the newly instituted 'spermatic economy' of nineteenth-century France and yet preserved the wife from these excesses; or to be a 'femme de lettres', thus refusing either of the other two options (which George Sand somehow managed to encompass; this accounts in part for her popularity!) and refusing to be 'woman' according to the current definition of that term, choosing therefore to be regarded as a monster by some and as a saint by others, to be marginal and therefore recuperate the freedom inherent in negation. This was the option chosen by Flora Tristan at the outset of her brief career. It was just the opposite of Rousseau's dictum 'that woman is especially designed to please man'.[23] And her stance would certainly have been condemned by her contemporary, Balzac, who announced 'A woman who devotes her life to intellectual pursuits is a frightful scourge'.[24]

Juxtaposing these two statements, we perceive all too clearly the double bind in which Tristan found herself. The first indicates the prevalent attitude regarding the duty of women. The second exposes an attitude toward rebellious intellectual women, an attitude that had been developing in France since the time of Molière, reaching its widest influence in the writings of Rousseau, whose admonition resembled Balzac's: 'An educated woman is the bane of her husband's existence, her children's, friends', servants', of everyone's existence'.[25] Mme de Staël, herself 'une femme extraordinaire', testified to the painful lot of the intellectual woman:

> ... public opinion seems to absolve men of all duties toward a woman who has a superior mind: he may be ungrateful, faithless, cruel to her, and public opinion will not bother to avenge her. Is she not an extraordinary woman? That says it all; she is left to her own devices, she is left to struggle alone against misfortune. The interest that a woman inspires, the power which protects a man, she can count on none of that: she leads her peculiar existence, like all Pariahs in India, in between all the classes to which she may not belong, because she is supposed to exist all on her own, an object of curiosity, perhaps of envy, and in fact deserving only pity! [26]

This powerful description of the complete ostracism that intellectual women already experienced at the turn of the nineteenth century, just after the century of salons, is a hint of the future mistreatment they would receive. It is perhaps significant that the one French woman with whom Tristan might have identified should close her self-description with a plea for pity. 'Pariah' was the very term Tristan would use to describe her own 'singulière existence'.

But if Tristan rejected the traditional female role espoused by the French patriarchy, she probably also refused to be 'a woman who lives by her brains', for her generation, imbued with a Rousseauist sensibility, would have 'preserved' her from an overdose of rationality.[27]

In the new hierarchy of values that evolved during this period of tremendous social upheaval, rationality was incarnate in the king and in the class he represented, the bourgeoisie. To rebel against the reigning mediocrity of the July Monarchy, artists chose to be ruled by the more 'noble' emotional sentiments traditionally associated with women. In order not to be co-opted by the materialistic society around them, and to register their protest against its brash disregard for the ideals of the French Revolution and of the July Revolution (even if they didn't choose to assert themselves through the intellect), women had begun to observe the limitations placed on them by their sex even in Madame Roland's more rebellious epoch:

> I am truly annoyed at being a woman. I needed another soul or another century. I should have been born a Spartan woman, or a Roman, or at least a French man ... I feel as if I were chained to a class and a condition which is not mine ... Everywhere my mind and heart encounter the barriers of public opinion, the fetters of prejudice, and all my strength is drained in the vain effort to break my chains.[28]

In this statement, the agony of the spiritual confinement of an intelligent woman is fully expressed. Tristan might well have made the same statement; it was her fight also. Probably because she realized this, she decided to be more than a 'femme de lettres'. After a brief excursion into literature proper with the novel *Méphis* (1838), Tristan decided to explore and expose the seamier sides of life in the London slums, as well as the condition of factory workers there in *Promenades dans Londres* (1840). And if this 'unfeminine' material wasn't enough, she soon took up political analysis and pamphleteering in the last book she published before her death, *Union ouvrière* (1843). Thus, from her early *Pérégrinations d'une paria (1833–1834)* (1837), which her publisher was able to present as a typical woman's travel journal despite its political content, she had moved herself to the point where obtaining a publisher was a major problem, far beyond the range of traditional French vituperation against 'les bas bleus' or 'les femmes savantes'. When we assess the reception of her work and the fervour with which she executed it, we should not underestimate the influence on her work and life of her increasing marginality, in a social and economic sense, with respect to contemporary expectations of women.

And yet, if French society seemed to offer women three choices – mother, whore or femme de lettres – its artists, poets, playwrights, composers and ideologists proposed still a fourth option, one which most closely approximated the life Tristan determined to live. For, in opposition to the materialist society they saw enveloping them, these men, in their secular religion which we now call Romanticism, envisioned

a kind of superwoman who would incarnate all the qualities that capitalist society now devalued: love, passion, sensibility, poetry and
mystery. Although these qualities were to be progressively incorporated
into the image of the proper wife, at first this vision of 'La Mère'
(Mother with a capital M) extended far beyond the domestic realm. The
attraction of this ideal conception of woman was based at least in part
on her incarnation of values which could not be properly integrated
into the new economic structure. Establishing her as an ideal, the
Romantics accomplished their revolt within the superstructure, offering
an impotent response to the material changes which were occurring
in the infrastructure. Their quest for La Mère took on a regressive, nostalgic aspect, so that when Tristan presented herself, as it were, as the
incarnation of these ideals, the Romantics were baffled. The abstract
version of La Mère was much easier to cope with than the reality, so
Tristan found herself an unwanted species even in this sphere.

Whereas for Romantic artists and writers the cult of the Mother led
to an impasse (they wanted to worship her but not to find her, for then
they would have to acknowledge the absence of an admirable male
father figure, and to take up their roles as sons), for Tristan this conception of her role was inspiring. She, a woman, could try to incarnate
this mystical, powerful woman deity, if she could find an appropriate
object, a child, one worthy of her love and devotion. She would find
this object in the proletariat.

Tristan's Martyrist Mission

But the problem of womanhood and of finding an appropriate role for
herself in a repressive environment was not the only one Tristan had
to face: her own class status was ambiguous, if not precarious, as her
family background shows us.

Tristan's early life is obscure. On the death of her father, Don
Mariano de Tristan y Moscoso in 1807 or 1808, we know that for Flora,
age three, 'paradise' was lost. The house and garden in Vaugirard, the
noble presence of her father, the visits of her father's friend Simon
Bolívar – her mother later reconstructed these elements of the past for
Flora, who had been too young to really appreciate them. Parisian Marie
Thérèse Laisney Tristan maintained a precarious foothold in the prosperous past by reminiscing with Flora about a world the child had never
known; her father's aristocratic Peruvian family came alive as her
mother read his letters aloud and embroidered her recollections.

For Madame Tristan, the impoverished present must have seemed
ill-deserved and grim beside that illustrious past. Because their marriage
was never properly consecrated, on her husband's death his family in
Peru ceased all recognition of her, and sent no funds. Moreover, the

French government, at war with Spain, confiscated the house in Vaugirard because it had been registered in her husband's name and he was considered a Spanish national. Madame Tristan found herself alone with two young children and her memories of the past. She went to the countryside, where it was cheaper to live, remaining there until Flora was 15. She then returned to Paris, perhaps hoping to marry Flora off, or at least put her to work (her son having died by this time).

Flora's education was therefore entirely in her mother's hands. Given her mother's fixation on their 'noble' past, Flora must have received an education not unlike that of the children of the '92 émigrés, who returned to France after the Revolution to find their lands had all been confiscated. 'Her mother encouraged her in the worship of a father who had died too soon, and in addition she spoke to her in glowing terms of the nobility and wealth of the Tristan family.'[29] Thus, Flora, like many of her generation, matured in the shadow of the past, but unlike others, perhaps, she had to make her way amidst the legendary grandeur of three figures from this past: her father, Simon Bolívar and Napoleon.

Against this background of past heroic glories and riches, the Tristan ménage lived very poorly in the Place Maubert. Like many émigrés, they lived only on their memories. For Flora, the memories were slight: the proof of the past came to her only from her mother's lips. But these same lips which recounted her fortunate 'inclusion' in the glorious past also revealed her unfortunate exclusion from contemporary French society. During the Revolution, Flora's parents had been married in a private ceremony by a priest in Spain, but in legal terms the marriage had not been registered. Considered a bastard by French society, she discovered this social truth about herself at 15, after the mythic foundation of her origins had been laid; it was the reason that the family of the first young man with whom she had fallen in love refused to allow the marriage.

> Thus, the descendant of a family of the high-ranking Peruvian nobility, whose pride had been inculcated in her by her mother, was, in the eyes of the law, a bastard child who could not be accepted by a respectable French 'petit bourgeois' family.[30]

We can imagine how this bitter truth must have affected Flora Tristan. And, while her father remained safely removed, in the realm of dead heroes, her mother, the living proof of their original transgression, was painfully present. Tristan made few references to her mother in her writings, but in these allusions she revealed a very deep ambivalence. In the introduction to *Les Pérégrinations d'une paria (1833-1834)* – referred to hereafter as *Pérégrinations* – which records her meeting with her father's family in Peru and includes a scathing analysis and indictment of that society, Tristan tells of her mother's second sin:

> ... we came back to Paris and my mother forced me to marry a man whom I could neither love nor respect. I owe all my troubles to that marriage; but as my mother has never ceased, since then, to show me her deepest regret, I have forgiven her and I shall refrain in this narration from speaking about her. (*Pérégrinations* I, p. xxxvi)

But she was not able to maintain her silence, and later, in volume two, at the moment of her uncle's rejection of her plea for her father's inheritance, she bursts out angrily against her mother, remembering '... the harm you have done to me! ... Ah, mother! I forgive you for it; but the number of misfortunes that you have burdened me with is too heavy for one human being to endure.' *(Pérégrinations* II, p. 22)

From these statements, we can see how deeply Tristan felt her resentment, and how much her confused feelings for her mother might have influenced her views of women. Once it became clear that French society had rejected her, and that despite her father's noble background she was considered an 'untouchable', doubly damned given the restriction of the *Code Napoléon*, she must have eliminated Napoleon from the pantheon of heroes with whom she could identify. (It is questionable in any case whether women could be as entranced by that hero as men of their generation were.) Probably, based on this initial rejection, Tristan came to view French society as an enemy; its approval was to be coveted unconsciously, even as Tristan conceived a mission to punish it in order to make it behave more justly.

Only two admirable figures remained: her father and Simon Bolívar. Should she seek the legendary aristocratic image that her father represented, or the heroic republican grandeur of Bolívar? She sought in her Spanish origins – the very source of her ostracism – the source of her glory.

Her trip to Peru (1833–4) to seek a share in her father's aristocratic lineage and wealth must have disabused her of the glories of riches, as she perceived the ill use that was made of them, and the greed and corruption that they seemed to breed. Moreover, since this visit also destroyed any illusions she might have held regarding her father's family and their generosity or sense of responsibility toward her, the experience came to represent still another example of the betrayal she had experienced in French society. She assimilated the Tristan y Moscoso family into her project of revenge, despite her strong attraction to them and to her father's brother, Don Pío, who had behaved so ignobly toward her. At the age of 30 Tristan had to renounce any hopes of recuperating her ties to the upper class; she had to recognize finally that her mythic family heritage would never be restored, and that even as she continued to believe herself a member of the upper classes, in reality she was a member of a much lower social stratum. Tristan's own description of the paradoxical class situation in which she found herself and the self-hatred it engendered is found in *Pérégrinations*, the most overtly autobiographical of her works:

> Born with all the advantages that excite the desire of men, I had been shown them only to make me feel the injustice which deprived me of enjoying them. Everywhere I saw danger for myself, everywhere society was organized against me, and sympathy nowhere. *(Pérégrinations* II, p. 22)

She would reject identifying with her father or his family, then, and identify instead with Bolívar, whose example exerted an untainted attraction. His life combined the advantages of the Spanish past, the connection to her parents, and the metamorphosis from poor to rich for which she secretly hoped. She wrote about his life in 1838, in an article for *Le Voleur* entitled 'Lettres de Bolivar'[31] which included letters her mother had received from Bolívar together with the almost legendary story of his youth.

'Le pauvre petit Bolivar', whom her parents had known in Spain as a young man disheartened over the death of his lover, had turned up in Paris several years later transformed into the rich 'Bolivar de la Rue Vivienne' after his schoolmaster and guardian pronounced the magical words, 'vous êtes riche', and he discovered his family patrimony. But soon he found the life of the rich to be a 'complete vacuum'. When he denounced the hypocrisy of the Directorate, he was ostracized from French society, which declared him a Jacobin. Returning to Venezuela, he took on a more important task, that of the liberation of South America.

We can see in the Bolívar story the elements of 'rags to riches', of ostracism, and of rebellion that would attract Tristan. But how could she, a woman, hope to liberate her country, France? Maybe it would be wiser to begin with the disenfranchised groups – women and workers.

To try to understand the inspiration for Tristan's mission is not to belittle the magnitude of her energy and sacrifice. But we cannot overlook the forces that drove her. The aggressive energy that she had accumulated as a woman, a disinherited daughter, a disillusioned wife and a *déclassée* made her eager to fight all the institutions which had oppressed her, no small task! These were the Church, the state and the family, which, she recognized, were interlocking directorates, each reinforcing the power of the others.

As she began her struggle, she probably realized that society was pointing the guilty finger at her. What kind of woman was she? She had left her husband and children. In terms of the *Code Napoléon*, she was a monster. In part it was the internalization of guilt feelings about these matters that made her want to suffer so much, to martyr herself.

In certain historical periods, the most approved way women can express their feelings of aggression against a society which has deprived them of power is through a project of martyrdom, whose accompanying self-pity and self-immolation allow them to erase the guilt they feel about their own anger. Norman O. Brown points out that martyrdom is a complex project: 'Giving is self-sacrificial, self-sacrifice is self-punishment. Archaic man gives to get rid of the burden of guilt.'[32]

Tristan's concern for the plight of the working class and women was profound and serious. Yet it was also over-determined and had other than completely altruistic motives. Her self-righteous assumption of the role of saviour allowed her to recuperate her lost class position as aristocrat and perfect her image as Mother; at the same time she was able to work out her aggressions against the society which had denied her her rightful position. By identifying herself with the causes of the poor and women, with their suffering, she could release her rage against the rich who had ostracized her in France and in Peru. The profoundly martyrist mission she conceived allowed her to rebel in a way appropriate to her sex, and at the same time, to accumulate the self-pity and the pity of others she felt she deserved.

At the same time, this complex project allowed Tristan to prove to herself and to others that she had 'a strength not common to my sex',[33] as she wrote to Fourier, and thus she could dissociate herself from the image of powerlessness attributed to her gender. Moreover, under the cover of virtue, she could take her revenge, and transform society's accusation that she was a bastard, a poor wife and a neglectful mother, into praise by exhibiting a desire to be supremely virtuous, and declaring to all the world by her actions that she had 'a *need* to do good'.[34]

But even as we try to understand some of the profound psychological causes which themselves arose from social injustice and that led Tristan to conceive her role and her project, we should not allow these personal motivations to obscure the equally profound humanitarian feelings which inspired her, as did the social basis of her concerns.

From this brief analysis we can see that the project which Tristan conceived was unlikely to succeed. Nonetheless, it holds enormous interest for us, for the manner in which it was to be executed gives an accurate idea of the permissions and taboos of the society Tristan tried to transform. As we shall see, the complex factors of sex and class were to haunt and deform the project entirely.

2
A Feminist Statement

Tristan's 'Woman Alone'

In 1836, ten years after her flight from her husband André Chazal, Tristan published a little brochure, *Nécessité de faire bon accueil aux femmes étrangères* [referred to hereafter as *Nécessité*] in which she transcribed her personal experience as a solitary woman into a call for social action. This work foreshadowed the analytical thrust and style of her later works. With its publication, Tristan renounced the privacy she had so meticulously cultivated during the 1820s and hesitatingly became a public personage, under the initials F.T. Marking her return from Peru and in a sense the end of her wandering, *Nécessité* illuminates Tristan's stance at the beginning of her literary and political career and her determination to fuse the private and the public, the personal and the universal, theory and practice.

Although this early work is marred by inconsistencies and provisional solutions, its importance cannot be underestimated. The originality of Tristan's perception of women as 'an entire class, forming half the human race' is striking. Moreover, she saw that women's problem extended beyond national boundaries. Indeed, Tristan's ability to conceptualize about large segments of the population based on their economic status, and her call to organize women on an international level, are evidence that she had wider views than other contemporary proponents of social utopia.

In this first work, she attempted to expose the difficulties faced by women travelling on their own because of the treatment accorded them by French society. 'Travel' was her euphemism for mobility, and studying it offered Tristan a chance to expose precisely how restricted contemporary French women were. Although her remedy was only minimally effective, her analysis of the problem was important.

Tristan recognized the inconveniences suffered by women of the two upper-class groups (both subject to social, psychological and even economic pressures), but her sympathies were largely with the third

19

class, in which she somewhat unluckily had found herself – 'the most
numerous, the most interesting and the one on which all the misfortunes seem to accumulate'.

She had experienced the discomfort of the other two classes, when
as a young woman she travelled as a lady's companion to two English
ladies, and also when she stayed with her father's family in Peru. But
on the whole, Tristan's past tied her most closely to this third group.
These were women who came to Paris after having been seduced and
abandoned, to hide their shame, or who had fled their husbands and
sought to lose their identity in the anonymity of the large city; or else
they were foreigners from other lands who fled home to begin a new
existence. Tristan's sympathies were clear.

> ... because the betrayed girl would not have been abandoned if she
> had been *rich*, the slandered foreigner would not have been forced
> to leave her country if she had been *rich*: only the weak and the
> unfortunate are ever deceived and attacked. Very few *rich* women
> find themselves in the cruel situation of having to leave their
> husbands, because they are used to living more or less apart from
> the very first. (*Nécessité*, p. 9)

It is significant that already in this early work Tristan chose to
focus on the economic as well as the social basis of women's difficulties. Still, it was in abstract terms that she described the solution to these
difficulties and the plight of these women, 'those unfortunate creatures'.
What emerged from this depiction was a romantic vision designed to
arouse pity for the victim of economic necessity: 'No ray of hope
shines on their horizon; and crushed under the weight of their woes,
they finally contract that morbid sensitivity'. (*Nécessité*, p. 9) Yet
Tristan, full of sympathy for these women pushed onto the 'path of
vice', provided no real solution beyond the formation of a kind of 'trav-
ellers' society'. (Ibid.)

At this juncture of her career, Tristan's solution was paternalistic.
She imagined that her depiction would arouse enough pity to stimu-
late the foundation of a charitable organization to help 'these forsaken
young women [who] waste their lives in the isolation of their cold,
gloomy little rooms, and die in the springtime of their existence'.
(Ibid). Because her analysis of society was still based on the perspective of the Enlightenment, her solution was to eradicate ignorance and
replace it with a religion of love. If only she could expose the problem,
she could rid society of the twin evils of egoism and materialism. Her
perception of the cause was essentially romantic and literary at this
juncture: 'And that disgraceful, inhuman society, prouder of its despicable triumph than Lucifer of his beauty, has then exhausted all the
resources of its infernal genius to close off all avenues (to women) so

that its victims should never be able to climb out of the abyss in which it has plunged them ... And that is the present order of things.' (*Nécessité*, p. 11)

So, too, was her vision of woman and of the family a romantic one. She regarded women from a Saint-Simonian perspective, one which derived in part from Rousseau and paradoxically would feed anti-feminism throughout the nineteenth century. She defined women as 'that part of humanity whose mission it is to bring peace and love in the heart of society'. (*Nécessité*, p. 24) This definition described a perfection few women were able to attain. Moreover, it rationalized their exclusion from the productive sphere of society just at the moment money was declared to be the central value of French society. In taking over the notion that it is woman's mission to guide society along the route of progress, that 'women are poetry and art' (ibid.), Tristan defined the first role she would choose to play. But, as we have seen, the contradictions were already rampant.

In this feminist pamphlet, then, she endorsed the bourgeois ideology gaining sway during the July Monarchy. Her vision of the happy family at home was little more than a romanticized version of the home she had never had, and one which no amount of experience would ever completely dispel from her imagination. Indeed, she seemed to envy those 'who live in the house built by your fathers, you who enjoy all the comfort life has to offer, who are surrounded by your family'. (*Nécessité*, p. 11)

At this point, she romanticized the provincial woman, an image which her *Tour de France* would finally dispel. Tristan imagined that a profitable exchange could take place between the provincial and Parisian women. But, even as she described her divine inspiration ('Our purpose is a holy one, therefore we hope God will give us words'), Tristan had to admit that her writing was based on observation, not inspiration: 'We can only speak from experience.' (*Nécessité*, p. 4) Thus, she could 'paint a faithful picture of all the suffering to which the woman [who is] alone and a foreigner is exposed'(ibid.), a picture which subsequently would become even more realistic. It is significant that as she would do later, Tristan here chose to present her *own* experience, transformed into material impersonal enough to fit the demands of a political pamphlet.

Nécessité was one of the earliest attempts to portray the specific situation of woman at the beginning of the July Monarchy, when the French economy was in a stage of transition toward industrial capitalism and when the role of woman was not yet firmly fixed in the home. Tristan was determined to show that love was not the only problem in women's lives, as many contemporary novelists pretended, including her contemporary and more illustrious rival, George Sand.

Still, the essay revealed a confusion about the process of history common to many of the social utopians, one which Marx would later criticize. Beginning with the motto '"Help one another," Christ' (*Nécessité*, p. 1), Tristan revealed an optimistic faith in philanthropy, based on the mistaken notion that the division between rich and poor was caused by ignorance and by greed, and was a moral problem that could be resolved by knowledge and good will. Sharing the age of Enlightenment's faith that progress could be attained through reasoned (and impassioned) discourse, Tristan conjured up a cosmetic remedy for the plight of women on their own: the founding of societies to welcome and help them. Nonetheless, despite these ideological limitations in this her first piece of political writing, Tristan also gave evidence of the kind of perception that would lead to her future importance. She envisioned her project as part of a much larger one, the erection of a new society, a process begun during the French Revolution: '... the foundations of the old society of the middle ages have crumbled ... a unanimous voice ... demands new institutions capable of adapting to a new era'. (*Nécessité*, p. 3)

The new society must be constructed according to the changing needs of its constituents. Her belief was that unity was necessary, 'because, divided, they (the suffering masses) are weak, incapable even of fighting against the last throes of a decrepit and dying society'. (Ibid.) The verb 'to fight' contradicts the notion of peaceful change implied in the Christ quote, whatever the ideological consequences. However, the reference to a 'civilisation décrépite' seems to prefigure the optimism of Marx, who in 1848 would announce that capitalism contained the seeds of its own destruction.

Thus, the introduction to her essay betrayed a confusion (shared by the young Marx) between the romantic notion of history as organic change, a natural process, and the scientific, socialist concept of change arising out of a dialectic opposition of historic forces. The contradictions in Tristan's thinking are evident: Why should the masses have to organize and fight if indeed there exists an organic process of growth and decay implied in the use of 'to collapse' and 'to die out'?

Tristan On Her Own

In this first publication, Tristan, the autodidact, flaunted her awareness of the writings of Fourier and Saint-Simon (alluded to as 'génies supérieurs') (ibid.), but then engaged in a daring satirical critique of their limitations. Because she had acquired much of her insight into the process of history and the need for collective effort from the work of these two philosophers, her criticism of their methods seems surprising. Yet, already in this her first work, Tristan boldly began to elaborate the outlines of the critique of utopian socialists that she would later develop more fully, one which prefigured that of Marx and Engels:

> But the shortcoming of our age is to generalize too much: thus one loses sight of practical applications; one dreams of perfect schemes, which will probably only be put to effect two hundred years from now. Our purpose here is not to offer another brilliant utopia by describing the world as it should be, but to show the path which can lead us to the realization of the beautiful dream of a universal paradise. (*Nécessité*, p. 4)

Indeed, at this early stage of her career, Tristan was already proclaiming her pragmatism, her originality and her superiority: 'We must not allow our theories to be associated with the moral utopias which arise everywhere and soon collapse.' (*Nécessité*, p. 13) In part, she may have assumed this position for practical reasons: by 1835, the Saint-Simonians had been rendered impotent by their own excesses and by repressive legal measures, and the Fourierists faced an uncertain future.

Yet this desire not to be 'assimilated', to work on her own while calling for collective action seems problematic, especially at this early stage. For, while Tristan's bold critique of their idealism was well-founded and just, it was also a means by which she isolated herself, rendering her own political success more unlikely. By pointing out false friends she may have sought to reveal her mission. But by isolating herself, she identified herself as the pariah.

In *Nécessité* we find the first instance of the pariah theme which would run through all of Tristan's writings. The appellation 'pariah' is commonly perceived as a stigma resulting in social ostracism. Before Rousseau, isolation was considered to be an evil in itself. However, Romantic ideology developed the notion that if society was evil, then isolation was worth seeking. The pariah could be outcast not because of a defect, but because of her or his superiority. This other, more positive meaning of pariah can be found in Madame de Staël's description of the plight of the 'femme extraordinaire', which we have seen above. Tristan may have chosen (consciously or not) to mimic Mme de Staël and her 'femme extraordinaire'. As a pariah, she could recuperate her lost status in a socially acceptable way.

Tristan's sense of isolation was also warranted from a historic point of view. In late 1834 when she returned from Peru, she understood the universality of her problems: she shared certain grave handicaps with all women, but as one who sought change, she became an outsider. In contrast to women in Peru, she had enough freedom to permit her to become the liberator of her sex. But the mood of France had changed in the interim.

The excesses of the Saint-Simonian sect on behalf of the movement to re-establish the primacy of sexual needs had set the feminist cause back enormously. By calling for the free expression of sensuality in that early bourgeois period, Enfantin, who took his ideas from Fourier, found himself attacked on all sides and finally placed in jail. There he determined to focus his energies on the safer and more abstract search for a spiritual 'femme guide' in the East.

Those sensible enough to recognize the danger of both options left the sect and joined the growing Fourierist clan. But this group, led by Victor Considérant, perceived the real necessity of clearly distinguishing itself from its predecessor and, in the process, tabled its feminism, as it were, until the future. It opted for a concentration on the safer elements of Fourierist doctrine of the reorganization of work by means of 'phalanstères', or communities based upon a kind of selective socialism, experiments within the bounds of bourgeois society dependent upon that society for material help.

Thus her assertion in 1835 that 'women feel that a new epoch is beginning for them' (*Nécessité*, p. 15), seems tardy. On her return Tristan would have found the energetic and vociferous Saint-Simonian women gone, or absorbed into the Fourierist fold. Nonetheless, she set out to restate the problem of women as she had come to know it through her travels, and to pose a temporary solution for it. (That she never tried to implement her plan can be attributed to her recognition of its limits and to the material fact that her own personal problems became so pressing that they prevented her from attempting to go beyond literary expression. For it was at this time that her husband Chazal had begun to hunt her.)

In *Nécessité*, Tristan was echoing the rhetoric of the feminist Saint-Simonian journals published from 1832–4 under the titles *La Tribune des femmes*, *La Femme nouvelle*, and *La Femme libre*. But by the time Tristan returned to France, these journals were extinct. (In part, we can attribute their demise to the increasingly repressive laws against organizing and against the press, but also, as we have seen, the movement led by Enfantin had been divided. Disgusted with Enfantin's excessively abstract search for 'la Femme messie' in the East, some women left to join Fourierist groups. Others accompanied him on this fruitless quest and were still in Egypt at the time of Tristan's return.) Yet the successors to these early feminist journals existed: Eugénie Niboyet's *Conseiller des femmes* [1833] and her *Mosaïque Lyonnaise* [1834], and Madeleine Sirey's *Mère de famille* [1833].[1] These journals continued to discuss the importance of women's role in society, but Tristan seemed to be completely ignorant of them. We can only speculate about her connection to these movements and their journals.

Indeed, Tristan's efforts to form a society to help foreign women and women on their own were reported in *Le Citateur féminin*, founded in 1835, on which Eugénie Niboyet also collaborated. Announcing Tristan's pamphlet, it took her project seriously, and called upon its readers to lend it their support.[2] Jules Puech, Tristan's biographer, asserts that this journal went ahead and founded such a society that year, and attributes it to Tristan's influence. If he is right, why was Tristan never involved in either society, her own or theirs?[3] This isolation seems to prefigure the exclusive role that Tristan was to create for herself.

The intensity of Tristan's call for amelioration of women's situation makes her lack of contact with contemporary feminist movements all the more curious. We do not know whether Tristan attended the Saint-Simonian meetings before her departure to Peru in the early 1830s, but we do know that large numbers of women did attend, and that Tristan's knowledge of the doctrine is beyond dispute. Although she seemed to have few intimate women friends, she was in contact with Angélique Arnaud, Pauline Roland, and Hortense Allart, all of them very close to the Saint-Simonian movement.

But even if she had no direct contact with the movement at that time, one wonders why she presented her *société* as the only hope and didn't mention existing societies for the association and education of women, such as those founded by Clorinde Roge (Chevalerie de la Femme [1833]); or Eugénie Niboyet's Société de la Morale Chrétienne [1830]; or the Saint-Simonian 'Association pour l'instruction populaire' founded by Marie-Reine Guindorf and Désirée Veret (Gay) [1833].[4]

It is possible that Tristan was unaware of these societies, but her total lack of contact with or mention of other feminist activity in the 1830s seems strange. Later, in *Promenades dans Londres*, we are struck by the brevity of her description of her meeting with Anna Wheeler, one of the only socialist women Tristan was to encounter in England, and a feminist; nor is any meeting with Désirée Veret Gay mentioned. Gay, a close friend of Wheeler's, living in London at the time of Tristan's visit, had been one of the most active feminists in the 1830s, and it is strange that Wheeler would not have introduced Tristan to her – unless, of course, Tristan's own interest in feminism had waned or she preferred to see herself as all alone at the head of a movement not yet born! How interesting an account of her meeting with these two socialist-feminists would have been! Omissions such as these cast doubt on the purity of Tristan's feminist project. (See Chapter 5 for a fuller discussion of this omission.)

A perceptive journalist whose identity (and gender!) remains mysterious, Herbinot de Mauchamps,[5] attacked Tristan on this very point. Presumably a feminist speaking as a male, he seemed to think that Tristan's image of herself as pariah was inaccurate and even self-serving, although he recognized that it had some basis in fact, and described her as a person 'who is always spurned by society like a pariah'.[6] Even so, he objected to her claim to exclusivity and solitude in the feminist struggle, and called her unjust because she dared to proclaim her solitude as a feminist in her next book, *Pérégrinations d'une paria (1833–1834)*, when in fact numerous feminist voices had been raised. There she contrasted her own advocacy with the reality '… that not one woman dares raise her voice against a social order which, by depriving them of a profession, makes them dependent and at the same time forges their shackles through the indissolubility of marriage'.[7]

Although Mauchamps passionately subscribed to her attack on the illegality of divorce (she was one of many women who presented petitions to reinstate divorce in the period), he could not tolerate Tristan's pose as loner. He reminded Tristan that on the feminist front she had mentioned only Mme Dudevant, and even then disparagingly:

> Eh, Madame! have you forgotten *La Gazette des Femmes*, and Mme Hortense Allart, Mme A. Dupin, Mlle Hermance Sandrin, etc. If some Fourierists, Republicans, or others have offered you their admiration without supporting your cause and that of women, it is regrettable for you and for them as well; but believe me, there are not only women but also men (and I proudly count myself one of them), who are demanding, openly and sincerely, justice and equality for all men and women.[8]

We must accept this interpretation by her contemporary as at least partially true. Whether Tristan's vision of herself as pariah derived from the urge to self-dramatization (certainly a good journalistic technique), self-deception or real ignorance is unclear at this early stage, but it is important to recognize that already in *Nécessité* Tristan, bravely and perhaps foolishly, chose to speak from a rather isolated and distant podium, even as she extrapolated the experience of all single women from her own. In this first work, it seems as if Tristan's construction of a certain image of herself was well under way.

3
The Manifesto of the Pariah

Tristan Courts Fame and Disaster

To analyse the reasons for the failure or success of a creative effort, we must understand the social, economic and historical constraints it confronts as well as those the individual places upon him or herself. These feed each other. To analyse a literary 'failure' is to illuminate the kind of literary success each society permits.

The case of women is special in regard to the normative social, economic and historical factors. Women break taboos as they move outside their assigned private sphere into the realm of public action and creative effort. Often, they must construct a self-image to justify this 'deviation' – a self-image that permits it, but may also inhibit it, ensuring its failure. The following account of Tristan's construction of a self-image, a myth of herself and her project, is meant in no way to diminish the originality and heroism of her effort, but rather is an attempt to explain her failure within its socio-historic context.

With the publication of *Nécessité de faire bon accueil aux femmes étrangères*, Tristan began to consider her destiny in larger social terms. She had been reading Fourier and lost no time in writing to him, enclosing her little brochure which, as we have seen, obliquely criticized his work! Her letter to him reveals much about her self-perception in the period immediately preceding her début as a *femme de lettres*. Exhibiting none of the humility traditionally associated with women, she fearlessly addressed herself directly to the great master himself in 1835. From her letter, it is clear she sought contact and an outlet for her enormous will to do good. 'You will find in me a strength not common to my sex, a need to do good, and a deep feeling of gratitude for all those who will give me the means of being useful.'[1]

If we look closely at this deceptively simple statement, we can see that, even in this first effort to gain support, Tristan engaged in certain forms of self-sabotage. By describing her effort as 'not common to my sex', Tristan praised her own capacities while denigrating those of

27

other women, a significant portion of her audience. Clearly, she wanted to distance herself from the other members of her sex and from the societal image of women she so hated. But, even if Tristan felt a disdain for her sex, she was still trapped in the realm of activity it permitted women. For example, she expressed her desire for action as 'doing good' and 'being useful', both traditionally 'feminine' formulations of public participation. Although she mentioned to Fourier that she hoped he would introduce her to 'two or three ladies who share our ideas', above all she wanted to meet the 'chefs de l'école' – Fourier, and Considérant, his heir apparent. Though largely unknown herself, she identified with them, boldly placing her own theories on a level equal with theirs, and referring to 'nos idées'.

Tristan's description of her character is significant at this early stage. Despite her 'imperious need' to meet others interested in Fourier's work, her 'melancholy and somewhat disagreeable character' made social rapport difficult for her. It seems as if she felt herself to be totally isolated.

Fourier was obviously intrigued by the letter and the pamphlet he received from this intense young woman. He tried twice to find her without success. Her explanation reveals still another aspect of her material (and psychological) situation: 'For the last two months since I moved ... I have been so troubled and afflicted by family matters, that I have found it impossible to find a moment to bring you my new address.'[2]

Upon her return from Peru in 1835, just as Tristan took the first steps to ensure herself an independent existence outside of the traditional female sphere, her husband André Chazal determined to assert his conjugal rights. He became increasingly aggressive and finally, in desperation, attempted to assassinate her in 1838. Infuriated by her seeming freedom, suspicious that she had received a large sum of money from her Peruvian family, resentful that his wife should have left his domicile to become another George Sand, he attacked Tristan at her most vulnerable point – their daughter Aline, whose early life hardly predicted the legacy she would leave Western culture, namely her son Paul Gauguin. Although Tristan had relinquished their son Ernest to Chazal's guardianship, he now began agitating for possession of Aline, to whom Tristan felt especially attached; for Tristan had fled Chazal while pregnant with her.

A brief chronology of these years indicates that at the very moment Tristan was writing her first book – *Les Pérégrinations d'une paria (1833-1834)* – publishing her first articles and letters, and meeting some of the most illustrious utopian socialists of her time (Robert Owen, Fourier, Considérant),[3] she was incessantly troubled by the actions of Chazal. The true position of women in French society at that time was clarified for Tristan through these personal experiences. Justice was on

Chazal's side when he assaulted her in the streets. Since she was his wife, this was his right. But even so, there were limits. If she was powerless to prevent his successive abductions of Aline, when the child complained that her father had made sexual advances and, it seems, raped her, Tristan was finally able to move justice to her side. But only for a short time. After three months, Chazal was released from prison based on evidence given in his *Mémoire,* which attacked his wife's morals.

With the publication of *Pérégrinations* in January 1838, introduced by Tristan's full account of her domestic troubles, his fury only increased. The court permitted Tristan a *séparation de corps* at last, but this left Chazal free to contemplate murder. Tristan was moving into a circle of writers and painters now. It must have seemed that social action was futile, so she decided to write a novel in which she could express her social concerns in aesthetic form. On September 8, 1838, six months before the publication of *Méphis,* Chazal tried to kill her, but the bullets were not fatal, although one lodged permanently in her chest. Her contemporaries, once they realized it was not George Sand who had been shot, began to take interest in the 'Spanish beauty', Flora Tristan.

This biographical information illuminates the specific kind of problems that faced a woman who tried to liberate herself from the traditional female role during this period, and evokes the atmosphere in which Tristan struggled. It would be both unfair and inaccurate to try to deal with the literary production of a writer without considering the sometimes overbearing psychological and economic circumstances under which she had to write. Not only does Tristan's experience stand as evidence of a particular societal malaise in regard to 'liberated' women, but to some extent it was the material against which she dedicated her life and work. The actual conditions under which she lived and worked and the stance she took toward her own life-material cannot really be separated from the way it transformed her literary projects.

Tristan's Martyrist Project

In composing *Pérégrinations,* Tristan had decided to discuss her own situation, in part, because she recognized that it mirrored the situation of all women:

> A great many women live in fact separately from their husbands ...
> It is therefore not to myself that I have attempted to draw attention
> but to all women who find themselves in the same situation, and
> whose number is increasing every day. (*Pérégrinations* I, p. 48)

Here Tristan painted a rich tableau fusing the genres of mémoire [memoir or petition], travel tale, and political pamphlet. Published in 1838, several years after her return from the visit to her father's family in Peru which provided material for the book, this literary effort marked the second stage in the construction of the image of herself as the pariah, and the first account of her initiation into the exigencies of that role.

In the introductory sections, where the author was intent upon establishing the proper view of her project and proper relations with the reader, her intentions were clearest, although their real significance must be sought beneath the professed purpose of her book, which was to instruct and improve the lot of the Peruvian people. Her manner of presenting this charitable effort, her organization and her omissions, lead us to suspect a secondary, unconscious project of vengeance and martyrdom beneath the expressed desire to 'rescue' the Peruvian people from the destructive aspects she had observed in their society. For, as she wrote, Tristan managed to cut her ties with nearly everyone. At the end of the three introductory sections she stood alone in her chosen pose as the fearless truthseeker, willing to suffer ostracism and scorn for her brave and honest words. She would continue to maintain this stance and, like others of the Romantic generation, she seemed to find solace in her suffering. But the valorization of isolation derived also from her confusion of her class and sexual identity, and its effect was therefore magnified.

In *Pérégrinations*, this pose of willing martyrdom was to be the shield with which she concealed certain realities about herself, a self-image that allowed her to carry out her project guiltlessly. (Because of this veil, she could never understand the true nature of her project, her class hatred, and therefore could never formulate a means for attack without the crippling subterfuge of martyrdom.)

Thus, although we must take careful account of the the myriad aspects of the fusion of genres which *Pérégrinations* presents, the originality of its treatment of these genres and of the raw material of Peruvian life, we must first of all view the book as an elaborate justification of her intense desire for rebellion and for revenge. Only then can we understand how Tristan and others who chose to conceal their efforts behind Romantic heroics doomed to failure.their vision of social change.

In the three prefatory sections of *Pérégrinations*, Tristan broke with each social group with which she had something in common, elaborately constructing a suicidal image of herself as isolated martyr. First, in the opening dedication 'Aux Péruviens', Tristan severed all ties with Peru, her father's country, and with her family and friends there, although she insisted this was not her intention. Tristan told her former hosts that despite 'such a warm welcome' from them, she must report faithfully what she observed in their country, even though in so doing she might seem to them to be a 'monstre d'ingratitude'. (*Pérégrinations* I, p. vi) In spite of her critical attitude, she decided to dedicate the book to them in the hope that the more intelligent and less vain among them would recognize that her criticism was meant to help them. 'I believe that you might find some benefit in my narration ... No one desires more sincerely than I do your prosperity ... '. (Ibid.)

Her relatives might indeed question her sincerity as they read on. Her philanthropic pose and patronizing air certainly offended them. Undoubtedly she was accurate in her discovery that, as she charged, '... In Peru, the upper class is thoroughly corrupt, its selfishness leads it, in order to satisfy its greed, its love of power ... into the most anti-social undertakings.' (Ibid.)

It it was mainly her uncle's egoism, his cupidity, his love of power and his refusal to give her her rightful inheritance that she had encountered in Peru. In attacking the society at large, she could surreptitiously attack him as well, for he was one of its highest officials and most powerful men. The vengeful aspect of this project becomes transparent: Peruvian society was, in spite of itself, to be rewarded by this book, but simultaneously her uncle would be punished.

In these opening pages, Tristan's construction of her image as a martyr was well under way. From the rhetoric of the dedication, the rewards of the image are clear: she should be admired for carrying out this difficult and unrewarding task. To tell the unpleasant truth publicly to friends and relatives who have treated her so well is bound to be misunderstood and to incur the unjust animosity of those who cannot recognize her good intentions. Already in the introductory material, then, the outlines of a pattern that will become familiar are discernible. The labyrinthine possibilities of the 'gift' are becoming apparent to Tristan. By hiding beneath the halo of benevolence, she will be able to execute her project of vengeance in a manner appropriate to her sex. Through her sacrifice, her own pleasure will be served in the way women are permitted to experience it, through suffering.

In choosing a martyrist project as her mode of action, Tristan had confined herself to the realm of sacrifice prescribed to women by her society. Yet how different she would be from her contemporary fictional sister, Eugénie Grandet! Of Tristan it could also be said, as Balzac said of Eugénie, 'She learned her destiny. To feel, to love, to suffer, to make sacrifices, will always be the theme of women's lives.'[4] But Tristan, a very real woman of the July Monarchy, at least tried to make sure that her own suffering left its mark on the societal organization that had caused it.

The Peruvians (i.e., her family) responded as she anticipated. Unappreciative of her efforts, they burned the book in Lima's public square, and the Tristan y Moscoso family cut her off from all funds. In this, they demonstrated their misapprehension of her 'good' intentions, and reinforced her feelings of isolation and ostracism, further justifying her proclaimed status as pariah. To some extent then, in this, her first full-length book, Tristan seemed to be elaborately ensuring the accuracy of her image as a pariah. The ties with Peru, with her father's family, and any connection with upper-class status and a life of ease, were indeed severed by its publication.

In the second introductory section, Tristan cut herself off from all those who had pursued similar literary projects, by valorizing a specific kind of approach and intention, one that she would be most capable of carrying out. She first distanced her literary effort from that of other memoir writers, who protected themselves from attack by posthumous publication. Tristan, by comparison, viewed herself as fearless. Because she had 'in her heart the martyr's faith', she asserted that she could be relied upon to tell the entire truth regardless of the repercussions, for she would not be 'stopped out of consideration for the opinion of others'. It is here that her curious perspective of the writer's mission is revealed. Tristan viewed it in much the same way as the constitution of a dossier for a trial:

> One might ask if divulging men's actions ... is always useful. Yes, I would answer, all those actions that are destructive, all those that result from an abuse of some superiority or other, be it from physical power or moral power ... actions that infringe upon the independence which God has dispensed to all His creatures without distinction. (*Pérégrinations* I, p. xxiii)

Tristan directly connected her task as a writer to her own social predicament: she must attack those who had deprived her of her rightful place and chance. Because this was her purpose, her scope would have to be wider. Since she identified with those who suffer, unlike most memoir writers, she determined to write about people of all classes, and not just 'the high-ranking ones in the social order'(*Pérégrinations* I, p. xx). (Indeed, her exposé of the full range of the female condition – as she observed it in Peru – is probably one of the first of its kind.)

But Tristan intended that her literary production be better and different from that of women writers in particular. In describing the specific tasks appropriate to women writers and the way in which these should be executed, Tristan disparaged the work of her more illustrious contemporary, George Sand. She accomplished this in a very contorted fashion, her argument riddled with an illogicality and inconsistency that betrayed her difficulty in expressing it. As we have seen, she first called on writers to publicize all excesses of social abuse. Then she qualified this recommendation: '... the same self-sacrifice which leads us to heap scorn upon the aggressor must make us throw a veil over the conduct of the oppressed person who seeks to escape his oppression ... ' (*Pérégrinations* I, p. xxiii).

She further refined this qualification: '... as long as the weaker sex, subjugated by the stronger, has to restrain the feelings that are the least restrainable in our nature, as long as there is no reciprocity between the sexes, to publish the love stories of women is to expose them to repression.' (*Pérégrinations* I, p. xxv)

Of course, Sand had based her work largely on this area of women's experience. But perhaps Tristan was referring to the danger of exposé implicit in memoirs. Fiction might afford a more appropriate shield. But in the next breath, she condemned fiction as pleasant but not conducive to social change: 'Novels have never motivated the actions of men.' (*Pérégrinations* I, p. xxvii) As if to focus her attack directly on Sand, she deplored the fact that although for the last ten years progressive writers had been calling for women 'to write about their misfortunes and their needs' (*Pérégrinations* I, p. xxv), not one had done so. Then she 'recalled' that there had been one, but she had published under a man's name, and written fiction. Thus Tristan attacked Sand's efforts on three counts: she published 'les amours des femmes'; she wrote fiction; and did so under a male pseudonym. Now Tristan, having denounced her rival, called somewhat inconsistently for women 'whose lives have been devastated by great misfortunes' (*Pérégrinations* I, p. xxvii), to speak of their suffering. The inconsistency of this admonition, and of the entire argument, supports our contention that these ruptures were part of an (unconscious?) attempt to establish a certain self-image: they justified her feeling of isolation and martyrdom. Although we may forgive her because her work revealed true feminist concerns wider than any that Sand perceived, Sand herself never did.

Tristan, an unknown, a young woman on her own, thus began her literary career by insulting the most powerful literary woman of her time, and perhaps the most illustrious feminist as well. Already in this preface, she had broken with her class, her sex, and her profession. Just as she did for the Peruvians, she would also do for Sand. She had dedicated the book to them; so, she sent an autographed copy of *Pérégrinations* to Sand. Whichever motive you choose – myopia, the will to self-destruct, or honesty – Tristan's act assured her subsequent martyrdom. Sand would never regard her charitably thereafter, and Tristan thus lost one of her more likely sources of support.

In the third introductory section, entitled 'Avant-propos', Tristan determined to make still another rupture, this time with social propriety. To carry out her promise of complete honesty, she revealed the precise circumstances of her marriage and just how badly her husband had treated her. And, to assure the proper identification of the cause of her misery, she further described him in a footnote: 'André Chazal, smooth-cut engraver and brother of M. A. Chazal, professor at the Jardin des Plantes'. (*Pérégrinations* I, p. xxxvi)

Tristan probably took great pleasure in this form of revenge. (This public revelation infuriated her husband. But in his *Mémoire*, six months earlier, he had already exposed many intimate details of their ménage in court and attacked her morals, accusing her of adultery and prostitution in order to exculpate himself from the charges of rape and incest.[5] The matter would not end with Tristan's more public reply here in the introduction to *Pérégrinations*. Later, at Chazal's trial for the attempted murder of Tristan, his lawyer would invoke passages from this book in order once again to accuse Tristan.

One could of course justify Tristan's presentation of these personal details on other grounds. They were relevant to the narrative and explained the difficulties she encountered in Peru because of the false identity under which she travelled (i.e., as a single woman). She assumed this identity because, as we have seen, under the *Code Napoléon* it was illegal for a wife to leave the house of her husband, and because married women travelling on their own were treated very poorly. Moreover, she thought that as a 'demoiselle' her chances for retrieving her patrimony would be better.

Much of the drama of the book derived from this lie about her marital status. The contorted nature of Tristan's description of her motivation for the lie indicates the extent to which she felt she had been victimized by her false position, by society and by the lie itself. She condemned 'the awkward situation in which I was placed by the lies that society's prejudices forced me to make'. (*Pérégrinations* I, p. xlvii) With this statement she dodged, as perhaps she was entitled to do, all responsibility for the deceitful position in which she found herself on the voyage to Peru.

But the lie to society was also a lie to herself, one which allowed her to make the final rupture with an image of womanhood she despised. To accomplish this, she had to break definitively with men. Like the preceding ruptures, this one was also initiated in *Pérégrinations*, this time in the text itself. This troublesome chore was doomed to incompletion. Various commentators are still trying to link her romantically to one or another male friend. (Unlike her contemporary, Sand, Tristan kept this aspect of her life very well hidden.)

This break with men represented perhaps the most curious aspect of Tristan's decision to paint herself as the pariah. For although in her self-portrait she may have rendered herself 'untouchable', in reality her physical beauty and the transparency of her own desires would have certainly made her very appealing, if also threatening, to men. Here is one description of her – there are many such – by Jules Janin, one of the leading figures of the social and literary scene of the 'juste milieu': 'That wonderfully beautiful woman, with sparkling eyes, coiled up in her chair like a snake in the sun, has the sharpness of reaction and appetites of a python.'[6]

Dangerously beautiful,Tristan herself seemed to sense how closely her various appetites were related, and how insatiable and destructive they were:

> But I am so ambitious, so demanding, so insatiable and so voracious at the same time, that I can never be satisfied with what is offered to me! My heart is like the Englishman's mouth – it is a bottomless pit where everything that enters is crushed and ground up before it disappears.[7]

But Tristan's huge capacity for love and the enormity of her desire had been rebuked very early. If her first expression of love had been wrecked by the discovery of her social status as an illegitimate child, the result of her next expression of affection was even harder to bear:

> The young man who was the object of my entire affection, even though irreproachably thoughtful ... was one of those cold and calculating men for whom a great passion has the appearance of madness: he was afraid of my love, he feared I should love him too much. That second disappointment broke my heart, I suffered terribly. (*Pérégrinations* I, pp. 47–8)

If her revulsion for the traditional position of woman had not been solidified by her own experiences before and after marriage, then certainly her mother's matrimonial experience and her father's lack of responsibility in guaranteeing his family's welfare must have made her deeply resentful.

It is probable that she conceived this project of rupture with the male sex as a sort of vengeance for all of these deceptions. To protect herself, she would choose, despite her protestations to the contrary, to reverse the roles, to enjoy herself as the desired object, and to project her own desires on to the others. One commentator recently described her manoeuvre this way: 'She belongs to a mythical region where no one can reach her, and,instead of being the seduced one, she becomes the seductress; she means to exert her influence for unprecedented purposes, she is taken in by her own equivocal game.'[8]

But this is just what she claimed she would not do at the outset of the description of this project of rupture. As in the other cases, this rupture with men in general and Captain Chabrié (captain of the ship which bore her to Peru) in particular also began with a declaration of good intentions.

I knew from experience the agony of loving someone who cannot understand you ... I had therefore promised myself to do everything in my power never to be the cause of such suffering, and to avoid, in so far as it should depend on me, inspiring feelings that I could not share. I have never understood the pleasure one can find in inspiring a love that one cannot reciprocate. (*Pérégrinations* I, pp. 49–50)

With this promise to prevent and repulse Captain Chabrié's love, she began to do just the contrary.

The contorted way in which this deception is carried out in the pages of the first volume of *Pérégrinations*, in the seams of the generic patchwork quilt of mémoire, travel tale and political tract, is an indication of how problematical a task it was for Tristan. In effect, she herself recognized that 'Two different persons coexisted inside of me' (*Pérégrinations* I, p. 167), a very physical being and a spiritual one. The first volume of *Pérégrinations* is the abortive attempt at the reconciliation of this struggle between these two beings in her, a reconciliation achieved through a repression of the physical side.

But two Tristans were involved in still another sense: the character in the mémoire who progresses with and learns over time, who is caught up in the development of experience; and the other, the narrator, who exists in the present and can distort and manipulate this first Tristan to fit her ideological, psychological and literary needs. One is the participant in the experiences of the travel book and of the mémoire, while the other is simultaneously fixing the image of the first and justifying her actions, in order that the composite image produced will be consonant with the philosophical and political statement on behalf of women advocated in the third realm of discourse, the political pamphlet. It seems as if the three mirrors offered by these genres were necessary for Tristan to reconcile the private, public and philosophical divisions within her.

In volume one, Tristan had freed herself to pursue a much easier task: to deal with the lives of other women, as an observer. In choosing such a vast object for her affections, she was less fearful of being betrayed. Or, as she put it later, 'Love humanity; that lover will not deceive you.'[9]

In volume one, she still had to extract herself from the other more treacherous love, that of men. Despite her protests to the contrary, at first she began by attracting Chabrié's love, and seemingly to enjoyed it: 'With each passing day M Chabrié's love for me grew, and I felt an undescribable sense of contentment at being loved by him ... I realized that I was truly loved. I felt a surge of delight at that discovery.' (*Pérégrinations* I, p. 86, 105)

But, as if guiltily catching herself, remembering the promise she had made at the outset of the description, in the framing of the project – not to solicit love she could not return – Tristan the narrator added, 'but this surge of gratitude was followed by the horrible despair which my situation engendered'. (*Pérégrinations* I, p. 105) There is an erroneous word here: why should Tristan feel 'gratitude', and not love, when she had earlier promised not to inspire love unless she could return it? The description of her excuse for the rupture bears a tell-tale resemblance to several descriptions of emotion felt by female characters in her next book, the novel *Méphis*. Note the passive voice, and the 'voix infernale': 'For me, to be united to a man who loved me, impossible! An infernal voice kept taunting me cruelly, saying: "you are married".' (Ibid.) Tristan's own sentiments seem to be absent from this description: it is the man who loves her!

But then Tristan may actually have solicited the love she knew she could not return, in order to protect herself, for as she admitted, 'Alone in the middle of the ocean, I had nothing to fear with his love.' (*Pérégrinations* I, p. 115) Alone amidst 19 sailors, it was perhaps natural that Tristan would seek his protection; but should she have made her intentions more clear? Finally she tells us what her real feelings for Chabrié were: 'The affection I felt for M Chabrié was not the passionate love ... ' (*Pérégrinations* I, p. 156)

Two other possible rationalizations were available to explain the inconsistency between her initial decision not to seek to attract men and her subsequent involvement with Chabrié. These both conceal from her as well as from us the project of revenge that may also have motivated her inspiration of his love. On the one hand, she could have recourse to the accurate description of the particular plight of women which forced them to make such false pretences of affection, described in political pamphlet style:

> Since women have no official functions in society, since only a very small number of professions are even open to them, they are in greater need of friendship than men. But let an affectionate woman find herself obliged to plead for kindness, the man to whom she turns will demand her love, and without any concern as to whether she is capable or willing to give it to him, he puts that price on the services of his friendship. (*Pérégrinations* I, p. 117)

This was certainly a rational approach, but when Tristan tried to convince Chabrié that he should be her friend rather than her lover, he replied with some justice, 'My dear Flora, your naïveté in every circumstance never ceases to surprise me.' (*Pérégrinations* I, pp. 120–1)

Naïveté would indeed be the narrator's other excuse for her character's deception of Chabrié:

> At that time I was still under the influence of all the illusions of a young woman who has seen little of the world even though I had

already known the cruellest suffering, but brought up in the countryside, in complete isolation from society, and having lived since
in seclusion, I had gone through ten years of misfortunes and dis-
appointments without becoming more perceptive. (*Pérégrinations* I,
p. 45)

This pose of innocence rings especially false since in the years after
she had left Chazal she had been supporting herself and had travelled
the continent – either as a lady's maid, as she asserted, or as a prostitute,
as Chazal charged. The first is probably closer to the truth, but even
so, Tristan had hardly led a sheltered life, at least not after her fifteenth
year. Could a woman nearly 30 years of age, who had lived in the
poorest districts of Paris, who had been married and then supported
herself, actually believe the following pretext for her behaviour?

I would squeeze his hand while putting his gloves on for him, and
often, while arranging his double cravats so as to protect him from
the cold, I would even kiss his brow. I enjoyed lavishing attentions
and little acts of endearment on him, as if he had been my brother
or my son. (*Pérégrinations* I, p. 99)

She could hardly have expected the old sailor to have interpreted
her affectionate behaviour as that of a sister or a mother. In any case,
once this love was cultivated, it had to be rejected if Tristan was to carry
out her project. She presented this rupture as a good action, a sacrifice
on her part, arranged to repair the damage that the woman he loved
before her had caused by abusing Chabrié. Tristan determined to
'... extract from his heart the love he felt for me'. (*Pérégrinations* I, p.
178) In this act, curiously enough, Tristan considered herself to be 'his
good angel' (ibid.), although she knew it caused him tremendous
pain.
   The rupture had to be carried out within the drama of the text, but
first Tristan-the-narrator had to justify the blatant and somewhat barbarous way she had exploited Chabrié's love for literary purposes; not
only had she exposed his feelings, but also his real identity. Again, as
in the prefatory sections on the occasion of each rupture, the narrator
assumed her charitable and sacrificial stance: it was she who would be
most hurt by these revelations. First of all, the task of telling the truth
is so difficult, she was certain to be misunderstood and resented for it,
but she would make that sacrifice for the sake of truthfulness. Here is
her justification:

I can feel now the difficulty of task I have assigned to myself, not
that whatever I have to say might be a cause of remorse for me; (of
course this is not so clear ...) but I am afraid that the portrayal of a

true love on one side, and of a pure friendship on the other will be, in this materialistic age, denounced as an improbability: I am afraid that I shall meet very few people whose soul, in harmony with mine, will believe my words. (*Pérégrinations* I, p. 99)

Despite all these fears, and the anticipation of miscomprehension, Tristan decided to take the risk, to be strong, to make the sacrifice: '... before I began this book, I examined carefully all the possible consequences of my narration, and however painful the duties that my conscience imposed upon me, my apostle-like faith has not wavered; I have not flinched at doing it.' (*Pérégrinations* I, p. 99) Of course the publication of this information would have enormous material consequences for Tristan, as she anticipated, but the 'spiritual' rewards must have been greater.

Now we are ready for Tristan-the-character to carry out the actual rupture in the text under the cover of an act of charity. Again, behind the scenes, the narrator has managed to transform a betrayal into an act of rescue:

Ah! It was only with God's assistance that I was able to carry out a project that exceeded human endurance; in undertaking to make Chabrié renounce his love, I ran the risk of losing his regard for me ... Well, I found the courage to do it!!! God alone understood the extent of my sacrifice. (*Pérégrinations* I, p. 318)

Elsewhere she describes her virtue this way: '... I have never flinched at any undertaking however painful it may be, when the hope of doing good was my motive.' (*Pérégrinations* I, p. 178)

But no matter how many times Tristan-the-narrator reiterated the good intentions of Tristan-the-character, there still remained the exultant and somewhat insensitive triumph with which both finally viewed the rupture. Now the identity of the 'character' could more easily fuse her identity with that of the narrator.

As soon as my decision was taken, I felt strong, free of any misgivings, and I felt the inner satisfaction that is so comforting of knowing that one has done a good deed. I felt at peace; I had just triumphed over myself: my good side had prevailed. (*Pérégrinations* I, p. 182)

Many questions arise from this explanation: what good did she actually think she was accomplishing by publishing these personal details, if not merely serving her own interests? Had there ever really been an internal fight, or had not she known from the outset that she would solicit Chabrié's attentions only for the duration of the journey?

Here, between the two Tristans, the narrator and the character, all is inconsistency and the truth is difficult to discern. But what is clear is that through this rupture Tristan-the-narrator had freed herself to pursue a project which would cause fewer complications: 'Entirely free of inner concerns I was able to devote myself to my role as observer.' (*Pérégrinations* I, p. 182)

The elaborate series of ruptures carried out in the prefatory sections and in volume 1 of *Pérégrinations* provides us with a view of Tristan's self-image under construction. Although Chazal's view of his recalcitrant wife is not to be trusted, his perception that she was constructing an image of herself seems well-founded. He questioned her motive. In his *Mémoire* (his self-defence), he quoted Tristan's profession of honesty:

> By embarking on the new path that I have just delineated, I am carrying out the mission that was given to me, I am obeying my conscience; I may be the object of hatred; but a truthful person above all, no consideration whatsoever will prevent me from telling the truth about people and events. (*Pérégrinations* I, p. 34)

He cited this passage from *Pérégrinations* in order to place its sincerity in doubt. Full of hatred and sarcasm, his charge nonetheless contained a grain of truth:

> The epigraph certainly attests to Mme Chazal's religious principles, and the phrase '*être de foi*' which she invented no doubt means one who worships truth and who would on no account ever consent to forswear it. Were it not so, one would have to conclude that Mme Chazal placed a sacred text at the beginning of her book in order to be able to dispense with moral or religious principles, and that she calls herself '*être de foi*' in order to denigrate or slander everyone.[10]

Tristan Makes Women's Fate her Subject

As the reader moves through *Pérégrinations*, it becomes clear that a pattern of purpose structures this seemingly random collection of events and observations. In the presentation of the raw material of experience, Tristan sacrificed simple chronological order to emphasize her own reading of past events and to establish a certain image of herself.

Not only did she alter the order of her experiences, but she chose her narrator's pose deliberately for a desired didactic artistic effect. 'Florita', as she was called by her Peruvian relatives, was hardly as innocent as she seemed. Her stance as the naïve concealed (from herself and from her readers) the fact that as well as being the heroine of a Bildungsroman, as Tristan pretended, she was also persuading her reader as she gathered material for her dossier. This material was of two kinds. The first was provided by her role as observer, which permitted her to record her own experiences and that of others she encountered – the 'characters' as we shall call them. This aspect is symptomatic of Tristan's mode of perceiving reality. Many of her characters' experiences seem to have been stamped with a familiar form: their ill-received gift of themselves and their subsequent wish for revenge.

The other kind of evidence came from Tristan's use of a 'dramatized narrator'[11] whom she calls 'Florita' (her Peruvian appellation), and who is engaged in recording the reception accorded her own appearance in the narration, as well as her self-conscious view of her own destiny in the light of this interaction. The various stances assumed by the narrator (as observer, as dramatized narrator and as commentator) reveal the way in which Tristan was coming to terms with a certain perception of reality, and beginning to articulate her role as an agent of social change. No fixed form – mémoire, travel tale or political pamphlet – was ample enough to contain these purposes, and thus the author relied on all three.

The structure of Tristan's account blends autobiography and cultural history. As she moved on in time, especially after the 'recognition scene' with her uncle in which all her illusions shattered (at the opening of volume 2), Florita increasingly extricated herself from the web of family entanglements and, thus, from the past. (In all probability, it was only after her uncle's refusal to provide her with economic independence that she conceived the idea of publishing her journal.) After she broke with her family, she could become an observer of society, thus protected not only from dangerous personal involvement with the people she studied, but also from certain truths about her own motivation. The stance seemed to offer a refuge, and even power: 'I felt I was carried away by an unearthly power, which transported me to ethereal regions from which I could perceive the things of the world in their true aspect.' (*Pérégrinations* II, pp. 37–8)

But even as she revelled in this detachment and its safety, the observer was being shaped by what she observed – was, to use Wayne Booth's term, a 'narrator agent' who, although she 'produces an effect on the course of action',[12] is herself influenced by what she sees.

Volume 1 is held together by the author's presentation of the motivation and justification for her journey to Peru and her subsequent account of it. As we have seen, this account involved her in creating an elaborate self-image consistent with her motivation. Even though this process involved the narrator in a continual series of ruptures with various sectors of society in volume 1, the author was already establishing the one bond that would sustain her through volume 2: her concern with women's fate.

If Tristan was handicapped in certain ways because of her sex (as a woman traveller), it also provided her with a privileged position. First of all, her own experience and her perception of reality led her to undertake a task rather foreign to most travel writers, to make an inventory of the various institutions which house and, too often, incarcerate women: the family, the Church, and the state. Tristan was to discover that the land inhabited by most women was that of servitude.

Masquerading as a single woman greatly facilitated Tristan's exploration of woman's condition in Peru. When married women compare their bondage to her seeming liberty, the reader, knowing her to be a married woman under French law, thus shares in the ironic and painful truth of Tristan's condition.

As a married woman, Tristan knew that statistics were insufficient to describe the actual suffering of women. Therefore she was determined to lift the veil of privacy covering the reality of married life.

> If one considers the great number of crimes that are committed every day and that are beyond the reach of the law, one will be convinced of the enormous improvement in morals that would result from exposing private actions. Hypocrisy would no longer be possible, and perfidy, betrayal, and treachery would not, under their deceitful guise, constantly usurp the rewards of virtue. (*Pérégrinations* I, p. xxxii)

Thus in her preface, probably written after the book itself had been finished, she promised a full study of married life, a 'picture of the misfortunes that result from enslavement' (*Pérégrinations* I, p. xxx), as well as a study of all forms of the abuse of power. The connection between her own predicament and that of other women, of autobiography and cultural history, resulted in an unusual travel tale, one geared to social change, which viewed culture from the side of the oppressed.

But *Pérégrinations* was not to be an abstract study. Rather, as Tristan's perception of the society in which she found herself sharpened, so her understanding of her own situation changed. Moreover, she did not view the plight of women in isolation but as part of a social context, not as an individual predicament but as one common to all women.

A Universal Truth: 'Marriage is Hell'

Peru offered Tristan examples of women whose courage, strength and independence she could admire. By contrasting their lives to her own, she came to understand the cause of women's difficulties in the world. In her own case, as long as she presented herself as an unmarried young

lady or as a widow, Flora was well-received, but she 'was always ostracized when the truth was learned'. (*Pérégrinations* I, p. xxvii)

Even before the fateful encounter with her uncle whose coldness
'freed' her to become an observer, Florita's persona, in her guise as the
innocent, began to discover the plight of women. Her own experience
with Chabrié had taught her the dangers to which a single woman was
exposed, and left her with a cynical world view: 'There is no such thing
as friendship in the world; there is only self-interest in the wicked and
love in good men.' (*Pérégrinations* I, p. 121)

Florita's next two encounters were with the species 'wife'. First, in
the colonial sector, Florita met an ex-slave who had become the wife
of her master. Then, from the sphere of patriarchal domination, she
encountered an upper-class wife, her cousin's widow, Carmen.

The ship's first stop on the island of La Praya offered Tristan a
glimpse of colonialism of the worst sort: La Praya's economy was
based on a human commodity, the slave trade. Florita's innocence was
striking. She encountered Monsieur Tappe, a French colonial who to
protect himself from his slaves had married one. To make certain she
could not poison him, he forced this woman (his wife, the mother of
his children, and his slave) to taste everything she served him first, thus
guaranteeing his own well-being at her risk. When he accumulated
enough riches, he told Florita, he planned to sell his wife and children
and return to France. Florita, incensed by his proposal, asked 'But, M
Tappe, that girl is your wife, before God: she is the mother of your
children; and you would put all these creatures at the mercy of
whomever should buy them on the public square?'. (*Pérégrinations* I,
p. 69) Indeed, he would. From this encounter, Florita learned that the
condition of servitude in its various forms extended beyond the boundaries of France.

As dramatized narrator, Florita had her third and last important
encounter before she met her uncle. It was another occasion designed
to reveal her naïveté. When her cousin Carmen professed her hatred
for life in Peru, Florita responded with an innocent question: 'Cousin,
if you hate it so, why do you stay?'. (*Pérégrinations* I, p. 296) As the truth
came rocketing back at her, shaking her out of her Enlightenment
optimism, the economics of freedom became clearer to her. Carmen
stayed, the narrator tells us, 'by the order of the harshest of all laws:
necessity'. (Ibid.) Liberty, as Tristan already knew, is not the result of
free will but is based on economic independence, the pursuit of which
had lured Tristan to Peru in the first place.

Carmen told her a truth with which Tristan was already familiar: to
understand how much women suffer, one must have been married.
Marriage is 'the only hell' (*Pérégrinations* I, p. 298), Carmen informed
Florita. On the basis of the latter's naïve questions, Carmen presumed

that her cousin was single. Therefore, she painted a detailed portrait of the evils her cousin had presumably not endured:

> It is easy to see that you have never submitted to the humiliating yoke of a harsh and tyrannical husband, obliged to accede to his every whim, to bear his unfairness, his contempt, his insults; that you have not been under the domineering influence of a haughty and powerful family, nor been exposed to the sinister cruelty of men. Unmarried, with no family, you have been free to do as you please ... There are very few women in such a fortunate situation: almost all of them, married very young, have had their capacities stigmatized, impaired by the oppression that their masters imposed more or less harshly on them. You do not know how many long years of suffering one is obliged to conceal from the eyes of the world ... (*Pérégrinations*, I p. 297)

Ironically, of course, Flora had endured the very difficulties Carmen described, with the exception of domination by a patriarchal family, and the reader's awareness of Tristan's real position increases the dramatic tension of this scene. But Carmen's 'soliloquy' is so long that one is forced to question the extent to which Tristan is articulating her own view of marriage here. Surely she wasn't taking notes during the conversation. Indeed, at this point it becomes apparent that a definite ideological and artistic form is being given to the raw material Tristan found, that she has exaggerated Florita's innocence in order to illuminate her growing awareness, thus making less obvious its hoped for didactic effects on the reader.

Carmen's story was that of the homely woman sought after for her money. Having no alternative other than marriage or the convent (like many of her sex and class in France), she chose marriage. Carmen's handsome and rich cousin then abused and humiliated her by living with other women. When she complained,

> ... she was told that she should consider herself lucky to have a handsome man for a husband, that she should tolerate his behaviour without complaining, these people finding that the ugliness of the wife and the beauty of the husband were sufficient reasons to justify the stealing of her fortune and the indignities which he inflicted on the unfortunate woman. (*Pérégrinations* I, p. 284)

After ten years of such a marriage, when he had spent her fortune and had contracted venereal disease, he came home to be nursed by his wife, who undertook the task with vindictive satisfaction. He died 16 months later, leaving her, at 28, an impoverished widow. When

Florita met her, she had been totally dependent on her avaricious father-in-law for some twelve years. At 40, only her sarcasm and wit brightened her bitter existence.

After Florita's encounter with Carmen, whom she categorized as still another 'victime du mariage', Tristan concluded that, 'So, women here, because of marriage, are just as unhappy as they are in France; they also find oppression in the bond, and their God-given intelligence remains inert and sterile.' (*Pérégrinations* I, p. 299)

This statement shows that Tristan's narrator was not as innocent as she pretended, that she understood and was intent upon proving her interpretation of the situation of women in France.

Amazons and Nuns

And yet as the reader moves on to volume 2 Tristan's pretext for the voyage, the quest for her father's inheritance, is still supposed to provide the suspense in the narration. But from the prefatory material, the reader knows that the uncle had already refused this demand by letter, and therefore Tristan's purpose in going to Peru takes on a certain martyrist cast. If recuperation of her family name, status and wealth was doomed from the start, then her real objective seemed to be to untie the blood knot, to convince herself that she was completely alone in the world, just at the very moment she had discovered her family and origins.

Indeed, once these expectations were fulfilled, and her uncle had rejected her request, Florita, her illusions shattered, seriously and overtly began to compile her dossier. As she observed the comic yet barbarous civil war which threatened her uncle's destiny, she began to contemplate her own. In the process of taking stock of society's injustices, Florita was transformed from the innocent who asked questions into the seer who gave the answers; her examination became more systematic, for she realized that her own destiny depended on her appraisal of the options available to women.

The subject of her next encounter, the Ravanas, contrasted sharply with Carmen's example of kept womanhood. They lived as a community of women, outside marriage, under the code of polygamy. For them, ugliness was irrelevant. Their physical appearance had nothing to do with their function in life: they were 'the camp-followers of South America'. (*Pérégrinations* II, p. 121) Without this troop of women, reminiscent of the Amazons of legendary fame, the Peruvian army could not survive. They supplied sexual services and performed domestic tasks. More important, they were the avant-garde of the army, transporting all its baggage, the tents, and the children, in all kinds of weather and over rugged terrain. They searched the encampment site, set up camp, got all the provisions together and awaited the arrival of the soldiers. If they found no food available in nature,

> ... they [would] fall upon the village like famished beasts, and demand food for the army; when it is given them willingly they do no harm, but if there is resistance, they fight like lionesses, and in their ferocious courage, they always overcome the resistance, they loot and sack the village, carry their booty back to the camp and share it among themselves. (*Pérégrinations* II, p. 122)

Like Carmen, once it is apparent that their demands are not to be fulfilled, they prepare their revenge.

These women incorporated both the traditional 'masculine' and 'feminine' functions, as described by anthropological studies. They sewed, washed, cooked and nursed the children, but they also acquired food by hunting or stealing, lit fires, and carried provisions and arms. Indeed, they were self-sufficient. Coming from the Western world, where capitalism was establishing itself based on a division of labour between the sexes, Florita was amazed by these women.

> These creatures are totally out of the ordinary; they live with the soldiers ... are exposed to the same dangers and endure much greater ordeals. When the army is on the march, it is almost always upon the courage and fearlessness of these women ... that its subsistence depends. (*Pérégrinations*, II pp. 122-3)

Unlike Carmen's, the fate of the Ravanas was not tied to one man, nor was it dependent upon their appearance but on their capabilities. These women guerrillas offered Tristan hope for women. She found in them striking proof of 'the superiority of women among primitive peoples'. (*Pérégrinations* II, p. 123) The 'feminization' of woman began to appear to her as a process rooted in history rather than in nature.

Impressed by the strength and courage of these women, Tristan-the-narrator realized that women have been and could still be 'superior beings'. She wondered '... would not the same hold true among more advanced peoples, if a similar education were given to the two sexes? We must hope that the time will come when the experiment will be attempted.' (Ibid.)

Through the examples of womanhood she encountered in her exploration of Peruvian society Tristan analysed the role played by the family structure and the differentiation of the sexes in the subjugation of women. To her the Ravanas seemed to represent an intermediate stage between legendary Amazon women and women such as Carmen: they served men yet retained their independence; they had not been consigned to the reproductive or decorative sectors of society. Yet Florita never communicated directly with the Ravanas: as Indians, they remained for her an anonymous group whose lifestyle she could only observe. No one woman emerged from the crowd. For Florita it was as if they were a remnant of an earlier form of society, and thus communication with them was impossible.

Next our narrator observes another, more modern and less liberated collective, one which still functioned in Tristan's France: the convent. Florita examines this collectivity through conversations with the Mother Superiors of the two major convents of Arequipa, with the nuns themselves, and especially with her cousin Dominga who, after eleven years in the convent of Santa Rosa, had managed to escape.

The Ravanas had offered an example of the capacities of women, but not a real alternative. Within the limits of Peruvian and French society at that time, marriage with God or marriage with man were the only two options available to women. If the story of Carmen's fate indicted marriage and the family as structures which incarcerate women, Dominga's plight accused the Church as well as these. Under the cover of these recorded experiences and observations Tristan could examine both institutions, the family and the Church, in terms of their material and ideological effects. She discovered that their oppressive structures are as dangerous as the ideas they propagate. Dominga's story makes this as clear in terms of the Church as Carmen's had in terms of the family. Here too the sacrifice is followed by revenge, but this time it is society's revenge. The narrator's presentation of Dominga's tale reinforces its ideological function, so that it takes on the character of a didactic lesson, first for Florita, then for the nuns in whose company she hears it, and lastly for us.

Dominga's suffering in the convent is initially presented in terms of Florita's imagining of her cousin's incarceration and escape from Santa Rosa convent. Visiting the convent, Florita observes its atmosphere: nuns ruled by the vow of silence and by a Mother Superior whose greatest wish is to return to Madrid and re-establish the Holy Inquisition, and who regards the escaped Dominga as possessed by the devil. Consequently, the Santa Rosa nuns fear speaking of Dominga. Then while visiting the much freer convent of Santa Catalina, Florita finally hears the account of Dominga's escape (only later did Tristan actually meet Dominga and hear the story from her lips).

Dominga had consigned herself to the convent as the result of a humiliating courtship; the young man deserted her to contract a more prosperous match. Beautiful, rich, and only 16 years old, Dominga cut her hair and took the vow: 'In her despair she saw no other refuge but that of life in the convent.' (*Pérégrinations* II, p. 183)

After three years in Santa Rosa, Dominga came to view her humiliation more rationally. She now regarded the convent as a prison, not a refuge. In her holy readings, she discovered the story of a nun from

Salamanca who, on the advice of the devil, put the corpse of a dead woman in her bed in order to convince the religious community she had died, and made good her escape. Dominga began to plot her own escape along similar lines. Eight long years of planning were necessary. Finally, Dominga found those who would aid her. With great courage, she succeeded in acquiring a corpse, burning it in her bed, and fleeing. Only after two months did the truth come out, '[b]ut the nuns of Santa Rosa refused to believe it'. (*Pérégrinations* II, p. 192) They continued to insist that she was dead.

Dominga's triumphant escape had a tremendous effect on the three nuns of Santa Catalina from whom Florita first heard the tale. She imagined that before too long they would themselves attempt something of the sort. Not until much later was the terrible irony of the story evident. When Florita met Dominga, who was still very beautiful, she was surprised to learn what the latter's freedom signified: '... she lives alone; and even though she is related to the wealthiest and most influential families in the country, no one dares visit her, the prejudices of superstition have still that strong a power over this ignorant and credulous people.' (*Pérégrinations* II, p. 275) According to Dominga, life was worse for her after she escaped because of people's attitudes. For them she was 'still *la monja* ... the spouse of God'. (*Pérégrinations* II, p. 278)

Apart from its documentary interest, Dominga's story is striking because of the way in which Tristan presented it. The textures of the various points of view of the story – Florita's, Carmen's and finally Dominga's – weave a more suspenseful account than pure third-person narrative would have done. In short, this story represents the process of exploration itself and transforms the reader into the explorer, moving from Florita's imagination to hearsay to the final, verifiable source of information: life lived. By withholding the most significant piece of information until the end, Tristan forces the reader to share Dominga's incarceration, the intrigue of her escape and the reaction to it, before she provides Dominga's ironic perspective, 'The woolen veil to which I was wedded is still on my head.' (Ibid.) Dominga, although technically free, feels enchained because of public opinion.

It is only after leaving her father's family domain in Arequipa that Tristan-the-narrator encounters a group she perceives as a modern and independent collectivity. It is then, on her own, that she begins to draw her final conclusions.

Modern Women vs. Slave Women: The Economics of Freedom

Apart from the consideration of several individual women, such as Dominga and Carmen, the *Pérégrinations* is, as we have seen, a study of women in various sorts of collectives. The move to Lima permitted Tristan's inventory of women's situations to change focus: from a military collective bound together by the need for survival (the Ravanas), to a religious one tied by vows of renunciation (the convent), her focus now turned to the study of a more informal grouping whose codes permitted greater mobility and freedom – the upper-class women of Lima.

This modern and independent collective of women might, she hoped, offer a model for change. In contrast to the Ravanas' industry, the absolute idleness of the Lima women seemed preposterous. Yet, whereas the Ravanas represented an earlier stage of society in which women had been totally integrated into the production process, the Lima women symbolized the disintegration of this function in a more modern setting.

They represented woman's new status at the centre of the process of consumption, their idleness proving their husbands' intrinsic merit and wealth, a role Thorstein Veblen would later immortalize. Whereas the Ravanas' dress was functional, if ugly, the dress of these women was beautiful. But its function was to prevent work and to allow for only one form of mobility, via their appearance. Although their dress was purely decorative, it had a distinct advantage over that worn by European women: the floor-length skirt (*saya*) and one-piece blouse and head-covering (*manto*) concealed their identity, permitting them to pass in the street unrecognized even by their husbands. It appealed greatly to Tristan, for she recognized what it offered them.

Although Tristan did not emphasize the obvious comparison with European women, at this point in the narrative they begin to loom in the background as the collectivity that is the real object of her study. In her treatment of the Lima women, it becomes clear that European women are the counterpoint, but of course Tristan's study of both groups was the first step in her own quest for independence.

The women of Lima, she writes, were generally 'taller and with a stronger constitution than the men'. (*Pérégrinations* II, p. 365) This physical fact distinguished them from European women of the upper and middle classes, for whom strength seemed obsolete and unattractive, according to nineteenth-century ideological injunctions. Without apparent difficulty, the Lima women raised six or seven children each, but then they had one or two nurses helping them. Obviously, Rousseau's *Émile* had not penetrated Peruvian society yet: the motherhood, breastfeeding and child-raising role was not central to these women's lives. In Lima's aristocratic society, childbearing in no way interfered with women's freedom.

Two other customs further increased their independence. First of all, the Lima women did not take their husband's name when they married but kept their own. (This aspect must have appealed to Tristan: regain-

ing her maiden name in France involved a complicated legal process.)
More significant perhaps was the exchange system: in marriage, the man
had to prove his love by presenting the woman with a substantial sum
of gold, by which she became independently wealthy. Lima women
'... can see proofs of love only in the amount of gold offered to them;
they judge their lover's sincerity by the value of the offering.' (*Pérégrinations* II, p. 380)

With such an exchange system in operation, it is not surprising that
the Lima women seemed so independent and mobile to Tristan. Their
psychological freedom was based on their economic independence, and
was illustrated by the freedom their dress, the *saya y manto*, permitted.
In this case, Tristan omitted discussion of the other origin of their
mobility, for obviously the presence of servants allowed them to put
on their costume and leave the house freely, 'acting in every domain
with the same freedom of action as do men, who simply put on their
hats and go out'. (Ibid.)

Tristan's fascination with the apparent freedom of these women
seemed to represent her nostalgic wish to restore the status and independence of eighteenth-century aristocratic French women. However
Tristan did perceive that the power of the Lima women was transitory,
and an empty power at that. Based on their ability to seduce men, its
magical effects were insufficient for the establishment of a more permanent independence: 'If ever they abandoned that costume without
adopting new moral principles, if they did not acquire talents to
replace the means of seduction provided by their disguise, they would
immediately lose all their power.' (*Pérégrinations* II, p. 375)

This had been the plight of French women: the *Code Napoléon* reinforced a new family structure, thus restricting women's role. But
Tristan's analysis did not carry her that far. Her admiration for the
women of Lima turned into a critique based on her perception of the
proper role of women. In rejecting them as an example, she rejected
the aristocratic notion of womanhood based on the illusory freedoms
granted by pleasure and appearance.

Tristan-the-narrator thus recognized that the power and independence of the Lima women was deceptive and transitory. They misjudged
woman's mission. In the margins of her critique of them, she began
to describe the role she would choose to fulfil: '... instead of being the
guide, the inspiration of man ... if she is only interested in attracting
him, in ruling over his senses, her power will vanish with the desires
she inspired.' (*Pérégrinations* II, pp. 373–4)

Like Wollstonecraft before her, Tristan believed that women must
educate themselves if they are to obtain real power, the power to
change the world. Thus Tristan turned from the collective of Lima
women to conclude her study with a portrait of the woman who had
ruled Peru until the recent civil war, La Señora Gamarra, La Prési-

dente. Tristan was to study this powerful woman at the moment of her defeat, and she saved this encounter for last, probably to offer her readers a lesson about the pinnacles and pitfalls of power.

First, as if to expand her exploration beyond the upper classes, Tristan visited a sugar plantation near Lima. This visit, which parallels the earlier stop at La Praya where the narrator had viewed slavery for the first time, as an innocent, is one which allows her to draw conclusions; not only does she interview the slave owner this time, but also the slaves. Here, indignation is superseded by analysis, for the narrator now considers herself to be an accurate chronicler, 'a conscientious traveller'. (*Pérégrinations* II, p. 383) She wants to report the entire truth.

In this, the first depiction of the perspective of people engaged in labour, Tristan juxtaposed their plight with the easy life of those who ruled them. She now perceived the economic basis of oppression here and the connection between the lot of men and women. (Tristan's future proclamation of an all-inclusive proletarian International, in which she linked the two causes of feminism and socialism, is prefigured in these pages.) Whereas in earlier sections of *Pérégrinations* she had focused on the plight of upper-class women trapped by marriage, the family and the Church, here she at last discusses the foundations of society as a whole.

Her terrible discovery is that slavery is the origin of society's wealth and also the evidence of the unequal distribution of that wealth. She had not yet formulated her solution to the problem, but at this point her hatred of it crystallized. Tristan's observation of woman's sacrifice at the plantation echoes the one recorded earlier at La Praya. This time it is the mothers who wilfully sacrifice their children to protect them from slavery.

The visit to the sugar plantation offered Tristan many contrasts: the prodigious vegetation and the misery in the eyes of the slaves; the palace of the slave owner and the huts of the slaves. The unreasonable and dogged logic of the slave owner who, argues that without the whip he can get no work from his slaves, is demolished by Tristan's observation that since the slave receives nothing tangible for his work, it is natural that he does not work. To the slave owner's complaint that slave women were killing off their babies, Tristan found a fitting reply as she studied the slave women he had imprisoned for this act. They looked at her as if to say, 'I let my child die because I knew he would not be free like you; I preferred to see him dead rather than enslaved.' (*Pérégrinations* II, p. 418) This time the contrast drawn between her own experience and that of others makes her see that the forms of slavery she has witnessed thus far were limited.

On her way back to the bathing resort to which she had been originally invited, she encountered those she referred to as 'free workers', fishermen who risked their lives to eke out a living. In their example

she perceived the evidence of slavery's downfall: free men endure
'... such dreadful hardships, to brave such imminent perils to earn their
living; I wondered if there really was any sort of work for which slaves
were necessary, and if a country where there were men obliged to do
that kind of work to live did need slaves.' (*Pérégrinations* II, p. 419)

She would not fully understand the evils of the new law of economic
necessity she observed here in the lives of these fishermen until she
wrote her study of industrial workers in *Promenades dans Londres*
(1840), where she finally came to understand how capitalist slavery
could be even worse than the kind she had observed in Peru.

This meditation on work is concluded by her return to the Lima
bathing society, to the ambiance of the class with which she identified
most closely. Shocked by the inactivity of the rich ('*far niente*, pleasures
and intrigue dominate their lives') (*Pérégrinations* II, p. 421), she found
their existence as empty as that of the women of her class, the Limeñas.

Tristan Finds a Model and a Calling

The question of to what degree the chronology of events in this narrative reflects Tristan's actual experience, and to what degree it has been
organized for didactic ideological purposes cannot be answered for
certain, but it seems more than fortuitous that she concluded her
exploration of Peruvian society and its women with the study of
Señora Gamarra, La Présidente, the one woman who stood outside traditional patterns. This woman had tried unsuccessfully to rule all the
individuals and groups Florita had observed during her stay. Gamarra
is the point at which the autobiographical and historical concerns of
the more mature Tristan converged. From being a person with no
options, contemplating suicide (*Pérégrinations* I, p. 191), Florita had
advanced to the point where she could articulate a political solution
to her malaise. Thus it is appropriate that she concluded with La Présidente.

In a sense Tristan the writer had kept us waiting for this meeting
throughout the book. It is perhaps more significant than her meeting
with her uncle, and more space is devoted to it. Since the early days
in Arequipa at her family's home (in the early part of volume 2) when
the war broke out and all the generals and the rich men of the town
were coming to Florita for advice, Señora Gamarra, President of Peru,
had seemed attractive to her. She admired this woman, and began to
conceive of a similar role for herself. Indeed, she realized that as a
woman in Peru she would not be able to accomplish this alone, but
would need 'a military man whose strength of character and influence
over his soldiers would make him able to help me; make him fall in

love with me, further his ambition, and use it for all my undertakings'. (*Pérégrinations* II, p. 106)

She began to search for such a man, and recognized him in Gamarra's secretary, Escudero, with whose aid, she imagined, 'nothing would have been impossible for me'. (*Pérégrinations* II, p. 259) At this early junction, Tristan avowed the personal and vindictive nature of her political ambitions: through politics she could express fully her deep desire for revenge on the society that had abused her: 'After having been victim of society and its prejudices, to try in my turn to exploit it ... to become like them, greedy, ambitious, ruthless, totally unscrupulous'. (*Pérégrinations* II, p. 103)

But such an image was inconsistent with the one she wished to project. Carmen's advice, echoing that of women across the ages, appealed to her more: 'Florita, why should we women bother with the affairs of the State since we cannot occupy any public office, since our opinions are received with scorn, and since the high personages believe us only fit to be their playthings or their housekeepers?'. (*Pérégrinations* II, p. 108)

It was at this point, with the possibility of action so difficult, that Florita left Arequipa for Lima, taking up her study of society anew, moving inevitably toward a more acceptable, literary solution to her problems. Finally, dissatisfied with the description of the myriad forms of woman's servitude, Tristan sought a political resolution.

Now, at the end of her journey, a 'fortuitous' encounter with Gamarra in the hour of her political demise permitted Tristan to examine the dangers inherent in her own political ambitions. Ironically, La Présidente's dress marked the transition from the values of the old world to those of the new. When Florita met her on the eve of Gamarra's exile, she was surprised to find La Présidente decked out in very feminine and European finery – inappropriate, it would seem, to her character and function. Gamarra's dignity, her harsh voice, her stern look, all these characteristics seemed contrary to and compromised by this dress. Florita asked her why she was dressed like such a doll; Gamarra, conscious of her ridiculous appearance, replied that her sister had brought her the clothes that morning and pleaded that she wear them: 'These dear people believe that I could retrieve my position if only I would consent to wear clothes imported from Europe.' (*Pérégrinations* II, p. 434) Doña Pencha Gamarra herself knew that this dress, representative of the new European notion of femininity, signalled the final ebbing of her power. She wore the clothes into exile, where she died shortly thereafter.

Even at the moment of the eclipse of her power, for Tristan La Présidente represented an example of the true capacities of women. Although at the opposite pole from the Ravanas in terms of power, she, like them, offered a blueprint of the possibilities open to women. Both gave proof of women's physical and psychological strength and endurance beyond Florita's imagination, perhaps because both were remnants of an age that predated modern notions of 'femininity'. Unlike the Ravanas, Gamarra refused all activity connected with the feminine image: she participated in no domestic functions; and included in her rejection of femininity was her rejection of love ('I respond only to the "sighs" of the gun, to the words of congress, to the cheering of the crowd'). (*Pérégrinations* II, p. 454) Florita observed that ambition had replaced love. Gamarra exhibited none of the other 'feminine' traits of gentleness, humility, or coyness, and she was rather ugly as well. But, then, Tristan recognized that these are characteristics that have no function for a soldier, and even inhibit his work. Nonetheless, the *lack* of these characteristics compromised Gamarra's work, according to Tristan. She became imperious. The effect of her total rejection of the 'feminine' was that it infuriated the men whom she commanded. 'Her behaviour was not in keeping with the customs of the country and turned everyone against her' (*Pérégrinations* II, pp. 454–6) – causing her to lose the advantages of being a woman, and making her a number of implacable enemies.

Finally, this woman, who had been a good ruler, was overthrown. The lesson Tristan drew from her example was that Gamarra might have succeeded in accomplishing Bolívar's work 'if she had not been trapped in a woman's body'. (*Pérégrinations* II, p. 453) Thus La Présidente Gamarra's example produced an ambivalent response in the narrator. On the one hand, it reinforced her fear of public life. Yet she could not return to the other option; to choose marriage and family was impossible for her.

> I could not but shudder at the thought that at one time I had contemplated holding Señora Gamarra's position, What! I thought, such were then the torments in store for me had I been successful ... I would also have had to endure sufferings and humiliations ... Ah, my poverty, my retired life, and my freedom seemed infinitely preferable to me ... I felt ashamed at having believed for an instant that happiness could be found in the arena of ambition. (*Pérégrinations II*, p. 443)

On the other hand, she could not resist admiring the example of Gamarra and her sacrifice:

> ... her courage, her heroic steadfastness in the face of the innumerable misfortunes she had to endure, made the unfortunate woman appear larger than life, and my heart sunk at seeing that superior creature, victim of the very talents that set her apart from her

fellow creatures, forced by the fears of a cowardly people to flee her own country. *(Pérégrinations II*, p. 450)

Discouraged, Tristan decided to return to France, still cherishing the notion of the good she might be able to accomplish if she were to obtain power, but aware also of the sacrifice involved. She had finally encountered a woman she could admire in Gamarra, and witnessed the rewards of the sacrifice born of such ambition. She sailed for France, occupying the cabin which La Señora had once occupied; and at the end of volume 2 we see her once more dramatically posed for her audience, 'entirely alone, between two immensities: the ocean and the sky'. *(Pérégrinations I*, p. 462)

No choice or commitment had been made, but from her presentation of Peruvian society and its women, Tristan had already indicated which options she rejected, which institutions she must fight, and which image of herself she could admire. By her ordering of random experience, by a clear focusing on certain segments of that experience, Tristan presented herself and her reader with one possible conclusion: the necessity for social change. How this should be accomplished, how the ideological views, aesthetic concerns and psychological needs of Flora Tristan could best be served, had not yet clearly been determined.

4

In Search of a Literary Solution:
Méphis ou le Roman d'un Prolétaire

Tristan Returns to Find a Repressive Regime

As we have seen, Tristan's personal life in the years after her return from Peru was enormously complicated by her fight to remain independent of her husband and to retain the guardianship of her children. Perhaps no better measure of the ideological pressures against her position exists than that recorded in the advice given her by one of her closest friends, a rather iconoclastic priest, painter and mystic, the abbé Constant, later known as Eliphas Lévi. His devotion to Tristan is evident from the eulogistic passages in his preface to *L'Émancipation de la femme ou le Testament de la femme paria*[1] which he published in her name after her death in 1844.

Like Tristan he believed in the superiority of women, but for him the true mark of this superiority was to be found in women's capacity for sacrifice. In the mid-1830s, when Tristan asked his advice on how to cope with the increasing aggressiveness of Chazal, he advised: 'Be a woman and forgive!/ Be a mother and suffer, if need be!'[2]

Tristan rejected this more traditional form of female sacrifice (i.e., to the family), although she continued to share Constant's view of martyrdom as 'une folie … honorable'.[3] In fact, her personal problems and the example of Señora Gamarra's defeat seemed to strengthen her desire for some great act of sacrifice in the political domain. But the repressive climate in France on her return from Peru probably retarded such an initiative.

By 1835 the incipient workers' movement had been temporarily crushed by the 'Loi sur les Associations' passed in April 1834: this law reinforced the 'Loi le Chapelier', which had not proven effective enough in preventing the organization of workers or in protecting the 'freedom' of manufacturers. The immediate result of this new legislation and the increasing judicial repression that accompanied it was to drive the Republican movement underground. The years 1835 to 1838 were to be '… quiet years in comparison to the previous ones (1833–4)

56

... No incident comparable to the Lyons insurrection in '31 or the massive strikes of '33 shook the country.'[4]

Tristan had left France with her head still full of the slogans and the glorious example of republicanism offered by the July Days; she returned, in early 1835, just in time to witness the trials of the leading Republicans of France. During her absence, the government had 'handled' the 1834 insurrection of Lyon in the style of the massacre of the Rue Transnonian in Paris, which occurred the previous April. Further repressive laws were instituted against the press. Once these infamous September Laws were in place, calm returned; the legitimacy of Louis Philippe was established:

> For the royalty those laws were more than a precautionary measure. They stated that henceforth Louis Philippe's royalty was unchallengeable, therefore legitimate; and that statement which had not been made since July was in itself a revolution ... because of its fear of disturbance, it (the bourgeoisie) declared sacred and immortal a regime born of an insurrection.[5]

If Tristan did not at first choose to seek a political outlet for her energies and frustrations, there was still a socially acceptable way for her to manifest her feminism, her protest against the injustices done her, and to earn a living: writing novels. *Le Siècle*, one of the leading organs of the press of the July Monarchy, satirized the fact that many women were choosing this option, one of the few available and respectable means of economic independence and intellectual assertion open to them. 'In general, the emancipated woman is an author, she writes novels in which the heroine is always an angel.'[6] This satire was probably directed at George Sand. Other women followed her lead throughout the 1830s. Tristan's example is unique, however, for although she too chose to channel her vision of social change into the novel, her feminism went beyond the realm of 'la liberté passionnelle' that confined the aspirations of Sand's women.[7]

Méphis (1838), Tristan's first and only novel, would never attain the popularity of Sand's novels partly because its concerns went beyond the 'love' problems of one couple and because it provided a much richer presentation of the schizoid nature of the female experience during the July Monarchy in France.

Méphis as Symptom of Personal and Social Malaise

As stated earlier, the 'failed' literary work offers us an important index to the aesthetic and social values of a period. Studying it requires a special methodology that focuses on the way in which aesthetic criteria have been overshadowed by other concerns. Such a work requires a different kind of reading, and provides another kind of information than do more successful artistic endeavours. It can even be argued that 'successful' artistic endeavours owe their acclaim to the fact that they are in harmony with contemporary social and aesthetic expectations. When personal and political trauma leads to ostracism, its translation into literature may also result in a work more 'interesting' than aesthetically admirable.

In the 1830s, the resolution of personal trauma often coincided with the working out of 'public' trauma. Its artistic form resembled an unassimilated mass of heterogeneous elements in which the borderline between private and public is not always clear, especially in an age when individualistic ideology based upon the nuclear family was becoming more important. The conflict between the desire for personal greatness (and individual expression) and the urge for group identification (and social solutions) was perhaps never greater than at this transitional moment in French history, and its influence on unsuccessful literature of the Romantic period is profound.

Even if the author is intent upon presenting this repressed material in an unobtrusive way, often the reverse occurs: the troublesome material signals itself through certain presentational slips such as repetition, omission, and inconsistency. In much the same way as Freud was able to detect within the 'manifest content' of a dream a guide to its 'latent content', when confronted with the unsuccessful novel, the reader must not accept the author's logic except as pretext, and must read the text that exists beneath the author's overt intentions to discover the real origins of aesthetic 'failure', and the truths it has to offer us.

But if such a study is to lead further than to the sources of the troubled psyche of one individual writer, it must show the social and historical roots of these sources, and show why in certain periods certain material will be acceptable or unacceptable. The mode of sublimation is economically determined as well, for as Reich put it, 'Side by side with the subjective urge, the form which sublimation takes is, of course, economically conditioned; it is above all a man's social position which decides whether he will sublimate his sadism as butcher, surgeon or policeman.'[8]

In this sense, the unsuccessful work of art is a richer find than the 'great' one for those who would mine the rich field where psychological, ideological and aesthetic concerns meet and confront history. That *Méphis* is such a work, an amalgam of the unassimilated experience, imagination and fears of its author and its age is not surprising if we consider the heightened physical, psychological and emotional conditions under which it was produced. In the three months after her husband's attempt to assassinate her, Tristan finished this novel with a bullet still lodged in her chest, one she carried with her to her death five years later.

The Battle over Fiction's Purpose

If writing a novel allowed Tristan a certain liberty with regard to exposing, under fictional cover, the personal problems that haunted her, it also imposed upon her certain aesthetic constraints. For the novel was a literary form whose pedigree was still uncertain. An intense debate on the validity of the novel as a genre flourished, especially in the first decade of the July Monarchy. This debate revealed the aesthetic and social concerns of a group of critics and writers for whom artistic choices represented vital acts of conscience as well as creativity. Here is an example of the contemporary critique of the novel's lack of fixed rules:

> A novel is a book, a poem, anything you wish; it is the most extensive literary form, the most convenient because it has no boundaries and no rules ... Perhaps that is why a novel is rarely a literary work: trying to be everything is the best way of ending up being nothing.[9]

If Tristan had entered a field where aesthetic freedom seemed to be the order of the day, it was a freedom constantly under attack. For the mainstream of critics during the July Monarchy, the following view, expressed by a critic of the *Revue des Deux Mondes* in 1836, prevailed:

> That surge of pride ... somewhat less fancied nowadays, the novel little by little renounces the pretentions which have so often made it seem ridiculous; it shows a tendency to become again what it used to be, a book easy and pleasant to read, and a spectacle to be enjoyed by the fireside.[10]

Even as critics who represented 'le juste milieu' solicited an art that they could comfortably enjoy, writers who had been influenced by the Saint-Simonian wave of the early 1830s continued to believe in the social role of art, and viewed the artist as a kind of priest. Such a one was Émile Souvestre, who in 1836 proclaimed his aesthetic priorities:

> ... if we are not mistaken ... the mission of the novel ... henceforth will be to vulgarize progressive ideas, to give them shape and set them in motion, in order, as it were, to set them up as authoritative examples to follow. Like the ancient epic poem, the novel will offer models to the people, it will summarize scientific subjects for

them, it will tell them which gods they must worship and will teach them their daily *credo*.[11]

Others attacked this concept of the purpose of the novel. Satiric novels were written to lambast the profusion of artists who viewed themselves as saviours of humanity: 'At no other time', Jérôme Paturôt says, 'have there been so many saviours of humanity. Wherever you walk you step on one.'[12]

One of the most vocal antagonists of *l'art utilitaire* was the aesthete Théophile Gautier who claimed that 'An ode is too light a cloak for winter', that one could write odes or novels 'which lead nowhere', and that, in fact, 'beauty ... has no useful purpose'.[13] His was a minority view during the July Monarchy, although it turned out to play a major role in the elaboration of the art of the later nineteenth and even part of the twentieth century.

Of course, there was a danger in *l'art utilitaire*, as Gautier had recognized. Even Benjamin Constant, who occupied the middle position in this critical debate and favoured a novel that would leave the reader 'filled with more pleasant, noble and generous feelings than before he started reading it', feared that such a purpose might overshadow the aesthetic perspective: 'Morality becomes the goal to which the author will, even unwittingly, sacrifice likelihood of incidents and verisimilitude of characters. He bends the former, alters the latter in order to make them coincide with his goal.'[14]

If the battle lines were not always clearly perceptible, the importance of the debate was such that it completely obscured the question that had provoked it in the first place: that of the validity of the genre itself. Yet in effect, the formal problems of the novel and in some sense of history were clarified by this dispute. For as writers lined up on each side of the fence, they were reacting to the greater social dispute taking place in the streets. In the wake of the dissolution of antiquated social structures and disillusionment over the unfulfilled promises of history, generic literary hierarchies would also be threatened.

It is clear that Tristan herself was preoccupied with these questions, even as she created the social and aesthetic solutions to them.

The Structure and Purpose of Méphis

Méphis is a difficult novel to define because of the complex nature and purpose of its conception. Its structure betrays the author's inability to tell a single story. What is presented instead is a series of stories involving the two main characters, Méphis and Maréquita – stories that elaborate a project destined for incompletion.

Before the central story of the union of these two characters can be carried forward, each character must take possession of the other's past. Thus the 'first' possible story, that of their relationship, is interrupted so that the past history of each can be recounted. *Méphis* is indeed characterized by a structure of repetition and rupture that reveals the author's hesitation before the fact of completion. Perhaps, like her character Maréquita, Tristan was haunted by the fear of consummation hinted at in this description of her heroine: 'She shuddered at the thought that she might fall in love again and promised herself to evade such perils at any cost.' (*Méphis* II, p. 88)

The project of their union (which would have fulfilled the traditional reader's expectations) is proposed initially in a negative way, as if to remind us of a certain refusal to comply. From the start, Méphis wants to distance his motives from those of a lover: '... I am not in love with you, nor will I ever be. I wish to continue being your friend, your adviser, the physician of your soul.' (*Méphis* II, p. 56)

Implicit in Méphis' declared intention to disabuse Maréquita of a certain conception of the role of woman is the author's project to write a kind of feminist *Bildungsroman*, by which she can re-educate the women of her time. Maréquita will learn that 'the heart must be killed' (*Méphis* I, p. 61), and that she must renounce the idea that life is meaningless without 'a great and powerful love'. (*Méphis* I, p. 56) She must learn that 'We have other things to do' (*Méphis* I, p. 159) than to restrict the meaning of life to love. Perhaps because this renunciation of desire and of the traditional role of woman is so difficult, it is delayed for nearly 400 pages.

The double 'return to the past' also bespeaks a desire for self-justification, a need to adjust the past for public consumption. Moreover, it betrays the traumatic character of that past, as well as a kind of masochistic pleasure in re-living it.

In fact, the main body of the novel deals with the recent past of Tristan's problematical adulthood, but behind this cover lies the deep desire to return to the past which preceded it, before these complications arose. This wish is expressed in one of the opening scenes of the novel, in a conversation between Maréquita and her servant, Mme Bernard (who resembles in many ways Tristan's own mother). Mme Bernard is a widow who has suffered 'reverses of fortune' (*Méphis* I, p. 37), and who is the first to be accused of the 'mal' from which Maréquita suffers. The latter blames Mme Bernard for her situation: '... you could have left me in the countryside where at least I could breathe freely, where I was at peace, whereas in Paris I feel stifled, and everything annoys me.' (*Méphis* I, p. 30)

Tristan's own mother had taken her daughter to the countryside where she had raised her until the age of 15, at which time she took her back to Paris. Within two years she had married her off. This resentment is only mentioned once in this manner, but it underlies in part the origin of the desire to return to the past expressed in the structure of the novel: a need to fix blame.

The bulk of the novel, then, is taken up with the presentation and consumption of the protagonists' past. Méphis' story, told by him directly to the reader, occupies most of volume 1 (some 300 pages), whereas Maréquita's tale, written by her and given to Méphis to be read (and therefore summarized for us by the novelist), takes only one third of volume 2, or about 75 pages. The remainder of volume 2 is occupied by the problematic union of these two characters. Haunted by intrusions from the past, this union is finally consummated – first in a moment of adulterous passion, and then, in death.

What is unusual in this presentation is the elaborate way in which the action of the present must be prepared for by a retrospective absorption of each other's past, for in this way Tristan offers us three novels within a novel. The significance of the delay can be explained also by a wish for androgyny, or the union of the sexes, which seems to be at the centre of the novel. For Tristan, the whole of human experience can only be viewed when both characters' stories are combined. It is clear from the errors, repetitions, and reversals that characterize the novel's presentation that both protagonists represent Tristan herself.

Neither the characters nor the situations in which they are involved betray a concrete material dimension; instead, they seem to be ideological props for the psychological and social analysis Tristan herself was working out. Because she identified so closely with her characters' hopes, their desires, and their fears (even in the last section, told from the third-person, omniscient-author point of view), she was not able to distance herself from them enough to achieve an ironic stance.

On their own, the stories of Méphis and Maréquita are deficient and incomplete, but the author hints that if some synthesis could be found for their experiences and ideologies, a complete story could be told, and the characters would be able to overcome their 'mal'. The novel finally seems to demonstrate, however, that union into an androgynous couple is impossible because the two characters represent principles that are irreconcilable. In this sense, Tristan anchors the androgynous concept in history.

The stories of Méphis and Maréquita reveal the double bind in which women were caught during the transitional period of the July Monarchy, and indicate the deep schizoid split within Tristan herself. Maréquita refers to an 'inner struggle' from which she seeks to 'emerge free'. (*Méphis* I, p. 71) Ultimately this can only be achieved by projecting her fear and self-hatred onto the two culprits to whom she assigns responsibility for her troubles: the rich and the Church. Incarnated by two characters – Torepa, a rich aristocratic suitor whose advances

Maréquita deflects, and by Xavier, a powerful priest whose 'influence' Méphis resists – these forces 'fatally' unite to destroy all possibility of resolution, except in death (the ultimate negation). The project for an androgynous couple or a 'femme guide', uniting the two principles of masculinity and femininity, must be postponed until the next generation at least.

We have already seen the way in which in the prefatory sections of *Pérégrinations*, Tristan successively cut herself off from various segments of society until she stood alone. The self-presentations of Méphis and Maréquita also serve to reiterate and rationalize their isolation from society. Their nearly symmetrical autobiographical sketches are descriptions of the mistreatment and betrayal they experience. Both stories lead to projections of sacrifice in the future, consolidated by the central myth of the charitable gift of the self on behalf of the suffering masses, a myth that will permit retribution against the rich. As René Girard perceived a century later, 'One defends the oppressed only to better overwhelm the oppressors. One worships Good only to better hate Evil.'[15]

This rule applies here. The stories of Méphis and Maréquita are a compendium of justifications for this desire for vengeance and its satisfaction. Perhaps this is another reason no single story can be completed: each is a part of the 'main' story, the quest for revenge.

In this, her only novel, Tristan's purpose is confused, but if we superimpose the image of her protagonists' struggles with the self, the other, and society onto the labyrinthian image of Tristan's own personal and historical situation, we begin to see that *Méphis* cannot be separated from her two-fold project of justifying her past and seeking her future. But since the project for the future feeds on the accumulated resentment from the past, it is thus doomed to remain a dream-vision outside the boundaries of the novel.

Male vs. Female in Nineteenth-century Paris

Tristan's situation on returning to Paris was similar to that of many young artists of her generation, complicated by the additional fact of her gender. Although in her novel she expressed this experience mainly through the male eyes of Méphis, his account is probably an accurate transposition of her own experience. He felt first of all the shock of the indifference and anonymity of the huge metropolis:

One must find oneself in Paris, without money, family, or friends to have any idea of what a poor and unknown foreigner experiences. The Arab in the middle of the desert is less out of the reach of a helping hand than the foreigner lost in a crowd that brushes against

him in the streets without bothering to find out if he is hungry, if
he has shelter, and if that very day he will not throw himself into
the river. (*Méphis* I, p. 161)

Méphis sensed the loss of community due to the new individualism
that facilitated France's evolution toward capitalism. Like many of his
age he planned to succeed on his own: 'I resolved to rely only on
myself.' (*Méphis* I, p. 150) But he soon discovered the difficulties of self-
reliance: '... without recommendations, the man who tries to make his
way ... will encounter a great number of difficulties.' (*Méphis* I, p. 162)

Méphis resembled his generation not only in these 'sociological'
terms but also in carrying with him a psychological burden: in this age
of upward mobility, the family continued to exercise its influence. On
the one hand, he was haunted by the fear that his real situation would
be discovered (as was Tristan): '... I had a weakness: the fear that
prying eyes would see into me drove me away from everyone; I feared
that my distress, the misfortunes of my family should be known and
should be viewed as a crime imputable to me.' (*Méphis* I, p. 163)

Implicit in this statement Méphis recognized that in the new society
to be poor was a 'crime': now that the 'cash nexus' had replaced the
old value system, the moral value of an individual was estimated on
the basis of his economic situation. Méphis' description of this phenomenon prefigures Marx and Engels' analysis in the *Communist Manifesto*, written ten years later:

> Furthermore, as money has replaced feudal and religious powers and
> the power of the people, it has become the measure of all merit, the
> source of all distinction; – no matter how you acquire your money,
> it is the amount you possess that determines the consideration
> you will receive. (*Méphis* I, p. 223)

In part, this statement explains why Tristan should have sought to
portray her own desires in male dress. During the 1830s, it was nearly
impossible for a woman to acquire power (or wealth) outside marriage,
and socially unacceptable for her to want it. Instead, women were
supposed to seek the accumulation of *moral power*, although this was
worthless in the new scale of values, as intelligent women such as Tristan
knew. Social constraints led women writers to declare their rebellion
against the limits imposed on their sex, and to express their desire for
power through male protagonists. Through Méphis Tristan could
explore and expose French society:

> ... the desire to have an intimate knowledge of the various classes
> which comprise society, in order to be able to carry the project on
> which I was assiduously working. With that object in mind, I

resolved to take up as many professions as my capabilities and circumstances would permit. (*Méphis* I, p. 230)

The ambivalence with which Méphis (and perhaps Tristan?) undertook this project is emphasized by several contradictions. Méphis is referred to as 'le prolétaire' although his experience in that class is limited to six months as a dockworker. He supposedly writes his 'tableau de la situation morale et physique du peuple en France et spécialement à Paris' (*Méphis* I, p. 226) without leaving the domain of the upper class. Over the course of the novel, the nature of his desire is further clarified: 'I always felt sure that I would one day find myself in a position to be heard, and then I could reveal to the nations the tricks of all sorts of which they are the victims.' (*Méphis* I, p. 291)

Later this project of enlightenment is expressed in a manner that clarifies its origins in revenge and class hatred. Near the end of his narrative, Méphis announces he has become, '... the secret leader of an army of workers, whom I could at will keep peaceful or lead to insurrection' (*Méphis* I, p. 321). This boast, unsupported by any anecdote or concrete detail, jolts the reader because it seems to expose Méphis' real desires so clearly. It is clear that it is not just knowledge or power that Méphis seeks: he wants to exploit both of these forces for his project of revenge. In the account of his work experiences that follows, with each formulation his position is elevated and his project of controlling and manipulating others for his own purposes becomes more apparent.

Indeed, Méphis' tale is a series of encounters which reveal a basic structure: close identification, then violent rupture. The objects of these ambivalent encounters are not so much the various stations (or classes) he enters as the powerful individuals at the centre of them. Each encounter seems to represent a projection of the fears and desires of the author in her own quest for a class and sexual identity, and therefore points to a personalized, 'novelized' interpretation of history, in which retribution dominates.

This process seems accurately described by Anton Ehrenzweig's definition of schizophrenia in terms of cubism:

The systematic fragmentation of pictorial space which Picasso cultivated at the height of his cubist experiences, comes dangerously close to the schizophrenic fragmentation, and the self-destroying attacks on the self ... A schizophrenic attacks almost physically his own function of the self and projects the parts of his fragmented self in the outside world which becomes in its turn fragmented and persecuting.[16]

This description seems to represent accurately the dynamic at work in the novel *Méphis*. The process of 'fragmentation' Ehrenzweig describes characterizes the autobiographical narratives of both major

characters, but is manifested differently in each account. For the lives
of Méphis and Maréquita are not entirely parallel, although they have
one structural feature in common: both are accounts of 'rescues'
followed by betrayal. It is important to analyse this common aspect of
their stories because such analysis explains the deep resentment that
motivates the novel.

Méphis' account includes only a brief outline of the initial betrayal
he experienced that resulted in his expulsion from the upper class. Once
the pretext for a project of revenge is established, a series of interrupted
elaborations of that project follows. In his story the 'fragmentation'
occurs in the process of his interaction with various sectors of society
in each fragmented attempt at revenge; through each negation, Méphis
builds his energy for the final reprisal, which is itself incomplete.

Maréquita's narrative, which follows Méphis' story, is entirely
consumed by the betrayal itself. This is Maréquita's only story, and the
'fragmentation' takes place in assigning responsibility for the betrayal.
The return to the book's earlier theme of betrayal emphasizes its
central importance. This story must be told once more, from a woman's
point of view, before the protagonists' union can be established. If
Méphis' story is one of expulsion from the upper class – leading to
poverty, a quest for vengeance and the subsequent recuperation and
renunciation of class status – then Maréquita's tale is an allegory of the
betrayal women suffer because of their lowered status at the hands of
men: here there is no revenge, only a smouldering hatred that avenges
itself through martyrdom, the only recourse available to women for the
recuperation of their lost self-respect. Clearly Tristan reserved
Maréquita's story for last in order to delay the representation of
material closest to her own experience and, therefore, most painful.

But if these stories of the past were painful, in a masochistic way they
were also pleasurable, for they resuscitated Tristan's 'lost paradise'
and reconstructed her expulsion in a way that placed blame properly.
Near the end of his narrative when he rediscovers his first love,
Clotilde, Méphis admits the pleasure he takes in his nostalgic return
to the past, for the future was much more uncertain: '... vague fore-
bodings hovered over my future. It seemed to me that henceforth, I
could no longer find happiness except in memories of the past.'
(*Méphis* I, p. 300) Taken together, these stories of betrayal represent one
of the few accounts available of the fragmented, schizoid experience
of the powerless during this period when bourgeoisie was in ascendance.

Méphis' Revenge

To study the quest for vengeance that pervades these narratives, we must
analyse the significance of the fairy-tale manner in which they are delin-

eated. A brief summary of Méphis' original 'fall' from the 'paradise' of
the upper class is necessary:

Jean Labarre (later to be known as Méphis), the son of a poor
sailor in Dieppe, rescues Lord Arthur, the son of rich, English Lady M.,
from drowning. She in her turn decides to rescue Jean from poverty.
She takes him with her to England and raises him alongside her son,
giving him equal opportunities for education and status. Lord Arthur,
who should feel gratitude toward Jean Labarre (known in England as
John Lysberry), instead grows increasingly jealous of this usurper of
his mother's affections.

When John Lysberry meets Arthur's cousin Clotilde and a project
of marriage between the two is announced, the ungrateful and per-
fidious Lord Arthur appears and reveals the real (class) identity of
Jean Labarre, the past he has tried so hard to conceal. Clotilde's family
nullifies the marriage plans. Just at that moment, Lady M. dies. Jean,
no longer protected, returns to Paris, fatally expelled from the upper-
class world of luxury and ease that marriage with Clotilde would have
guaranteed. Lord Arthur later marries Clotilde himself.

In France, Jean (now Méphis) struggles for survival. Material problems
occupy him, but he carries with him a repressed wish, characteristic
of those who have been ostracized. The manner in which he expresses
this wish indicates that his desire for vengeance is ambivalent: it is con-
tradicted by a sense of gratitude and a deep hope for reconciliation. As
in the earlier description of Tristan's own lie about her marital status
in *Pérégrinations*, here again the expression seems contorted, the causality and attribution confused by a wealth of relative pronouns and dependent clauses: 'I simply could not contemplate killing a man whom I
had snatched from the jaws of death, and who was the son of the
generous woman to whom I owed my education.' (*Méphis* I, p. 150)

The autobiographical aspect of this event is nearly transparent.
Close study reveals how Tristan transposed it to this novel, for this
account of betrayal is a condensation of many of her own experiences.
She had been excluded in various ways from membership in the upper
class on at least three occasions: first in France, when she discovered
her illegitimacy and couldn't conclude her marriage with the upper-
class boy; then in England, where she was, as she put it, 'obliged to
accept a position as ladies' companion to two English ladies who travelled';[17] and finally, in her attempt to join her father's family in Peru.

Perhaps Méphis' ejection from proper society was placed in England
because its remove from her own family history made it less painful
to recount. Yet her job as a 'dame de compagnie' must have been one
of Tristan's most humiliating experiences. Sociological studies of the
treatment of such employees in the mid-nineteenth century show
that under normal circumstances in this, one of the few occupational

options available to women of good family, these women suffered from 'incongruent social status' even as did Jean Labarre:

> She was a lady, and therefore not a servant, but she was an employee, and therefore not of equal status with the wife and daughters ... She is not a relation, not a guest, not a mistress, not a servant, but something made up of all three. No one knows exactly how to treat her.[18]

One of the ways that members of the English upper classes sought to resolve this difficult problem of a master–servant relationship with an employee who differed from them only in worldly wealth and not in birth, manner or education, was to hire a foreigner who would more easily tolerate being treated as an inferior, for they believed that '... foreigners are less tenacious of their dignity ... largely because of their ignorance of English customs.'[19] If Tristan was chosen on this basis, she would certainly have experienced great humiliation; and it is likely that she did. Méphis' description of a rich family for whom he works seems to reveal the displacement of this repressed material: 'The two beauties reminded me of reptiles that charm animals in order to prey on them; and I considered the father and mother to be the most abominably depraved beings that our beautiful civilization had ever produced.' (*Méphis* I, p. 223)

The only means of escape from such a situation would have been marriage, which would have firmly established Tristan's wished-for status. It is likely that Méphis' experience is a transference of her own, but Tristan drew a heavy veil over these years of her life, and such ideas cannot move beyond the level of speculation.

In any case, the revelation (the unmasking of Jean's origins and his subsequent expulsion) lead him to dream up a more acceptable means of vengeance, one that would simultaneously permit revenge and strengthen the chance for reconciliation. This plan is articulated by Méphis' in his wish 'to make Clotilde miss me' (*Méphis* I, p. 158), for Clotilde represented his wish to identify with and be admitted to the upper class. He was

> ... prompted by the desire to show Clotilde the man she had rejected succeeding, by means of the sole power of his genius, the steadfastness of his resolve, not only in surpassing others, but in leading them and in being honoured. I wanted Clotilde to miss me, and perhaps, because profoundly I still loved her passionately, I hoped without admitting it to myself to marry her as soon as I would have secured a position. (*Méphis* I, p.158)

More than any other, this passage reveals the true nature of Tristan's desires and the basis for her own exalted ambition as well as that of her protagonist, Méphis. Before this difficult project to attain greatness could be achieved, however, a more accessible solution, a more direct form of revenge, was needed to release the accumulated hatred and resentment. In part, Méphis finds this in the debasement of Clotilde and, not surprisingly, he accomplishes it by unmasking her, an act that literally kills her. The memory of the paradise of his liaison with her and the betrayal that the rupture represented had stayed with him: 'The memory of Clotilde still lingered in my thoughts ... Clotilde was the object of all my plans for success and fortune.' (*Méphis* I, pp. 294–8) And, although he insists that he blamed her education and not her for submitting to her parents' wishes, the manner in which she reappears in the novel indicates the depth of resentment he feels.

The fatal reappearance of Clotilde occurs at a *bal masqué* in Paris. Tristan's description of Clotilde is reminiscent of the remarks that were made about Tristan by her contemporaries.[20] (I have placed the more discordant details in brackets.) '... the beautiful Andalusian woman [with blond hair] ... the woman belongs to one of the most illustrious families [in England]. Her story reads like a novel, and everyone tells it as he pleases ... She was attracting the attention of a host of men who looked at her with admiration.' (*Méphis* I, p. 301)

Indeed, Tristan was at this time frequenting the Paris *bals*; her portrait by ex-abbé Constant appeared in the social calendar of the period, *Les belles femmes de Paris et de la Province*[21] published in 1839 and edited by such luminaries as Balzac, Nerval, Hugo, Gautier, Janin, Houssaye, Sandeau, *et al*. The significance of this fragmented presentation of herself is ambiguous and surely over-determined. On one level it represents a variation of the narcissistic theme, but in this sense Tristan's identification with Clotilde must signify her deep sense of guilt and her need to see herself punished. Or does the degradation of Clotilde indicate her hatred of women – or her desire for them? Most likely, it indicates all of the above, and therefore a deep confusion about her sexuality.

In any case, Tristan's representation of Clotilde shows that the author is imprisoned in society's perception of the dichotomy of good woman/bad woman. If at first Méphis perceives Clotilde as a pure woman, 'the virgin on earth' who 'exuded the scent of chastity' (*Méphis* I, p. 301), he is soon disabused of his error. On looking more closely, he sees her as 'the vulgar woman offering the pleasure of the senses', a prostitute. (Ibid.) He is shocked by her revealing dress and describes her conversation as 'no less indecent ... than the display of her charms'. (*Méphis* I, p. 302)

Méphis approaches Clotilde and 'sous trois costumes différents' (*Méphis* I, p. 303) is able to obtain her favours. This is significant because it corresponds to the three identities of Méphis – John Lysberry, Jean Labarre, and Méphis; and indicates Tristan's curious fixation on the motif of the disguise. Méphis describes the scene of Clotilde's degradation and his mastery with great satisfaction. At last his vengeance is legitimate:

> The very woman who, a few years before had contemptuously rejected me because pride had silenced the love in her heart, because she was of noble birth and I the son of a poor fisherman; – that woman had now placed herself in my power, at my mercy! – I could treat her like a prostitute, she had given me the right to do so ... I only felt contempt and hatred for her, I decided to take my revenge. (*Méphis* I, pp. 301–5)

In this curious passage, it is no longer clear with whom Tristan identifies. That a woman, especially a woman who considers herself a feminist, should take such delight in the degradation and humiliation of a member of her sex, is a paradox. Is she chastising her sex, or herself? Or, is she allowing herself the pleasure permitted only to men by her society – to take women, to degrade them, freely?

Méphis describes his encounter with Clotilde alternatively as 'a horrible dream' and 'a fantastic vision'. (*Méphis* I, pp. 308–9) The dynamic that underlies it will recur throughout Tristan's *oeuvre*. Once the Other has been humiliated, then the author of his punishment can take pity on the object of his degradation. Even though Clotilde's status as a prostitute is vindicated by the account of her choice of this vocation as a means of rebellion against her detested husband Lord Arthur, even though we come to recognize her as another 'victime du mariage', still her unmasking results not only in her moral humiliation but in a physical state that approaches total annihilation.

Once this vengeful project of destruction is accomplished, Méphis transforms himself completely. Now he will rescue her: 'God has sent me to you to save you!!!' (*Méphis* I, p. 308) Of course, this generous stance of the saviour can be effected only after vengeance has been achieved, and serves to rehabilitate Méphis, at least in his own eyes.

The lesson he draws from the encounter is even more curious. It bespeaks an ideology of self-repression, of sensual annihilation, and defines the only freedom allowed to women as the joy of asceticism, the total sublimation of real physical being. By this moral, Clotilde's destruction is justified.

> ... one is free only in as much as one can control his senses, then and only then can one follow the inclination of the soul. Whoever lives only for his senses can no longer share in any spiritual joy; his oppressed soul is indifferent, and feels imprisoned ... it only aspires to being relieved of its mortal coil. (*Méphis* I, pp. 305–9)

In her moments of sublimated exaltation on her *Tour de France*, Tristan would employ the language of the last sentence to describe her experience.

The encounter between Méphis and Clotilde is characterized by a basic confusion over roles. Which character is the patron and which the prostitute? Méphis' gloating comment, 'I had succeeded in becoming her master and forcing her to buy my love-making' (*Méphis* I, p. 306), shows how closely the two are related. Indeed, the excessive violence which characterizes the description of the scenes of unmasking – in which the upper-class woman Clotilde is degraded still further, from a debauched prostitute into a wild animal – seems to indicate the over-determined aspects of this tale of unmasking and seeming mastery. Perhaps because of the intensity of Méphis' (and Tristan's) attraction to and identification with Clotilde (and the class she symbolizes), Clotilde has to be transformed into a 'wild beast', the aggressive energy displaced from its real source (Méphis) to her:

> ... she uttered a piercing cry, gave me a blow on the chest which almost knocked me down and threw herself upon me as if to strangle me! – She had a prodigious strength! She bit my hands, scratched my face, tore my hair; and at the same time she was screaming shrilly and fiercely like a wild beast. (*Méphis* I, p. 311)

The violence with which Clotilde reacts to his attempts to remove her mask from her hand indicates how charged the question of identification was, and reveals that the two characters may be merely alternate aspects of the same character. Clotilde's final subjection to a status of nothingness, led away by the police to an insane asylum, signifies the partially successful termination of the vengeful act, sanctified by the aegis of the proper legal authorities, and Tristan's own deep desire to remain within the society she so detested, and yet to take vengeance on it.

Interestingly enough, the story of Maréquita's betrayal involves a reenactment of this situation, with certain significant changes. For, if Méphis' account is the story of the discovery of class consciousness, then Maréquita's represents the discovery of the significance of her sexual identity.

Maréquita's Undoing

Maréquita's is the story of woman's fall. In this it differs from Méphis' account:

What a strange contradiction! An All-powerful marriage, sanctioned by law, is fiercely opposed by customs; every young girl abhors tyranny, laughs at the ridiculous husbands depicted by novels and plays, *yet, all of them want to get married, since it is, unfortunately, the only way stupid prejudices leave open to them to enjoy a certain independence which family and society deny them* [emphasis added]. (*Méphis* II, p. 204)

However, the loss women suffered on their first gift of themselves, in a society that valued virginity (in women of a certain class), was probably more traumatic than the more subtle and gradual loss of liberty they experienced in marriage. We might say that in this first gift, on what Freud would have called a phylogenetic level, a woman experienced a life-long sense of 'thralldom'; her body, whether she willed it or not, was now considered to be possessed by the first man who entered her. For, under the rule of the virginity taboo, society demanded 'that a girl shall bring with her into marriage with one man no memory of sexual relations with another'.[22]

It is in the recounting of her original transgression that Maréquita's story undergoes the process of 'fragmentation'. Like Méphis, Maréquita also had a project of marriage (to a gentleman named Don Olivera) that would have ensured her membership in the upper class. He is described in a manner that recalls the description of Tristan's second love in *Pérégrinations*: both men fear the enormity of woman's love – '... and every time [he] entreated her *to love him less*'. (*Méphis* II, p. 43) But the union between Maréquita and Don Olivera is not destroyed by this disparity in affection. Instead, and as in Méphis' case, the marital project is interrupted by the intrusion of a jealous third party. The chevalier d'Hazcal (his name obviously an anagram of that of Tristan's husband, Chazal) desires Maréquita for himself, just as Lord Arthur had wanted Clotilde. He manipulates events so that her union with Don Olivera is irrevocably ruptured by contriving to get Olivera imprisoned, and then convincing Maréquita that only by giving herself to the Duc de V., an elder politician, can she save Olivera's life! Then Hazcal's treachery extends even further. Under the pretence of 'protecting' her, he marries her – his real intention being to possess her legally, so that he can prostitute her. (Tristan charged that Chazal had tried to do the same to her, as we have seen.)

The structural parallels are striking. Here too a 'rescue' is central to the story. Whereas in Méphis' account it was his rescue of Lord Arthur that permitted his entry into the upper class, in this case the rescue is not the pretext for union but instead becomes the cause of the rupture. Both events are parables of the ill-received 'gift'. Maréquita returns to Olivera once she comes to recognize the extent of Hazcal's treachery, but Olivera is too proud to accept her 'gift' with gratitude. He returns her 'gift' by humiliating and ruining her, much as Lord Arthur had done to Méphis. 'On learning that he had been protected and saved by Maréquita, his male vanity, his nobleman's pride, was wounded so deeply ... that his love for her turned into hatred.' (*Méphis* II, p. 58)

The scene of Maréquita's reunion with Olivera is parallel in many ways to that of Clotilde and Méphis, but there are important differences. Unlike Clotilde, Maréquita is *not* a prostitute, although she has exchanged her body to purchase Don Olivera's life. But Olivera receives her as if she were, and proceeds to attempt to humiliate her. When she refuses to offer the expected sexual favours, he tries to rape her. This last act leaves her with an indelible sense of his betrayal: 'Olivera's brutal behaviour and his monstrous ingratitude ... this deception left a deep anger in her heart.' (*Méphis* II, p. 87) Like Clotilde, at the end of the encounter she remains frozen, immobile. But this humiliation and degradation are only the last steps in the process. First Maréquita must discover that both of the acts by which society symbolically grants adulthood and selfhood to women – sexual union and legal marriage – result instead in a relinquishing of the self and servitude to a new master. From this perspective, man takes the place of Eve, and a new version of the story of the Fall can be written: it is he who tempts woman to commit the 'original sin', the giving of herself, for which she is to receive so little in return. It is in this first betrayal that woman's hatred of man originates.

The reaction of the two major characters to their ejection from 'paradise' is dissimilar, and reflects Tristan's accurate perception of the way in which sexual identity prescribed behaviour. Méphis responds with a project of revenge, to be achieved through regaining his lost status on his own; Maréquita emerges from the deception with her sense of failure and futility reinforced. As she says, '... our souls had not in the least been involved in what we had believed was love; unfortunately we almost always come too late to that realization, and it only serves to poison our existence.' (*Méphis* II, p. 151)

Her knowledge contains the seeds of a double hatred: of the Other who has tricked her, and who is unworthy of the sacrifice; and of the Self, who allowed the trickery to occur, who is constantly being robbed of 'ses biens'. She consequently does not seek further risk, but seeks to maintain what she still has left by withdrawing to a safe place, by avoiding all involvement. Already, Tristan seems to say, the lines that bind male and female fate have been drawn.

By Maréquita's gift of herself, the 'rescue' seems to have been accomplished, but she finds herself doubly enthralled: she has awarded her virginity to a man she doesn't love, the Duc de V., and her hand in marriage to one for whom she feels no affection. Later she describes the legal contract binding her to Hazcal in words Tristan herself often used to describe her own situation: 'I am indissolubly bound to the contemptible being who has so ignominiously deceived me.' (*Méphis* II, p. 69) But even more than she resents men Maréquita comes to resent the Church, which sanctifies this right to subjugate woman: '... the Roman Church, by making marriage an indissoluble union, and keeping for itself alone the privilege of dissolving it, made a slave of woman and placed her under the protection and the domination of the priest.' (*Méphis* II, p. 55)

Maréquita's experience seems to encompass the entire realm of possibilities available to women, for whom the exchange system is based on sex and reproduction. She is the proof of her own assertion that woman 'is considered by man as solely intended for his pleasure and for reproduction'. (*Méphis* II, p. 56) She is successively wife, prostitute, rape victim, and a pious woman. Once their stories converge, Méphis will try to transform her into a *femme forte*, capable of acting instead of reacting, of expressing her passions, but because of the false education given her by the Church, Maréquita will be unable to achieve the perfection Méphis seeks in her.

Ironically, it is only through her experience as a 'real' prostitute that Maréquita seems to feel that a fair exchange has been accomplished. Toward the Duc de V., who takes her virginity (and saves Olivera), she feels gratitude. Is it because he is a representative of the aristocracy? Is it because their exchange was without pretence or trickery? Although the sexual experience itself is represented as traumatic ('Maréquita experienced the most agonizing mental tortures one can imagine, it was as if her soul were stifled') (*Méphis* II, p. 58), the duke himself is presented as a generous person who really cares for her: he insists on giving her 'a life annuity'. (*Méphis* II, p. 61)

In some ways it is obvious that the duke represents for Tristan the generous person she had hoped to find in her uncle Don Pio. Despite his refusal to recognize her legitimacy, she probably continued to feel a kind of Oedipal attachment for him. In the novel, Maréquita has the Duc de V.'s child. Conceived outside marriage, the child is nonetheless given the duke's name and his protection. Significantly the birth takes place in Spain, the site of Tristan's parents' illegal marriage. The account transcribes rather transparently Tristan's own complex about her birth and fulfils her own wish for legitimacy.

Thus, as in all the encounters in the novel, this one has been overdetermined. Although she feels for the duke 'a feeling of dread and revulsion' (*Méphis* II, p. 60), because he has taken her prized virginity outside the proper realm of exchange, that is, love, he is one of the few men who treats her decently.

Méphis has a strikingly similar experience with a rich duchess, his patron's wife. Probably also his first sexual venture, it is not characterized by duress; nor is his body an object of barter. For him, too, it is the occasion for a peaceful interlude. A child is also conceived of their adulterous union. Guaranteed her family's protection, it enters the upper class legitimately at birth.

A curious pattern of resemblance and dissymmetry distinguishes these accounts of adulterous alliances. In these two exchanges, sexual liaison is portrayed as the only viable means of entry into the upper class. For Maréquita, the entry is more violent: the Duc de V. succeeds in taking her virginity against her will. Méphis' more peaceful entry is accomplished by his liaison with the duchess, who is represented as a Madonna but is in fact a saintly older woman who gives birth to Méphis' child. Transposed to the world of visual arts, this birth leads the duchess to transform Méphis' painting, the *Femme guide*, into a Virgin Mary who more closely represents her own vision of womanhood.

The disparity between Méphis' and Maréquita's case is striking. Its significance is revealed later in the narrative, indirectly, when the stories of the two major characters converge. In the final sections of the novel, Méphis' desire to transform Maréquita into a living version of his painting, the *Femme guide*, is evident. The results of his effort remind us of his earlier liaison. Maréquita comes to resemble the Virgin Mary, and rejects the life of action and pleasure for one of sacrifice and renunciation.

There are also striking parallels in the accounts of the marriages of the two main characters. Maréquita's experience as wife (to Hazcal) is much less positive than her experience as prostitute. At first, she feels grateful to him for having arranged Olivera's rescue (through her sacrifice to the Duc de V.) and for saving her reputation by covering her with his name in marriage. She feels she should '... show him at least some gratitude. Despite all her efforts, her heart, as if instinctively, refused any expression of affection, and although living under the same roof, she saw very little of her husband.' (*Méphis* II, p. 64)

Thus, in the one realm of female experience in which sexuality was considered legitimate, there was a total absence of contact.

Méphis is also the victim of a 'mariage de convenance', and like Maréquita refuses his legitimate wife's demands for intimacy. Both of these marriages, based on exploitation and not on true sentiment, are the sources from which the agents of fatality arise: the hatred and resentment felt by Hazcal and Méphis' wife hasten the tragic dénouement of the novel.

Maréquita at first remains with her 'vieux père', whose title at the outset of the story is 'grand-père'. (This seeming error of the transformation of *grand-père* to *père* is significant. At birth Maréquita's family consisted only of a mother and this grandfather.) Soon, however, she discovers that her antipathy to Hazcal is well-founded: he had invented the plot to endanger Olivera's life in order to capture Maréquita for himself and prostitute her to pay for his gambling. Maréquita's fury is unleashed on discovering Hazcal's trick. Tristan's description of her reaction seems excessive: 'Her hair stood on end ... then her mind started to wander, she had the impression of being dragged down by a fallen angel into a loathsome abyss; she could hear the hissing of serpents – the sickening fumes of hell sent her senses reeling.' (*Méphis* II, p. 66)

This description, characterized by religious and sexual symbolism, reveals her fear of being consumed by the Other. However, it occurs outside any *sexual* context, not at the moment of her ignominious gift to the Duc de V. nor of the attempted rape by Olivera, but instead at the instant she discovers Hazcal's real intentions, and his betrayal of her.

The only other nightmarish description of this kind occurs toward the end of the novel, when Maréquita again feels that the exchange is unfair, that she is being betrayed and used. The similarity of expression is striking – again it is marked by the confusion of religious and sexual imagery. The nightmare vision returns to haunt her when she suspects Méphis' infidelity, and fears that her boundless gift of her love to him will not be returned in full:

> ... a single thought takes possession of her mind; it is an evil spirit relentlessly pursuing her; he encircles her with serpents he holds in his hands, hisses in her ear words that further intensify her ardour; shows her in the distance the enchanting prospect which the *unfortunate woman desires, which she so fervently longs for, but which is always beyond her reach* [emphasis added]. (*Méphis* II, p. 161)

This time the vision is linked by the narrator to the earlier event of her original gift: 'We have already said it, since the fatal night when, in order to save her lover, she had given herself to the Duc de V. ... she would at times behave in a manner akin to madness.' (Ibid.)

What is established here is that for Maréquita (and for Tristan) woman's original gift of herself will *never* be received with the appropriate gratitude. It will always exceed what is demanded and therefore be doomed. Maréquita's description of her love for Olivera predicts this fatality: 'My love for you was too great and could not be satisfied on this earth.' (*Méphis* II, p. 52) Instead, on an individual and an institutional basis, this love will be requited only by condemnation and betrayal. Yet woman will always seek to establish the ideal exchange, one in which she is not betrayed, in which her gift is fully appreciated. In a materialist society that provides an unequal terrain for the battle of the sexes, martyrdom is certain for the kind of woman whose 'vision du monde' is based on this parable. It is the only way by which woman can assure her divinity even while she is being degraded.

And yet woman is condemned to try constantly to re-establish her original innocence and, thereby, to reconstitute the value of her gift. So it is that when Maréquita, fleeing from Hazcal, returns to her true (and first) love, Olivera, she conceives of herself as a virgin once again 'in as much as it was not of her own free will that she had spent the night with the Duc de V. ... she was forced to do so.' (*Méphis* II, p. 74) Yet in Olivera's view she is no more than a prostitute: since she is already soiled, he determines to use her as well. Thus, the man for whom she has sacrificed herself totally decides to take her by force. In what must be one of the few representations of rape in nineteenth-century literature, Tristan presents her heroine '... bathed in sweat, her temples ablaze, her pulse throbbing, her hair a mess, her clothes dishevelled.' (*Méphis* II, p. 75) Thus the final rejection of her original gift convinces Maréquita that, as Tristan was to put it later in a letter, 'All is deception with men nowadays.'[23]

In order to avoid this deception, Tristan recognized that it was necessary to avoid danger, to repress her need to love. Recurring statements in *Méphis* underline the difficulty of the struggle against the erotic self, especially after the original betrayal: 'From the age of 16, Maréquita had successfully fought her ardent nature and her intense need for effusiveness and love.' Other descriptions underline the difficulty of the self-repression: '... she shuddered at the thought that she might fall in love again and promised herself to evade such perils at any cost.' And: 'The unfortunate woman had been so deeply hurt at the time of her first love that she dared not give free rein to her ardent nature.' (*Méphis* II, pp. 158, 88, 146)

Utopian Players

Méphis offers us a rare example of the shape and texture of a *Bildungsroman* written by a woman during the 1830s in France. If the novel was technically limited by Tristan's own distance from the real work-a-day world, perhaps her lack of experience enhanced its other aspects. By her refusal to immerse her character in one milieu, she expanded the novel's scope. Her attempt is important because it provides a compendium of the various illusions and deceptions which her generation faced. Moreover, by her decision to portray the active principle – the character who learns through experience, as a male – she accurately reflected the split consciousness with which a woman author would have to approach the task of writing a *Bildungsroman* in a society whose sexual division of labour was becoming increasingly well-established.

If we study the two narrators' tales closely, it becomes clear that Méphis represents the 'reality principle' for Maréquita. As the male he has greater mobility; he can test all her theories out in the society from which she has withdrawn. Successively, his experiences shatter Maréquita's illusions, leaving intact only their common 'illusion', that of the Mission of Woman.

First of all, when he returns to Paris, Méphis seeks to become a journalist. Besides his desire to write about his observations, he shares Maréquita's Saint-Simonian illusion about the power of journalism and of art. 'As for frightening the powerful, I can assure you that they are very successful in doing so; caricatures, satires, plays are the only restraints capable of curbing the powerful of the earth.' (*Méphis* II, p. 33) But when Méphis tries to enter the world of journalism, he finds it corrupt and unworthy of his efforts. He condemns it, although he continues to conceive of it as a realm in which he might manifest his will to power and influence, much as did Tristan herself.

> ... but the latter (newspapers) were fearful of my strong words; the truths that I revealed seemed revolutionary to them, and either because they had serious objections, or because my courageous style exposed the triteness of theirs, or because my point of view, too lofty for the usual mediocrity of their paper, frightened them, they categorically refused me a place in their columns ... they stole my ideas ... and reduced them to their own level. (*Méphis* I, p. 219)

The state of journalism was also documented by Balzac, who showed in *Les Illusions perdues* (Lost Illusions)) the disparity between the hopes it nurtured in the young generation and the deception and resentment it engendered.

Tristan's main characters, Méphis and Maréquita, also share an illusion about the power of art. Maréquita believes that art offers real hope for social change, and defines it as 'the only brakes that can contain the powerful of the earth'. Therefore, in the properly organized society, 'artists would be the leaders and guides'.(*Méphis* I, p. 33) She believes in the power of art to change the world, but she has had very little experience. Apart from a few allusions to collaboration with her artist-friends, only one example of Maréquita's experience of art is given. It is perhaps the only completed *story* in the book, and represents Maréquita's only entry into the realm of 'work' (or art).

This scene opens the novel but remains outside of it, almost like a vision of utopia, and is the occasion on which Méphis first sees 'la belle Maréquita', at an aristocratic *soirée* where she exhibits 'the magical power to captivate her audience at will'. (*Méphis* I, p. 9) In this 'apparition', Maréquita's beauty, her voice, her song and her gaze make her seem to be 'in communication with Heaven!!!'. (*Méphis* I, p. 13) Her eyes 'flashed fire!' and she seems to incarnate ideal beauty and to personify the romantic artist *par excellence*, a superior being, inspired.

She sings three songs. The first, 'A Young Girl's Heart', makes all the young women in the room stand up, their eyes filled with tears, their beings charged with emotion, almost as if they were at a Saint-Simonian meeting. The next song, 'The Cry of the Masses', a 'call to the courage of the oppressed' written by a young Polish patriot, entrances her audience: 'the more enthusiastic ones tried to touch her to make sure she was a *human being*.' (*Méphis* I, pp. 12,11)

If the first two songs have feminist and socialist shadings, the last song represents the apotheosis of the romantic malaise. Unlike the first two, it incarnates an anti-social strain. Called only 'The Daughter of the Ocean', it depicts the martyrdom of the romantic artist, condemned to ostracism, isolation and anonymous death, consumed by self-pity and self-absorption, 'to be misunderstood and sorely tried'. (*Méphis* I, p. 15) Sung in Spanish, this song represents the plight of Tristan herself, the problem of her name: her wilful concealment of her identity ('I was called the daughter of the Ocean'); her illegitimate birth ('do not ask where I come from'); her time of birth ('I was born in the midst of the storm' [the French Revolution]); her sense of being superhuman ('Let no one speak to me of love. I do not belong to this earth'); of being unable to communicate: 'My affections and thoughts/Are unknown to the inhabitants:/I do not understand their language,/They cannot understand mine.' The refrain that runs through the song, 'I leave no trace behind me' (*Méphis* I, p. 15), refers to the fear of anonymous death, the desire for immortality.

Maréquita's songs thus range from the subject of women, to that of revolution and back to the self, and so represent the inherent contradictions within Romanticism itself. Although the novel's first scene seems to promise a conventional Restoration novel, it contains many odd elements. For Maréquita is not represented merely as a beautiful woman; she is also an artist and in a sense therefore a 'messiah'.

And as the Romantic artist *par excellence*, she suffers from an undefinable and incurable malady. She has no connection with the material world and lives on the pension provided her by the duke. While others regard her as an 'être d'élite', she is told, 'God showered his gifts upon you so that you should guide others and not be guided.' (*Méphis* I, p. 69) Still, Maréquita has no direct experience with the art world outside of this enchanted aristocratic circle: she appears, she intoxicates her audience, she disappears.

In this first scene, Tristan seems to subscribe to the contemporary 'utopian strain of mesmerism' that influenced Fourier, Saint-Simon and Owen as well as the Romantic writers, because it provided 'the richest source of the irrational', a facile means of achieving power, or the illusion of power. The belief that 'the mind's faculties could be read in one's face and could bring others under one's influence by projecting fluid from the eyes'[24] was a source of fantasy for writers such as

Gautier, Hugo and Balzac, who, alongside the utopian mesmerists, were able to construct a new hierarchy of power and faith based on this mysterious gift of influence existing outside the realm of wealth or birth.

Yet, although Méphis shares Maréquita's gift, the power to dominate others 'par le regard', when he tries to exercise it in the world of art, he has less success than she. But her limited experience in this milieu hardly prepares her to critique it. Méphis would immerse himself more fully.

Art and Progress

If his first ostracism from 'paradise' occurs through no fault of his own, Méphis initiates the second. For in the world of art, the stratum of society he enters next, power cannot be exercised on the basis of birth; ideas and skills are the foundation of its hierarchy, and the value of these is much more relative. Here at last he can demonstrate the superiority he feels is rightfully his. But ironically in this novel, Tristan's first real venture into the realm of 'art', her major character attacks the tenets of the artistic milieu and breaks with it.

If Maréquita's singing at the opening of the novel represents the 'successful' functioning of art as a means of overpowering an audience, in order to influence them in the right direction, Méphis' experience in the art world results in the opposite: expulsion and denunciation. Maréquita triumphs with her superiority and her exclusivity; Méphis tries to do the same. The presentation of his rupture with the artistic community in the chapter 'Atelier de Girodet' is intended to prove the worth of Méphis' own excellent but misunderstood qualities.

In assessing Tristan's sources for the 'Atelier' chapter, it should be noted that she had a long-standing connection with the art world. Her husband André Chazal was a lithographer, and her first job had been as an 'ouvrière coloriste' in his studio. It is possible that through her brother-in-law, a minor painter of the period, she had come to know Girodet. Also, in the 1830s some of her closest friends – the ex-abbé Constant, Ganneau and Traviès, for example – were minor painters. (Each is known to have done at least one portrait of Tristan.) Moreover, one of her closest friends, Jules Laure, who is said to have painted the only portrait of her she liked,[25] was a student of Ingres.

Méphis' entry into the art world is depicted in a curious manner that reveals Tristan's confusion about her own sexual identity and that of Méphis. Méphis first enters the studio as of his niece's guardian. Before long, the niece, who was meant to be Girodet's model, has vanished and Méphis himself has become the master's model. Only in the third stage does Méphis become a painter. First his status is that of *mother*, then, of sexual object. If the pretext for his first transition is odd, then the representation of Méphis as model is even stranger. Not only are feminine qualities attributed to him, but the manner in which he poses for Girodet, and the latter's fascination with his beauty, seems rather odd.

This sequence bears close resemblance to Tristan's own description of her desire to be properly portrayed. In one of her letters to her painter friend Traviès during this period, Tristan refers to her desire to be represented: '... one of my greatest desires is to have a close likeness of myself painted. That is why I had it done more than 20 times, and 20 times it was a failure.'[26] In the novel, Méphis insists too much on the opposite desire: '... even though being a model was totally antithetic to my active and restless nature, I pretended having an insatiable desire to see myself painted in every position. I would sit for hours.' (*Méphis* I, p. 171)

In fact Tristan was possessed by an insatiable desire to see herself represented. She described her concern that Traviès capture her likeness: 'We shall have to spend long hours talking about various subjects so that you may fully grasp my character.'[27] Indeed, Tristan's desire to be represented was so intense that it seems to signify a stronger urge than the need to 'see' herself; perhaps, in reality, it derived from the ultimate narcissism, a desire to possess herself. From this perspective, the novel *Méphis* represents a playing out of the many contradictory aspects of her personality and a mirror of her confusion about her sexual identity.

After the sequence as a model, Méphis is somewhat arbitrarily 'transformed' into an art student. At first, he views this experience positively. He has replaced his desire for Clotilde (and the upper class) with the desire to create: 'Clotilde had faded from my memory ... the exhilaration of the artist had so deeply penetrated my emotional faculties.' (*Méphis* I, p. 176)

Soon the reason becomes clear. As an artist, Méphis has a power and a freedom he never had before: 'How can I describe to you the happiness and exhilaration I felt at finding myself in possession of two large canvasses on which I was free to draw all that my mind had conceived? ... those months were perhaps the only happy ones I ever spent in my life.' (*Méphis* I, p. 174, 176)

The positive aspects of this experience are short-lived, and culminate in a duel over aesthetic priorities. Méphis espouses the Saint-Simonian conception of the role of art and of the artist:

To my mind the arts are the means of communication between God and man; art is religion – prophets, poets, sculptors, painters, musicians are its priests! Masterpieces, the Revelation! For me, religion is *teaching*! ... to pursue art for art's sake is to separate oneself from the Creator and His creation, it is to renounce imitating God's marvels, which can only be approached through the harmonious connections between the useful and the beautiful. (*Méphis* I, p. 171)

Méphis' tenacity and the insistence with which he asserts the supremacy of his ideological position result in a painting contest in which he poses his visual representation of his theories against that of his rivals, the rest of Girodet's students. For Méphis, as in Tristan's own experience, it is the case that 'They all were always against me.' (*Méphis* I, p. 172)

The dispute is ostensibly between two schools of aesthetics: 'l'art pur' versus 'l'art utilitaire'. To depict the quarrel between these aesthetic doctrines in the visual arts, Tristan transposed the debate that was actually taking place in the world of letters. For the dispute in the realm of art was situated mainly within the area of technique, rather than that of content, and was between advocates of colour, led by Delacroix, and advocates of line, led by Ingres.

The paintings of Louis, Méphis' personal enemy and Girodet's favourite student, seem to be a composite of the work of both Delacroix and Ingres. Louis' two paintings, which respectively symbolize 'man: strength' and 'woman: pleasure of the senses', deal with subject matter that interested these two masters: in the one case, a man taming a horse, in the other, a Venus, an odalisque.(*Méphis* I, p. 160)

It is important to observe the moral terms in which Méphis expresses this aesthetic debate. We learn nothing about the style, the line or the colour, of Louis' paintings. All reference to technique has been omitted. Only the subject matter is described and we have to infer the rest from the moral indignation with which this is accomplished. Méphis' manner of reproducing the painting verbally transcribes an *angoisse* that seems excessive to the situation. Overt sensuality in him evokes a puritanical outburst, especially in the description of the *Venus*, in which a seemingly objective description turns into a moral judgement:

One of the pictures represented a young man of gigantic size, taming a wild horse; the other a naked Venus or an odalisque, reclining on black satin pillows; in the background was a sumptuous red velvet curtain with gold fringes and tassels; the nude was surrounded by splendid incense burners whose aromatic whorls of smoke lent an atmosphere of voluptuousness to the picture; vases filled with beautiful flowers, turtle doves billing and cooing, little cupids with lascivious expressions and indecent postures, hovering above the bed; and finally in order to achieve a perfect illusion, the expression and the posture of the woman showed, as well as a painting can do, the sort of sensation she experienced. (*Méphis* I, p. 179)

Although the first tableau is hardly described here at all, its iconography is deeply imprinted in Tristan's psyche and associated also with sensuality. Much later in her *Tour de France* she would use practically the same image to describe her process of self-repression: 'To calm my rebellious flesh takes an enormous effort and several days. Ah! miserable flesh, so like a spirited, untamed horse! There is a power in my body … which rules over my mind.'[28]

It is as if Méphis, like his creator Tristan, cannot tolerate this expression of luxury, of unrepressed sensuality. But since he is supposed to be a male, and to come from a humble sailor's family, there is nothing in his past that would explain this kind of reaction. Rather, it is the injunctions from Tristan's own feminine, upper-class upbringing that are transmitted here. Méphis' definition of his rival's philosophy illuminates Tristan's puritanical association between sensuality and debauchery: '… sensualism was his philosophy; he glorified the senses, wallowed in debauchery, and the licentiousness of his life was consistent with the materialistic views which he expressed in the motto he had adopted: the senses, nothing but the senses.' (*Méphis* I, p. 178)

Clearly here Méphis equates sensualism with debauchery. After he has expressed his contempt, he can regard Louis with pity: 'Poor young man who can only see in man the driving power, and in woman sensuality'. (*Méphis* I, p. 180) Such painting does not represent 'teaching', just sensuality. Therefore, Méphis offers his own paintings as an example of the proper use of art. One is a painting of an austere bishop; kneeling at his feet is a medieval baron-warrior, who prays to the bishop to bless his sword. Its title is *The Past. The Power of the Priest and Brute Force are Destroyed*. The other is a painting of the 'femme guide de l'humanité' entitled *The Future. Intellectual Power Replaces Brute Force*. In this painting, the idealized woman (whose description resembles Tristan's) leads humanity up a steep and rocky path. She is dressed in white; the 'femme guide' has long black hair and 'une expression angélique', and Méphis views her as 'source of life and prime mover of progress'. (*Méphis* I, pp. 181–3) Behind her is a crowd of people, including Rousseau and Bernardin de Saint Pierre: the deities of the Romantic pantheon, transformed into believers of Méphis' ideology. They were:

> … exceptional enough to recognize the enlightening influence of woman's advice in their life, and to admit that it is the moral role given to her by Providence in order to counterbalance men's physical strength … it was the destiny of men to be guided by women. (*Méphis* I, p. 183)

But while Méphis is thus elaborating a description of the ideological content of his painting, Louis and the others are studying the image of the woman whom Méphis regards as 'the idealization of woman as I perceived it' (*Méphis* I, p. 181); they find her to be the opposite of the *Venus*. Louis describes her as 'That thin and pale woman with a stern expression on her face, and loose-fitting garments' (*Méphis* I, p. 183). For him, Méphis' art represents a kind of asceticism and renunciation. But Méphis takes pleasure in his representation: 'It is a delight, an ecstasy which detaches him from materialistic life; he forgets society, its pretentions, and freed from the demand of the flesh, he lives solely for the activities of the mind.' (*Méphis* I, p. 175)

But his joyful experience as an artist is doomed to a violent finish. Girodet's students find that religion and their Master have both been insulted. Méphis interprets their reaction in a familiar manner. They are 'vexed at the superiority of my work, and tried to find faults with me'. (*Méphis* I, p. 184) Méphis is commanded to destroy his paintings and his refusal results in a fight which then leads to a duel. He realizes that despite the superiority of his views and his affinity for art, he will have to renounce it: 'I realized that it would be impossible for me to pursue my artistic career as I felt it should be, and the thought drove me altogether mad.' (*Méphis* I, p. 188)

Probably the effect of this renunciation is so strong because Méphis recognizes that the art world is the only means of access to status without birth or wealth, and also the only socially acceptable mode of rebellion against society – if it is closed to him, there is no other means. Thus, the excessive reaction: Méphis feels himself victimized, martyred for his ideas: '... men shower abuse on me, my master dismisses me, my comrades attack me because I want *to teach*! ... I wanted to show through my work that I was *truly a religious person, truly an artist*!' (*Méphis* I, p. 188) (In another section of the novel, Maréquita's encounter with a would-be suitor, the decadent aristocrat Torepa, provides still another reason for the intensity with which the renunciation of art is effected in the 'Atelier' chapter. *Age* is a factor: Tristan's society attended genius from its youth. Torepa is 30 years old, and Maréquita's criticism of him for not becoming an artist is blunted by the social fact that he is too old to do so: 'It is true that it would be rather late to think of becoming an artist.' (*Méphis* II, p. 19) Tristan wrote *Méphis* at the age of 35. Perhaps she wondered if she were not too old to be making her entry into the art world.)

This 'Atelier' chapter as it stands, inserted into the narrative of Méphis' past, resembles less a chapter of a novel than a short story or a representation of a dream. Only its subterranean unconscious threads will be picked up again in other segments of the novel, the themes of sacrifice, martyrdom, and exclusion. To interpret this chapter, one must go beyond the realm of art, although, as we shall see, Tristan accurately perceived certain aspects of the contemporary art scene. The significance of Méphis' expulsion from Girodet's *atelier* is reinforced with such violence that it has to signal more than is at first apparent. Although it is probably an accurate account of the hardships that dissident artists faced, the manner in which it is presented seems over-determined, and probably indicates the psychic roots of the social malaise: '"To damage my painting[!]" I exclaimed; "but you, miserable dauber, I would rather kill you than agree to change the slightest shade" ... It took all the control that I was used to exerting over myself not to crush him under my feet.' (*Méphis* I, pp. 186–7)

Is this a rendition of Tristan's own feelings about the art world? Or is it an outlet for the transference of her feelings of hostility toward the upper classes, a displacement of her urge to use violence against them for misunderstanding her worth and her intentions, for not seeing that she is really one of them, in the best sense? The answers to these questions are not clear; but it is important to point out that historically, Tristan's representation of the *atelier* was partly correct. In her depiction of the kind of censorship exercised by masters in their studios, she did capture an aspect of the power they exercised. It was not excessive to view the increasing control on the new-found liberty and will to self-expression among artists of this period by salons, museums and, indeed, by the art critics of the burgeoning press, as an attempt to censor and modulate this freedom of expression so that it would serve the ideological needs of the new social order.

> ... starting with the Restoration, a real surveillance and pressure system is put in place at all levels: the academic institution places the artist in the forefront and crowns him like a demigod while matching homage with rigorous control, since it assumes the right of the exclusivity of exhibition, the sanction over the distribution of the works. In a word, the domain of the imaginary is mapped out.[29]

Moreover, given this system, it was probably accurate to characterize the infighting among artists as equally violent. For during the post-Revolutionary period, the 'traditional sources of patronage collapsed'[30] and Méphis correctly criticizes the intensity of the artists' drive for success. In effect, Méphis' experience in the *atelier* bears witness to the increasing egoism and individualism which have been attributed to Romanticism[31] and which marked the artists' entry into the realm of bourgeois business relations.

Interestingly enough, Méphis' duel was to be echoed later in the century in a cartoon depicting Ingres and Delacroix exiting from the Institute, jousting over their divergent aesthetic doctrines: line versus colour.[32] It was well known that Ingres viewed Delacroix as 'the enemy'.[33] That these two painters should have built up such hostility between themselves and their followers provided the illusion that the interests they represented were diverse. But this quarrel would produce nothing revolutionary in terms of changing society, for both camps were, as Tristan seemed to perceive, allied to the basic tenets of the status quo: force and materialism.

And yet to transfer the animosity she felt against them on to Girodet and his students is in a sense to accuse a false enemy. For neither they nor their 'materialistic' painting are the real enemies: rather they are a symptom of the fetishization of reality within their society. Indeed these artists are, as Méphis charged, merely concerned with the formal aspects of art, and not with the significance of the reality they are engaged in reproducing. On the other hand Méphis himself is guilty of an abstraction. For although his paintings do introduce the dimension of history, of change over time, they do so in a very vague manner; and because of the vagueness it is difficult to discern whether he has not simply replaced the romantic nostalgia for the past with a simplistic nostalgia for the future, whether indeed the notion of progress itself, advanced in such a manner, is not just another deception.

It can be argued that Méphis' aesthetic fails to promote social change precisely because he does not seek to analyse the actual social realities in which it is entrenched. Instead, it seeks simply to bypass and replace that aesthetic code with another code whose moral basis is more affirmative, in the naïve hope that the attraction of the idea will suffice. Tristan, and Fourier before her, had recognized that to change society it was necessary to change the position of woman from that of the subjugated to that of an equal. But could a new myth based on woman's superiority lead to such change?

If we look closely at the two genres of painting represented as antitheses in the 'Atelier' chapter, it becomes clear that one is simply the reversal of the other, and that the possibilities that either mode could limit or change society are rather small. In fact it is probably accurate to view both conceptions of art presented in *Méphis* as consonant with the interests of the new capitalist system. For the false satisfaction of instincts and the repression of instincts are both aspects of the capitalist economy of instincts. In presenting Méphis' solution as the only solution and in endorsing it with such force, Tristan chose to replace one master–slave dichotomy with another, this time with woman on top. But she did not explain how this victory of morality over force was to be achieved. Instead, what she began to do in this chapter was to elaborate for herself a myth of her own redemption and elevation. Perhaps that was why her character Méphis likes the freedom of art so much: dreams of power and glory can be realized there so much more easily.

What is significant in Tristan's presentation of the artistic scene of the July Monarchy is that she recognized the danger of the major aesthetic code that was then establishing itself, and she tried to demystify it. By its formalism such art, whether practised by Ingres or by Delacroix, was so preoccupied with technique that it gave no thought to the kind of social relations its depictions helped to institute. As such, this art was a necessary adjunct of capitalism in the sense that it made the connection of force and of pleasure seem natural and necessary, and disregarded all moral consideration. *Jupiter and Thetis* by Ingres and *The Death of Sardanapulus* by Delacroix are the crowning examples of the way this art beautified the new codes of power, patriarchy, plunder and materialism.

By refusing the aesthetic of utilitarianism, this art seemed to revolt against the dominant materialist forces in contemporary French society; but in fact Tristan's critique of this art already prefigures its co-optation into the ethereal realm of pure art. Its exponents would be allied to reactionary forces in the crucial battles of 1848 and 1871. (The portrait she draws in this chapter of the art world of the July Monarchy must have interested her contemporaries, despite its personal overtones; it was published in one of the leading art journals of the period, *L'Artiste*.[34]

Tristan's confused acceptance of the opposition between the body and the soul indicates to what extent she was caught up in the dichotomy prescribed by the moral economy of her time: how else could she recuperate her lost class status (as an illegitimate child), and her lost human status (as a woman, Eve)? The confusion that is at the centre of the novel derives from this dichotomy.

For once Tristan had accepted the duality implied by the opposition between good and evil, and transferred it to her conception of woman (as in the description 'vulgar, sensuous woman, offering pleasure') (*Méphis* I, p. 301), she internalized the bourgeois morality that permitted capitalism to exist and flourish, and renounced the possibility of transforming her society through the creation of an aesthetic of social change. Marx's description of the way in which moral categories are a remnant of aristocratic ideology, masking real economic relations, describes accurately the intellectual model that inhibited Tristan's revolutionary consciousness: 'Just as *in reality* all differences become merged more and more in the difference between poor and rich, so all aristocratic differences become dissolved in idea in the opposition between good and evil. This distinction is the final form that the aristocrat gives to his prejudices.'[35]

It is clear that Tristan, although she had insight into the connection between the situation of women and that of the worker, was a victim of moral obscurantism, especially in her view of woman. Apart from her own terrible marital situation, she was severely marked by the experience of being a woman on her own, a woman who refused to act in the way prescribed by her society. At the same time, her husband

was constantly accusing her publicly of prostitution and adultery.
This, taken together with the fact of the legal condition of women in
the years following the *Code Napoléon*, must have encouraged her
moral reading of social reality. Unfortunately, the contemporary
injunctions on free expression of the senses led her to proclaim on
behalf of the enemy and to fight a false foe.

Her confused class status also encouraged this limited, 'moral'
assessment of reality. Wilhelm Reich's description of the internalization of the repressive structure of capitalism is relevant here: 'As a result
of the economic measures adopted by the ruling class, this production
relation becomes anchored in the psychical structure of members of
society, in particular, of the ruled class.'[36]

In this Tristan represents precisely the opposite view from that of
George Sand, who at that moment was glorifying the life of the senses
and motherhood, and who, not ironically, was to be much more
popular with her contemporaries. Yet, even in Sand's writings (especially *Lélia*), we sense the malaise that led intellectual women of the
period to proclaim against sensuality. It is as if, because of social def-
initions, the faculties of intelligence and sensuality were not supposed
to co-exist in women of the July Monarchy. Tristan's description of love
emphasized the way in which this area of women's experience had been
distorted:

> The driving force behind all human virtues, behind the gratification
> of the soul, when perverted by pride and debased by the senses,
> becomes the poisoned wellspring of countless hidden debaucheries,
> of the repulsive vices displayed in city streets, and of the crimes that
> fill the prisons. (*Méphis* I, p. 314)

Méphis' Education in Prison

The next scene of the novel depicts Méphis' stay in prison after the duel.
It is marked by contradictions that reveal Tristan's confused class
status and limited perception of the economic mechanism governing
French society. Framed by two stock descriptions, it is full of the exag-
geration common in descriptions of prisons during the Romantic
period. On the one hand prison is hell: .

> The memory of my time at the Conciergerie is like an infernal
> vision! There never was among Satan's cohorts more treachery and
> brazenness than I found among the band of criminals, counterfeiters,
> thieves, murderers with whom I was jailed ... The world holds
> nothing for them but the sinister poetry of hell: orgies in their
> dens, the savage satisfaction of revenge, misery of solitary con-

finement and penal servitude, escapes, fights, their existence is but chaos. (*Méphis* I, p. 197; 209)

Yet in between these descriptions one finds the assertion that 'We led quite a merry life in that prison. Not a day went by but that pretty young women decked out in their best came to the visiting room.' (*Méphis* I, pp. 206–7) And indeed, the prisoners Tristan presents are rational, intelligent and for the most part sympathetic individuals. How then do we explain the hyperbolic and inconsistent descriptions above?

In part, we can attribute these descriptions to the stock vocabulary of the time, and the popular fascination with prisons and prisoners. For Tristan and her contemporaries these prisoners were daring and admirable creatures who followed their own will. As such, prison symbolized a kind of forbidden yet marvellous place. Here, at last, our hero Méphis is welcomed. In this domain, his leadership is recognized. He identifies with his fellow prisoners, yet remains apart, superior.

I understand your hatred for a society that has trampled on you with both feet; in your situation the only course of action was *revenge*, since society denies you any means of making peace with it; I have experienced all your misfortunes, all your sufferings, for I have been a victim like you and yet I refuse to join you in your revenge. (*Méphis* I, p. 214)

Tristan had to make the character with whom she identified so closely reject such an overt declaration of vengeful intentions. We can also ascribe his decision not to join in their project to his identification with the upper class. The description of Méphis' arrival in prison clarifies this: 'From the moment I agreed *to come down to their level*, they lavished attention on me and showed me the respect and deference that *the true outlaw* never fails to offer to the one he thinks possesses the talents of a *leader*.' (*Méphis* I, p. 198)

Here, another appealing aspect of the prisoners' milieu is identified. It provides a class structure in which Méphis' nobility is instantly recognized. 'Ah! No one is better able than he to understand the need for a leader! ... without a leader, there is no unity, no order, no strength, no safety.' (Ibid.) The intense attraction which the prisoners' programme of vengeance held for Tristan becomes apparent from the strong language she employs to describe their attack on Méphis' project. Rather than join them, he decides upon a means of action which would permit him to retain his superiority and yet not cut him off from the upper classes outside prison, to '... first enlighten your enemies ... to show them that it would be in their interest to forgive you, to treat you as brothers.' (*Méphis* I, p. 214)

The prisoners reject this notion of cooperation between classes as naïve and impossible; they denounce it in no uncertain terms:

> ... the sheep and the wolf cannot live in the same den; others before you have held the same opinions but their efforts were fruitless; the rich, the powerful fleece us everyday so as to leave us with the bare minimum; and they buy themselves beautiful things with the spoils from the poor proletarian ... Child, the rich, the powerful are *evil incarnate on earth*; and you will not persuade Satan to submit his impure brow to the baptismal waters. (*Méphis* I, p. 215)

It is clear from the strength of the language employed here that the prisoners' position is one that strongly attracted Tristan. Indeed, her experience would lead her to adopt a similar stance, as she traversed the roads of France near the end of her life, and discovered that, in fact, the bourgeois could never be the true ally of the proletariat.

In prison, then, Méphis finds people whom he admires and who regard him with appropriate respect, for he approves of their hierarchical form of social organization. Yet, to narrate this utopian interlude, Tristan returned to story-telling, the method that predominates in the novel. It allowed her to avoid the more difficult and more painful style of action in the present and to emphasize and justify the deep resentment society had engendered in her.

The prisoners' stories resemble parables. Each depicts a different stratum of society, a different form of mistreatment, and a different lesson. The first is told by the character who represents the class that through its amoral accumulation of money dominates the society of the July Monarchy: the bourgeoisie. At 72, this wily man, a rich thief, reports that he learned his trade in jail, that prisons are the schools of thievery for the young.

More interesting are two other accounts, one given by an 'enfant naturel' of a 'grand seigneur', the other by a proletarian. The first, 'Prince Oscar', has been denied his rightful inheritance (like Tristan) by the premature death of his father, who left behind unsigned a document that would have legally protected him. 'Wonderfully handsome' (*Méphis* I, p. 200), Prince Oscar thus finds himself burdened with the background and tastes of a rich person, but with no means to live like one. Not surprisingly, Méphis feels the most sympathy for this thief. Prince Oscar's credo is a curious mélange of the ideologies articulated by Méphis, Maréquita and the Saint-Simonians: 'Had I been born a royal prince ... my name would have been blessed by artists, scholars, women, the poor and especially industrialists; because I can assure you I would have promoted commerce.' (*Méphis* I, p. 203)

This fallen noble, so beautiful, so well-dressed, is the only person who understands Méphis' painting of 'la femme guide de l'humanité'.

His story evokes Tristan's own confused sense of origin and sexual identity, as well as her search for a means of expressing the conflicting class loyalties within her. Despite his noble sentiments, Oscar finds himself in jail because of his own weakness for luxury. His story is an indictment of society for having deprived him of his rightful inheritance and his accustomed mode of life.

The third story is told by 'Conrad le sombre'. In her presentation of Conrad, Tristan's confusion about Oscar's class (and her own) is apparent. 'Conrad, like Oscar, the prince, belonged to the lower classes.' (*Méphis* I, p. 204) Obviously Oscar's membership in the lower class is only the result of his lack of funds; psychologically and sociologically he is a creature of the upper class, like Tristan.

In Conrad, we find the novel's first real representative of the 'peuple'. A locksmith, Conrad incarnates the honest man who finally learns through experience that honesty doesn't pay. His sons died for their country in the war; his wife has died of sadness. Alone, he begins to realize how much he has given to and how little he has received from society. He turns to thievery. Somewhat gratuitously, he speaks Tristan's own words, warning the rich of the certainty of revolution unless there is change:

Monsieur Lysberry, if they do not want the people to revolt, to destroy everything, they must make them happy, or keep them from learning how to read, because, from the moment they are able to understand, from their reading, that their condition has not improved, that the freedom with which they have been lured is but an empty word, that they remain the very humble slaves of the rich, then we run the risk of seeing them fall upon the rich. (*Méphis* I, pp. 205–6)

Conrad's explanation of how he became a thief seems out of place, an intrusion of the author's own views on the character's identity. Would a thief actually speak these words, would he be concerned enough to warn the rich of their eventual danger? Hardly. Once again Tristan's own confusion about class allegiance emerges.

The three prisoners represented in this chapter are ciphers, not real characters: they reproduce the various stages through which Méphis has already passed (disinherited rich boy, worker) and will pass (rich thief). They also represent the alienation and objectification with which Tristan views certain aspects of her past, and of her society. What Méphis (and Tristan) admire in the prisoners (besides their violent expression of resentment) is their method of organization. 'Criminals are the only ones, so far, to have understood the principle of association; they all belong, from the mere little pickpocket to the cleverest outlaw, to an admirable hierarchical system!' (*Méphis* I, p. 210)

This passage echoes the Saint-Simonian doctrine of capacity and hierarchy. Tristan never really rejected these concepts. In fact, her positive presentation of them reveals how deeply committed she was to the aristocratic system of which they are the foundation.

It is in prison that Méphis becomes aware of the process in which he is engaged: 'Each phase of my life was a new initiation for me; each pain, each disappointment helped me to understand men and things.' (*Méphis* I, p. 212) Tristan also experienced a similar process. Evoking her political mission as a writer, Méphis renounces the career of artist: '... when the people have no bread to eat, and no useful education to help them, when they are destined for a life of despair, of crime, in short, for the scaffold, how can I *educate them with my paintings*! Before showing them an allegory, it is necessary to make them understand words.' (*Méphis* I, p. 213)

Tristan herself was engaged in making this kind of decision at the time she wrote *Méphis*. Could art provoke real social change? For Méphis, at this point, the answer is no. Rejecting art as too abstract and removed from reality, he decides to dedicate his life to enlightening the poor about the causes of their condition. And yet at this juncture in the novel, Méphis himself has had very little experience in the world.

Méphis' Study of Paris (and Himself)

Méphis' career is varied, but although his story is called 'Histoire d'un prolétaire', he actually spends very little time in the ambiance of that class. When he emerges from prison, he tries his hand again at journalism, again unsuccessfully. Impoverished, he at last 'visits' the lower classes as a dock worker, but this occupation soon proves too difficult for him. Within five months, on the pretext of his health and his interest in making a study of the diverse classes of French society, he moves back into the class in which Tristan herself felt most comfortable – the upper class. Somewhat gratuitously, Méphis has learned two important lessons: from his brief experience as a worker, he learns that the proletariat is 'the slave of property'; and in the stamina and sacrifice of working women he has detected 'the superiority of woman'. (*Méphis* I, p. 249, 228) (We see that as early as 1838 Tristan was beginning to link these two problems.)

Clearly, Méphis is propelled through the various strata of society by psychological and ideological concerns rather than by the need to survive. In his next experience he serves the upper classes, first as a horse trainer, then as a fencing instructor. Here he learns the law of economics: 'how easy it was to appropriate other people's money with impunity, while giving something of very little value in exchange.' (*Méphis* I, p. 231)

Another brief interlude is spent as a medical student. This experience teaches him the way in which poverty and the city itself corrupt the future leaders of society. He proposes a kind of *phalanstère* (which resembles the modern American university) in which men (and women) could study under much better conditions. In each of these instances, Tristan renders the lesson Méphis learns rather than the texture of his experience.

As a male he has greater freedom to act, and these 'acts', as well as the cast of opposing characters, permit us to assess the full range of Tristan's own fantasies and to observe the way in which her personal and social concerns intrude on the aesthetic dimension of the novel. In fact, Freud's description of the process of reversal is fundamental for understanding the special way in which women choose to enunciate some of the urges which society has declared taboo for them: '... reversal, or turning a thing into its opposite, is one of the means of representation most favoured by the dream-work and one which is capable of employment in the most diverse direction. It serves in the first place to give expression to the fulfilment of a wish.'[37]

We see this principle of 'reversal' in operation especially in the context of Méphis' quest for a way to manifest power in his society. Each encounter leads him to attack a certain power structure, and subsequently to appropriate its methods of influence. He had rejected the sensuality prevalent in the art world as manifested by Girodet's students, and the criminality common to the prison community as manifested by Conrad, even while adapting some of their methods to attain power (and social change), but there was still another centre of power from whose organization he could learn: the Church. In his next position as a duke's secretary, he meets the Jesuit, Xavier, and determines to learn the secret 'of the coterie of priests'. (*Méphis* I, p. 265)

Apart from the hatred Tristan felt for the Church because of its influence on women, she shared with many liberals of her day a justified fear of the resurgence of its power.[38] In the years after the July Revolution, there was a strong anti-clerical sentiment. Memories of Charles X's use of religion to restore monarchical power were still fresh. In the wake of the deception of the July Revolution, however, new beliefs were needed. Also, fear of disorder was leading to a religious revival: 'While the national guard arose all over the country to defend property against anarchy, there was a religious revival everywhere.'[39]

Not only the supporters of the new regime were responsible for the resurgence of religion, but also those who opposed the new order paved the way for its return with their mystical utopian theories.

The rehabilitation of spiritual power by the Saint-Simonians who, while condemning the Roman hierarchy were great admirers of it ... [T]he mysticism included in all the socialist propaganda, all those 'spiritual states' and all those moral elements announced a religious revival which the defeat of Bourbon clericalism, its main obstacle, had made possible.[40]

Tristan shared this tendency to mysticism, although she was violently anti-clerical. Brought up as a Catholic, despite her hatred for the Church she recognized its attraction. As we shall see, in her depiction of its power she shared the view of her contemporaries who perceived it as a demonic force. One of them, François Génin, wrote an attack on the Jesuits in 1844, charging:

> They had been banished, they had broken their ban; there they are now, in the midst of society, ready to take their revenge on it, brazen, impudent, their eyes flashing fire, and their lips thundering out menace and anathema. They preach in Paris, all over France; they invade the salons, the cathedrals.[41]

A 'demonic force', the priests' party aroused enormous fear. Génin regarded and depicted this group in much the same manner as did Tristan: 'Liars by nature, scrupulous followers of Machiavelli's precept … under the guise of fathers of the Faith … like spiders, they secretly get down to work again.'[42]

As in the earlier examples of Méphis' encounters with various centres of power in French society, here too Tristan represented the concerns of her contemporaries but exaggerated them to fit her own preoccupations. As in the 'Atelier' chapter, Méphis at first identifies with the central figure and then expresses extraordinary antagonism toward him. The two chapters are linked first of all by the reappearance of Méphis' painting, the *Femme guide*. This painting, which symbolizes Tristan's own ambition as well as Méphis' vision of the role of woman, has a curious way of resurfacing. At first it is used in the novel as the pretext for Méphis' expulsion from the *atelier*, and the cause of the duel that leads to his prison sentence. Then, in prison, the painting (which he presumably carries with him) evokes the admiration of Prince Oscar, the déclassé aristocrat with whom (Tristan and) Méphis seem to identify so closely. On leaving prison, Méphis, desperate for money, tries to sell both his paintings, but succeeds in selling only *The Bishop*, the art dealer refusing to purchase the *Femme guide* unless Méphis is willing to transform it into a *Holy Virgin*. Méphis refuses.

In this later chapter, the painting *is* transformed into the Virgin by Xavier, the Jesuit, and the duchess, his sister. The inference is that given the opportunity the Church and the aristocracy will reinstate traditional Catholicism. Méphis is infuriated by this act and nearly leaves the duke's employ, cursing Xavier for his role in the destruction. But then, learning from the duchess that Xavier's real intention is to make

Méphis a member of the *Grande Congregation*, he decides to stay on, and learn the secret of the power of this organization.

The deep ambivalence Tristan felt toward her own sex and toward the manifestation of power is clear in this section from the inconsistent way she represents Méphis. On the one hand, Méphis mouths the Fourierist dictum about judging character on the basis of the treatment of women: 'Maréquita, if you wish to know the real worth of a man, find out first how he behaves in a love relationship.' (*Méphis* I, p. 283) On the other, he is prepared to imitate the Machiavellian behaviour of Xavier, the character he seems to oppose so strongly. Observing that the duchess' brothers (both Jesuits) use her as 'an instrument which they completely controlled' (*Méphis* I, p. 268), Méphis determines to do likewise. 'I was able to use her against her own brothers' (ibid.), and like Xavier he has no scruples about inspiring love in a woman without loving her. Although Tristan probably meant this ironically, as a critique of her main character, because she seemed to identify so closely with him, this critical aspect doesn't come across clearly enough. Actually, Méphis' Machiavellian tendencies here prefigure his designs on Maréquita, and are consistent with his name. Yet because both characters ultimately represent the schizoid aspects of Tristan herself, she presents them in a confused way.

That the duchess, an adulteress, should want to transform the *Femme guide* is not ironic, since she herself comes to represent the Virgin Mary. Through a kind of 'immaculate conception', in a relationship devoid of sensuality she conceives Méphis' child, and dies in childbirth. (Her husband, Duke D., will pretend paternity and legitimize this child.) Her relationship with Méphis is idyllic: she is described as an angel, a suffering saint. A victim of a 'mariage de convenance', married to a debauched duke 30 years her senior, her adultery is condoned. In death, perhaps, she has made the proper sacrifice for her transgression, and her passing is lamented. Méphis feels only pity for her. One of the rich, 'covered with diamonds, velvet and lace' (*Méphis* I, p. 255) she languishes in boredom and unhappiness. (A favourite theme of the period was the 'suffering' of the rich. One use of this theme was to prove to the poor that their covetous envy was unwarranted, and to cover the writer's deep desire and jealousy with a more acceptable motive.) That the duchess is depicted as one of the few 'good' women in the novel, with whom no taint of debauchery is associated, shows the extent to which Tristan, like her character Maréquita, identified with the Catholic version of suffering womanhood.

Such a representation is possible also because all Méphis' erotic and aggressive energy has been 'displaced' in this section onto Xavier, the Jesuit, who is the central figure in the chapter. All the sensuality that should have been present in his adulterous liaison with the duchess has been transferred to Méphis' relationship with Xavier instead.

As in the 'Atelier' chapter, here too the dichotomy between 'sensuality/ asceticism' is central, but whereas in the earlier chapter these opposites were represented by the diverse paintings of Louis and Méphis, here the dichotomy exists within the character of Xavier and is represented with great difficulty and inconsistency. If, as he insists, Méphis does not preach 'mortifying the flesh', why does he have such difficulty when describing those who live 'a life of dissipation' (*Méphis* I, p. 305)?

The inconsistencies occur in the various contradictory descriptive portraits of Xavier. In the first portrait, he is represented as an ascetic: '... trained from childhood to repress all his feelings, he had successfully achieved total control over his strongest emotions.' (*Méphis* I, p. 264) The next portrait reveals him to be the opposite: 'In a word, he was a man of passions and sexual appetites.' (*Méphis* I, p. 281) The confusion here between asceticism and sensuality is not surprising – for as Reich has pointed out, '... the more intensively a character trait has developed, the more readily it will change into its opposite ... Sensuality easily changes into asceticism.'[43]

Subsequent descriptions of Xavier seem to transform him into a woman, and indicate to what extent sexual identification was becoming a problem for Tristan in the novel:

> ... his appearance was graceful and handsome ... his light-hearted tone, his often high-spirited cheerfulness, his satirical turn of mind, the passionate expression in his eyes, his voluptuous lips, his pretty neck ... his beautiful white hands, his small elegant foot, a number of pretty little nothings, while giving infinite charm to his personality, made him the most attractive and the most dangerous creature woman had ever seen ... Xavier resembled those beautiful courtesans whose expressions fascinate, whose smiles entice; on seeing them your senses are roused, but the rapture lasts but one moment; soon the atmosphere of vice drives you away. (*Méphis* I, pp. 264, 282–6)

If we did not know that these descriptions were attributed to a man, they might easily confuse us.

By the time this series of portraits of Xavier is complete, he has come to represent debauchery and sensuality in much the same way as Louis' *Venus* painting and Clotilde have, although at the outset he was depicted as 'the intelligent priest'. (*Méphis* I, p. 269) These inconsistencies and the obvious bisexuality of the portraits betray Tristan's own difficulty in accepting the repressive moral economy of her age, and perhaps her own bisexual inclinations as well. For in this chapter she achieved the wish she would express in her letter to Olympe six months later: '... for a long time now, I have wished to be passionately loved by a woman – Oh! how I wish I were a man in order to be *loved by a woman.*'[44]

In these passages, Tristan seems to have transformed herself into Méphis in order to experience this love, and she has projected her desire onto a feminized Xavier. Moreover, this love has been doubled: the duchess (under Xavier's influence) loves Méphis although he feels nothing more than friendship for her – 'He [Xavier] had no trouble discovering the passion I inspired in her; it was one of those exalted, feverish loves' – and Xavier's own project for Méphis is described as a seduction: 'they wished to seduce me.' Xavier has been depicted as a woman, a seductress, but he still conceives of Méphis' role in much the same way as Méphis sees Maréquita's: 'He saw in me the man destined to lead others.' (*Méphis* I, p. 271, 268, 279)

If this chapter is characterized by sexual confusion, it is also marked by another example of the 'identity of opposites'. These characters have a common goal, although the author is at great pains to point out the difference in their ambitions. It is perhaps also because Méphis identifies so closely with Xavier's power that the latter seems so 'seductive' at one moment and so 'cold' at the other. Here is Méphis' desire: '... he must have had under his clerical frock a hidden but real power, which was a most attractive means to succeed. My mind was tormented by the desire to penetrate such a prodigious secret.' (*Méphis* I, p. 263)

In expressing their ambitions, Méphis and Xavier begin more and more to resemble one another. One wants to fill the role of 'new prophet'; the other speaks of 'the holy mission I have to accomplish'. And when they describe their projects more fully, the similarity between them is astonishing, even though Méphis is keen to point out that '... the clever Xavier had some shortcomings. I could understand much more than he understood himself.' Here is Xavier's conception of his role: '... I envisaged the fame I would acquire, the powerful influence I could obtain over the people by destroying the entire structure built on Christ's teachings and by explaining the pure moral principles to be derived from them.' Méphis' is quite similar: 'I always felt sure that I would one day find myself in a position to be heard, and I could then reveal to people the many tricks of which they are the victims.' (*Méphis* I, pp. 276,279, 280–1, 276, 291)

This confusion of sexual roles and missions for self-aggrandizement and social reform explains why the eventual rupture between the two has to be so violent. On learning of Méphis' defection from the Jesuits, Xavier, like Clotilde, 'was going to jump at my throat to strangle me'. (*Méphis* I, p. 292) René Girard has pointed out that the proximity of the mediator increases the hatred and the violence:

The closer the mediator gets to the desiring subject, the more the possibilities of the two rivals tend to converge and the more insurmountable becomes the obstacle that divides them ... The desiring subject wants to become his mediator; he wants to steal from him his very being of perfect knight or irresistible seducer.[45]

Whereas the earlier encounter with the art world was in some sense terminated by the duel and by Méphis' victory over his opponent, and his resentment of Clotilde avenged by her humiliation, *this story remains unfinished* – just as Maréquita's relationship with the aristocrat Torepa, whose courtship she rejects, remains unfinished. Both are projections of the desire of Méphis/Maréquita: Torepa representing power attained through birth and wealth, the aristocracy, and Xavier power through influence and the Church. Tristan's representation of these power structures is consequently deeply ambivalent. It will be through the return of these repressed desires that the novel will finally terminate, with the death of the two major characters.

In the process, Méphis finally discovers that the secret source of the Church's power is identical to that of the criminal world: organization and hierarchy. The *return* to this conception of power through control and organization indicates what an attraction it held for Tristan. It explains in part her rejection of sensuality, for the latter represents disorder and loss of control. Although she had appropriated certain ideas from Fourier, such as the notion of Harmony, the Phalanstery, and, to some extent, the belief in freedom from constraint, she was much more deeply attracted by the structure underlying the Saint-Simonian project: hierarchy and organization. However, in subscribing to this aspect of the Saint-Simonian doctrine, Tristan bound herself (as inextricably as did Enfantin's disciples) to the other social institutions whose power derived from their hierarchical structure, namely the Church and the aristocracy.

On a conscious level, however, Méphis refuses to draw on these sources to realize his wish for power – he must instead turn to other means of attaining it. When he learns that the other means to power that was institutionalized during the July Monarchy is money, he determines to acquire it. And, since the desire for power itself was unthinkable (especially for a woman), it had to appear under the cover of a benevolent cause. So, in the last phase of his account of his past, Méphis describes his experience as a banker in the following terms:

... a man truly devoted to the interest of the people, motivated, as was Christ, by that love of humanity which makes one brave anything, [who] endeavours, with the ordinary means at his disposal in the world, to acquire wealth in order to use it for the service of his fellow-beings, his ambition could not be more praiseworthy indeed ... and in that case the end justifies the means. (*Méphis* I, p. 318)

As we have noted earlier, Tristan may have intended her portrait of Méphis as a caricature of the male principle and of the social reformer of her time, but because these roles held such attraction for her and because she identified with her characters' desires so closely, this irony was undercut and muddled.

In devoting his energy to the interests of the 'peuple', Méphis could realize his wish for power – without giving up the notion of hierarchy. Such a role would allow him to play God, the martyr and the generous aristocratic patron. Once more, this project returns as the desire to publish a journal to spread the 'véritable morale' that is defined as 'personal freedom, and the equality of rights without any distinction based upon sex.' (*Méphis* I, p. 319) Before long this project is forgotten however, and Méphis describes himself as a much more active revolutionary. In a passage that reveals Tristan's own desire for power, Méphis sees himself as '... the secret leader of an army of workers whom I could, at will, keep peaceful or lead to insurrection'. (*Méphis* I, p. 321)

Perhaps because this role approximates Tristan's own wish too closely, it must be repudiated. Thus, without any transition, Méphis is transformed into what seems to be a caricature of a Fourierist. In this role he travels 'in order to disseminate my doctrine of reforms' (*Méphis* I, p. 322), but meets only with other businessmen and manufacturers of his own class. As he grows more rich and powerful, Méphis faces only one problem. It arises from the source of his new wealth – his wife (by a 'mariage de convenance' which he had contracted 'in order to put my vast projects to effect'). In a curious way, the benefits of this arrangement are perceived as a sacrifice on Méphis' part. He accepts the disturbance of 'my peace of mind in order to attain the power that has replaced all others, that of gold'. (*Méphis* I, pp. 320–1)

Here, as in the Xavier episode, woman is again viewed as an instrument for the attainment of power, but here the woman, a banker's daughter, demands reciprocity, an even exchange.

Then that shameless woman revealed her thoughts to me. She had chosen me, she said, because I was young and handsome! and since she was paying me, I was to make, at least, a show of love, and lavish on her the cares, attentions and courtesy, that a woman demands of her lover! (*Méphis* I, p. 324)

Since, in this section, there is no Xavier to absorb Méphis' erotic energy, it has been transferred to his wife, and in this passage, Méphis himself is transformed into the object of desire. Once again, perhaps, this characterization permits Tristan to watch herself being admired.

In this curious transposition of sex roles, the wife has assumed the qualities associated with Maréquita's husband, Hazcal: like him, she is older than her spouse, and is characterized by 'hardheartedness ... selfishness ... tastes altogether materialistic'.(*Méphis* I, p. 224) Here, as in the *only other legitimate marriage* in the novel (that of Maréquita and Hazcal), the motive for union is purely material, and, like Maréquita, Méphis also feels his role to be that of a prostitute ('she was paying me ...'), although his wife's demands are certainly more 'legitimate' than Hazcal's project of full-scale prostitution for his wife.

Indeed both these transactions indicate the extent to which Tristan connected legitimate marriage with prostitution, and recognized the plight of the economically dependent person in any exchange. In her own marriage, the situations which Méphis and Maréquita face were combined. In the first place, Chazal knew that he had rescued her from poverty and, like Méphis' wife, probably also expected gratitude at least in return. Here is Chazal's description of Tristan's situation when he found her:

> The poor girl living in a garret, in the most dilapidated house in a street where the best are not worth much (rue du Fouarre, near Place Maubert), enjoyed, as we chatted in the evenings, my helping her with colouring the perfumer's labels which were her only means of subsistence; she also appreciated my sending her some wood.[46]

Moreover, he charged that rather than being constrained to marry him, Flora Tristan, '... the little colourist ... seemed to be looking forward to the time when she would no longer be a worker but would become head of a prospering business.'[47] But if we give heed to Chazal's charges, which are legitimate in some sense, for indeed Flora's marriage certainly improved her financial condition, we should also see the other side. When Chazal's own financial problems became too grave, he probably attempted, as Flora charged, to prostitute his wife, as does the character Hazcal: '... he made an ignoble proposition to his young wife. As a last resort, he intended to prostitute her.'[48]

All of these marriages – fictional and real – are described by Tristan in the same manner: as a constraint 'to carry the yoke of such a vile creature'. (*Méphis* I, p. 324) Méphis' sympathy for men 'condemned to marry a rich dowry' (*Méphis* I, p. 325) seems displaced: the real anger has been transferred from the humiliation a wife feels within the more usual relationship of woman's economic dependency.

Although Maréquita flees Hazcal as soon as she learns of his project, Méphis, like Tristan, decides to tolerate for a time this person 'whom I despised, with whom I could no longer bear to live'. (*Méphis* I, pp. 357–8) But Méphis attributes his 'sacrifice' to a wider goal than that of the well-being of his immediate family: 'my desire to be useful to my brothers made me tolerate everything until that day with a religious resignation.' (*Méphis* I, p. 325)

Economic realities soon intruded on the arrangement, however: in the years after the July Revolution, the economic crisis leads Méphis to bankruptcy and smuggling. In this last episode of his story, the original 'fall' from paradise is recalled, then reenacted, and concluded by a new version of the betrayal. Méphis returns to Dieppe to take up smuggling, and realizes how the seemingly insignificant rescue of Lord Arthur had changed his whole life. The logic of the causality described is again convoluted: 'Without that incident I would never have left my village; a sailor, like my brothers, I would have been ignorant of the world, I would never have thought of fighting its enemies.'(*Méphis* I, p. 335)

Just at the moment of this retrospective meditation, another man jumps into the sea, this time to commit suicide: Méphis once again performs a rescue. At first, this act of charity benefits him. The man, a captain, agrees to work for Méphis, and to sell him his ship for purposes of smuggling. Here again Méphis' desire for power is transparent. He describes this interlude as one of the happiest of his life: '... I had absolute control over 15 men ... the devotion they showed me, the fact that their fate was bound to mine, all that carried me along ... and justified my behaviour in my mind.' (*Méphis* I, p. 341)

Even after Méphis has earned more than enough in this illegal manner, however, greed pushes him on. He keeps gambling for higher stakes. Finally, he is betrayed by the very man whom he rescued: a repetition of the original betrayal occurs. Only here it is clearly money that is lost:

... what a painful impression that betrayal has left in my heart; twice, at the risk of my life, I rescued a man from certain death; the first, milord Arthur M. ... caused me to be spurned by the woman I loved, and ruined my life ... Twenty years later, I saved the other exactly in the same spot; he repaid me by an abject betrayal, and left me a broken man ... What kind of awesome power can thus push men to act with such monstrous ingratitude? (*Méphis* I, p. 352)

Tristan's character decides that 'society corrupts them'. (*Méphis* I, p. 352) The description of this betrayal and its indelible impression constitutes another item in Méphis' dossier, which justifies his desire for vengeance.

As we have seen thus far, although Tristan does not render the texture of her character's experience, she does use him to explore society and to comment upon its injustices. Through his eyes we perceive the deep psychic and social strains which marked her epoque and her own malaise.

Womanpower in Nineteenth-century France

To say that *Méphis* suffers from the flaws of a first novel is too easy. As we have seen, Tristan's purposes in writing this novel often worked against each other: to denounce or reform; to blame or to pardon; to confess or to conceal; alternatively and simultaneously, these goals drove her, producing an unshapely book that nevertheless illuminated boldly her problems as well as society's.

According to Freud, in our dreams (or in our novels) a personal agenda may reveal itself. It can be detected in time sequence as well as in repetitions or contradictions. If a novelist's manner of characterization and point of view are an indication of the stability of the writer's ego, then Tristan's handling of these tasks is revealing. Although she resorts to dualist dichotomies in representing her characters, they often speak with the same voice, the same expression, the same vocabulary and style; whether the source be Méphis, Maréquita or the narrator, these similarities are disturbing. The characters distinguish themselves from one another by minimal ideological differences, and these are often inconsistent.

Especially in her treatment of the time sequence Tristan reveals how problematic it was for her to deal with the present, and to bring the relationship between Méphis and Maréquita to its consummation. Replete with recurrences, reversals, and errors, their convoluted accounts of the past do much to explain their present status and future project. Taken together, their stories of the past describe a common perception of a world in which 'everything is tainted with scorn, filled with bitterness'. (*Méphis* I, p. 316) Neither character can survive on his own in the face of this enormous resentment. If a 'personal myth' exists (Charles Mauron describes this as 'the most frequent illusion in an author'),[49] it may well relate to her characters' common project for revenge against the perpetrators of the 'monstrous ingratitude', of not appreciating their various gifts of themselves.

Each character has, however, a tragic flaw that prevents the successful mission of revenge. Méphis is Machiavellian: he acts according to the law that 'if you want the end you must not stick at the means' (*Méphis* I, p. 333), and thus is not worthy of emulation. In an ironic footnote pointing to the origins of his ideology, Tristan shows her antipathy to this aspect of Méphis, a character with whom she otherwise identifies closely: '[S]ee Victor Cousin's philosophy classes, Theodore Jouffroy's and Guizot's works, in a word, the whole school.'(*Méphis* I, p. 333)

Lacking his energy and ambition, Maréquita can do nothing; she represents the passive principle, although she often denounces its effects: '… she resented her need for other people's approval, cursed the education she had received and the ties which still bound her to a society she loathed.' (*Méphis* I, p. 70)

In writing this novel, Tristan was less concerned with aesthetic merit than she was with the exploration of the labyrinth in which psychological needs, social problems and theories for change intertwined. Appropriately, Tristan added 'ou le prolétaire' to the title of *Méphis* when she listed her works in the frontispiece to *Union ouvrière* (1844).[50] For although Méphis is not a true proletarian, he nonetheless represents that class's desire, which is at the centre of the novel. Tristan correctly associated the desire and anger of the working people with that of women, because in her society both shared the status of have-nots.

Méphis is an extraordinary novel, then, because it represents the 'untouchables'; and their portrait is that much sharper because it is over-determined. In Tristan's attempt to define her own sexual and class identity, she explored the social definition and implications of sex and class. The dualism in the novel represented by the two characters at its centre clarifies Freud's view[51] that all dreams are dreams of ambition or eroticism, and demonstrates that we cannot simply ascribe dreams of ambition to men, or of eroticism to women. Often the wish for one is expressed through the wish for the other.

Méphis and Maréquita offer us an index of the limited options available to Tristan's bisexual selves; their problematic search for a means of action and power reveals the way in which her society circumscribed freedom along sexual lines. Their myriad and contradictory purposes illustrate the conflict Tristan faced and the way that class and sex both determine a woman's response to her expression of power in any given historical period. Reich formulated the problem at the level of the superego this way: 'The superego of a woman in the age of Plato was fundamentally different from that of a woman in capitalist society.'[52]

Indeed, in Tristan's society, the only valid way for woman to attain power was through martyrization, self-sacrifice and renunciation. By these self-destructive means, she could accumulate moral power, the only power available once the avenues to material wealth were closed to her. Intelligent women recognized that moral power was no longer as valuable in a capitalist society: by revolting against materialist society, they also revolted against their powerlessness.

Such a revolt would be doomed to failure, however, if it was based on moral premises. For the valorization of the virtue of past ages would only serve to replicate these virtues, which had no exchange value in capitalist society, and further entrench this 'feudal remnant'[53] in women, thus making it all the more unlikely that they could accumulate the kind of power necessary to change the order of things. Tristan still fell prey to this 'fatal' defect of the romantic period – despite her perception of the reality of the effects of class and sex identity: '... there was a great consumption, during the romantic period, of women victims.'[54]

That Tristan herself should have created still another 'femme victime' in Maréquita is not so surprising given her epoch and background. If we glance back at a letter she wrote to her then husband-to-be, the earliest document we have of Tristan's conception of her role and her difficulty in filling it, we can gauge the conflict she faced: '... I want to become a perfect wife, I probably shall not be able to, I want to make you so happy ... I want to treat my mother as I would like my children to treat me, in a word, I want to be kind and gracious with everyone, be learned but in such a gentle and pleasant manner that every man will want a learned wife.'[55]

Already here in this letter to Chazal of January 3, 1821 (which he reproduced as a 'pièce justificative' in his own defence), we see that Tristan knew how difficult it was to be the perfect wife, mother or daughter, and knew her true desire, to be a learned lady. In fact, at his trial, Chazal attacked her for failing to fulfil her 'feminine' role: 'As for the care our children required, she gave them but little, and left them entirely in Mme Tristan's care ... She never lived with Mme Tristan to whom she constantly showed a lack of respect.'[56]

Tristan's own ambivalence about her sexual identity and the responsibilities associated with her female status are clarified by a recurring error in the text. In reality, when she left Chazal, Tristan became responsible for her daughter and her two sons. When one son died, she was then in charge only of herself and her two children, one male and the other female. The three of them lived together, and at times she left the children with her mother for whom she must also have felt responsible.

Not surprisingly, in the novel Maréquita has no family to care for. It is Méphis who takes charge of his 'poor old mother, my good sister, and my sweet little niece'. The use of extra adjectives and the extra woman already indicates a possible transference of Tristan's personal emotions. More significant, however, is the fact that these three, for whom Méphis claimed he felt such responsibility, are lost in the text for over 100 pages of the narrative and for ten years of Méphis' life. All of a sudden when he returns to Dieppe to take up smuggling toward the end of the novel, he remembers them and goes to look for them, having forgotten that he brought them to Paris long ago. (*Méphis* I, p. 334) Later, after the failure of the smuggling enterprise, returning to Paris and to his difficult but wealthy wife, he contemplates suicide, and remembers his family: 'I thought of my poor old mother, my good sister and my sweet little niece.' (*Méphis* I, p. 358) In a burst of tenderness, he wants to go and embrace them for the last time. (In fact, what Tristan is probably transcribing here is the overbearing sense of responsibility her society made her feel she ought to have toward her family. Actually, like Méphis, she had roamed rather freely, leaving her children with her mother, or with a woman who took boarders. For her lack of maternal instinct, she was roundly condemned by Chazal, by George Sand and by French society in general.)

At this point in the novel, Méphis remembers where his family is: 'From the time of my marriage, the three of them had left Paris to settle in a village in the vicinity. They feared being an embarrassment to the wealthy pride of the family into which I had married.' (*Méphis* I, p. 358) Méphis' error in defining the whereabouts of his family and his ascription to them of the desire not to embarrass him – these elements betray Tristan's own difficulty in defining her familial duties and relationships.

Private and Public Demons During the July Monarchy

In the early years of the 1830s, the bubble of Saint-Simonian fervour burst because of a quarrel over the question of free love and its endangering the power of paternity. The schism this disrepute engendered among the *fidèles* ('faithful') represents the first stage of the demise of the Saint-Simonian sect. The doctrines of Saint-Simon and his interpreter Enfantin and the doctrines of Fourier and his disciple Considérant were often at odds on this very specific question of 'rehabilitation of the flesh'.[57]

For courageous women like Tristan and her friend Pauline Roland, who dared to try to live the utopian dreams and visions of their contemporaries, life was not to be easy. Could a new ideology of pleasure replace years of Catholic indoctrination which had instructed them to enjoy renunciation? 'I found myself naturally inclined to reject with horror a doctrine which could make me feel happy, or at least justify feelings which I had till then regarded as sinful'[58] is the way in which Roland describes her reactions to her discovery of the sexual freedom permitted by Saint-Simonism. Instead of dealing with this conflict, she decided to leave the provinces (and the married man to whom she was attracted) for Paris, to postpone coping with this new morality.

During these tumultuous years, women especially endangered themselves and their futures in their attempts to live by the contradictory doctrines of the day, and to incarnate by their example the vision of woman which these doctrines eulogized. Such women were caught in a myriad of double binds in this transitional period: Catholicism still exercised an important influence on women even after they had consciously decided to reject it. And because neither the socialist nor the feminist solution had been fully invented, many contradictions existed. After all, the notion of a woman saviour and the notion of sacrifice are both common to the ideology of Saint-Simon and Catholicism.

By juxtaposing Roland's statements about her predicament with those we find in *Méphis* we can illuminate the paradoxical situation in which creative women found themselves. Roland explained the bind she found herself in as a Saint-Simonian disciple: 'They must endeavour to prove that it is not in order to satisfy their passions that they have embraced the new religion.'[59] That is, true adherents had to show by their example that the doctrine 'rehabilitation of the flesh' could work and had to demonstrate this selflessly, by refusing to enjoy sex. A perfect example of the exalted repression of the time is indicated in Roland's platonic letter to another Saint-Simonian, Charles Lambert. It indicates the degree to which eroticism has been sublimated and transferred to the realm of a mystical union: 'You are truly there, in my heart of hearts ... I possess you more completely since you left. Therefore I am calm, joyful, happy, you are right here, you can no longer escape me. Forever and ever. Ah! yes, we shall live eternally in each other's heart.'[60]

We should remember that this was written by a 30-year-old virgin on the eve of her decision to 'sacrifice' herself to a young man who was in 'need' of her. Such was the exaltation of the time: this language is Tristan's as well. Moreover, its energy all comes from the difficulty of coping with the conflicting taboos of virginity and pleasure.

The problem of self-repression, or the question of how to express one's sexuality, becomes central in volume 2 of *Méphis*, in which Maréquita's story and her encounter with Méphis are finally elaborated. If, as Freud says, dreams are always either dreams of ambition or dreams of eroticism, what happens when a woman decides or allows herself to fantasize about both? When Tristan attempts to fuse the two dreams and the two realities in volume 2, we see why she has waited so long to try it. (How could she do other than fail? The expression of the dreams of power and eroticism in fiction and in real life were forbidden to women.) The way in which Tristan expresses this forbidden wish indicates the extent to which the society was successful in repressing both the creative *and* the erotic energy of women.

A survey of the statements which the narrator makes about Maréquita's sentiments toward men indicates the extreme ambivalence of Tristan's feelings, as well as their masochistic dimension. Nearly every assertion includes the extremes 'love/hate': other statements contain 'missed opposites' 'to know/to despise,' 'admirers/enemies,' 'husband-lover/slanderer'. (*Méphis* II, p. 83) Yet society had taught Maréquita that she could become a complete person only through denial of herself, through connection to a man. The obvious way out of this dilemma was to create

... an ideal love; with the help of that marvellous image in mind, she had had no difficulty in rejecting every man who presented himself to her; they all seemed so insignificant compared to the hero who was constantly present in her mind that she could not even bring herself to cast a pitying glance in their direction. (*Méphis* I, p. 147)

By the creation of such an unattainable ideal, Maréquita could implicitly reject all men and pronounce her contempt for them. Because none of them can measure up, they become much smaller, and in the process, she herself much larger and more worthy. And, to take her final revenge, she determines to identify herself only with Méphis, someone who has also suffered like herself. She gives him the task of presenting the 'vile and contemptible souls like that of the chevalier d'Hazcal or selfish and unfeeling hearts like that of Olivera' (*Méphis* II, p. 93) with the double spectacle of the suffering they have caused. Maréquita's identification with Méphis simultaneously celebrates her own suffering and punishes those who have made her suffer.

As if to prove the worthiness of the task she has set herself, Maréquita announces from the outset her certain knowledge that it will fail: her sacrifice thus makes the task the more noble and by inference enlarges her own grandeur. With her first appearance, at the Givry Ball, Maréquita has declared her martyrization proudly: 'Farewell! Had I come on this earth at a later time, I would/have found hearts to love me,/Souls to understand me;/But I was destined to go through this phase,/To be misunderstood and sorely tried'.(*Méphis* I, p. 15)

In *Pérégrinations* Tristan had already characterized the ideal person as one who is 'capable of those acts of devotion which the common herd calls madness'. (*Pérégrinations* I, p. 48) But in that earlier description a revealing transformation took place. First Tristan explained that her suffering had taught her what an extraordinary man she must seek; but when she gave examples of such men, these examples turn out to be female: Jeanne d'Arc and Charlotte Corday. Does she reveal here the secret of the impossibility of the consummation of her love on earth? For what better way to take revenge on the men who have infamously tricked her than to bypass ordinary men by pretending to seek the ideal man, or better still by seeking relationships with women, by deifying women, especially the only woman on whom she could rely, herself?

This interpretation explains in part why Maréquita greets the discovery of Méphis, the man worthy of her love, with such 'distress'. Union with Méphis is taboo, because he is first of all a man, and thus a member of the sex that has manipulated woman. Moreover, he represents a side of her character that according to social codes has to be repressed: the active principle. His approach to the world and to the Other is as manipulator; he seeks power and pleasure unabashedly.

Their union must be delayed until the last section of the novel, after each has rehearsed his or her litany of woe. And various excuses have to be found for the fatality that intrudes upon their union. The first obstacle appears in Maréquita's imagination. She has taken Méphis with her to a secluded cottage on the shores of the Seine, and there, at the moment when Maréquita seems to glimpse happiness, she has a nightmare vision: '... suddenly two menacing monsters would appear before her eyes, the despicable Hazcal and Méphis' wife.' (*Méphis* II, p. 147)

Her fear that their legal spouses would find them was common in women of her day, and rightly so, since by law husbands were permitted to murder their wives if they found them committing adultery. In the novel, however, the destruction of Méphis and Maréquita's union is not accomplished by their spouses but by a complex series of events coordinated by the combined forces of the rich and the Church.

It is significant that before this intricate assassination plot can be worked out, Méphis has to consign himself to death by relinquishing the principles for which he stands. But first, because of Maréquita's recurring fear of being discovered and of the risk she is taking, she makes the ultimate request of Méphis: he must prove his love for her by his willingness to sacrifice. Maréquita demands: 'Leave everything for my sake.' (*Méphis* II, p. 162) Once this demand is rejected, as it must be for Méphis to retain any semblance of his own identity, Maréquita begins to contemplate assassination. She envisions total consummation of their union and complete happiness for a limited period of time, after which she plans to administer poison to them both so that they can die in their sleep. Once Méphis has shown the insufficiency of his love, his unwillingness 'to sacrifice all for it', this 'betrayal' allows Maréquita to satisfy her pent-up urge for vengeance against men.

Thus, Méphis' refusal to model his desire on her needs provides an excuse for the rupture of what otherwise would have been the perfect union. Given the intensity of Maréquita's original distrust of men and her desire to avenge their enormous ingratitude and betrayal of woman, obviously the perfect union with man cannot be happily consummated. Méphis' betrayal provides the excuse for further development of the masochistic dynamic: 'Tired of playing the role of martyr, the desiring subject decides to become tormentor.'[61] Maréquita now contemplates with excitement the possibility of satisfying her demand for Méphis' total surrender, after which she will take her vengeance and assassinate him. The desire to kill him 'has an inexpressible charm for her'. (*Méphis* II, p. 169)

Before she can accomplish this act, however, the spouses do intrude, but adultery is not proven. Maréquita is frozen into death-like immobility (similar to the state she and Clotilde have experienced earlier).

For his part Méphis finally realizes that the only means of regaining Maréquita's trust and love is for him to accept her ideology of love and to accept her as she is. He must accept the fact that the women of his time '... felt incapable of expressing in any other manner the feelings with which their hearts overflow ... devoting themselves to the individual was the form heroism took among women at the present time.' (*Méphis* II, pp. 210–1) Méphis must therefore renounce his hopes for changing Maréquita or achieving social change through her leadership.

In order to arrange a scenario that would allow Maréquita to demonstrate her 'dévouement' and recuperate her love through sacrifice, Méphis manipulates his debts so that he will be imprisoned and Maréquita will have to rescue him. Once in jail, however, Maréquita's rejected aristocratic suitor, Torepa, and Xavier, Méphis' 'rejected suitor' from the Church, will conspire to murder Méphis. They triumph, although Maréquita does initially succeed in rescuing him. Consumed with grief over his death, Maréquita dies soon after. She has not been able to absorb him, so she is absorbed by him; she leaves to their daughter the task of publishing Méphis' writings, and this daughter will, Maréquita hopes, become herself the 'femme guide'.

For Romantics, these two deaths had a positive face '... superior beings reach the end of life much before ordinary people, whose senses are active and souls dormant. Their passage on the earth is only revealed after their death, and only then do people admire the path they have laid out across the desert.' (*Méphis* II, p. 143) The admiration of posterity, which comes after the life has been consumed, is supposed to give worth to the individual project, and prove that the suffering and martyrization have been worth it.

In sharing this Romantic fallacy, by which one's own greatness can manifest itself only through a *personal* mission which leads to suffering, failure and martyrdom, Tristan predicted the fate of her own attempt to assure her immortality through her rescue of the working class, which after all would have to be the agent of its own rescue. In the novel, such satisfaction is also elusive. The aristocrat Torepa repents for the murder of Méphis, but his is a private and personal act, one that will affect few lives. As for Xavier, he is left at the end of the novel consolidating his power. Thus, the novel presages Tristan's defeat and offers a misreading of history: it will be the rich who rule and not necessarily the Church.

But why should Maréquita, who considers herself the epitome of virtue, have contemplated destroying Méphis? In a very precise way, Méphis, like his namesake Mephistopheles, represents the tempter in this novel. Maréquita is correct in demanding to know his 'intentions about her'. (*Méphis* I, p. 356) He is the first man ever to criticize her, and it is his criticism that poses the first real threat to the identity she has created for herself. Méphis tempts Maréquita, and therefore

woman, to become all that she could and should become. He engages
in a thorough-going critique of the present condition of woman,
and his desiring of Maréquita is therefore also a desire to transform
her. Sartre's description of the process of 'love' accurately accounts for
the dynamic in which these two characters, in reality different aspects
of Tristan's own character, are engaged: 'The Other is for me simultaneously the one who has stolen my being from me and the one who
causes "there to be" a being which is my being ... Thus my project of
recovering myself is fundamentally a project of absorbing the Other.'[62]

This absorption of the Other is a fatal project, however, for it would
'necessarily involve the disappearance of the characteristic of otherness
in the Other'.[63] As such it would result in a negation of the very basis
of existence of the self. And yet it is just such a project that is carried
out in *Méphis*. In this sense, the novel represents an indictment of the
fatal quality of love that Flora Tristan views as '... an absorbing, exclusive passion ... with its intolerable tyranny ... which binds two lives
together so strongly, and so much identifies one with the other, that
they must both be destroyed in order to be separated.' (*Méphis* II, p. 149)

This combat is represented as a struggle between two doctrines of
love: Méphis', which implies the retention of individual autonomy and
freedom of action, and Maréquita's, which implies the total absorption
of both lovers in each other. The action of the novel demonstrates the
internal struggle between the socially defined 'male' and 'female' principles within Tristan. Méphis will surrender his selfhood, which exists
in terms of his ideal of reasonable love, to Maréquita's need for all-
consuming passion. His Otherness will be absorbed. At first, he glimpses
the power of this passion with admiration:

> While criticizing the selfishness of such a passion, Méphis admired
> its intensity; he was struck with reverence, as if he were in the
> presence of one of those mighty hurricanes which uproot trees, tear
> down houses, convulse the Ocean and cover the beaches with
> broken down ships and wounded bodies. (*Méphis* II, p. 166)

His description of his fear of this kind of love is equally powerful:

> The one (of those passions) he feared most was love; he knew that
> once man falls prey to this passion he cannot control himself; that
> unwittingly he is ruled by the will of another, that he loses his per-
> sonality which becomes absorbed in that of the loved one. There-
> fore he considered it a sign of weakness and pusillanimity to give
> way to feelings of the heart. (*Méphis* II, pp. 28–9)

Even though Méphis glimpses the destructive power of such an all-
encompassing love, and even though this kind of love runs counter

to all his principles, he finally succumbs to it, and before long woman has her revenge. Méphis' resistance is futile: 'He obeys as the slave obeys his master.' (*Méphis* II, p. 31) Thus he forfeits his priorities: of accomplishing his worldly projects, of considering the happiness of the masses before that of the individual, of transforming Maréquita into the strong person with whose help he can change the world. Because his position represents the one that Tristan admired most and tried to live by, the process of his relinquishing it constitutes a strong condemnation of the woman who leads him to it, as well as an indictment of his weakness in succumbing to it.

The similarity of Tristan's own predicament to that of both Méphis and Maréquita can be seen from her description of her own struggle against herself. In a letter to her friend Traviès, Tristan confessed the effort it had been to act on the strength of her beliefs:

Ganneau. I have already told you that I loved the soul of that man in a very special way. My soul has never felt in any other soul the sweet comfort that his has given me ... However, true to my opinion, that one must mercilessly cut the individual to pieces, on the eve of my departure I offended Ganneau most cruelly! One day I shall tell you the inner tears I shed at seeing the perspiration dripping from his brow. But by the living God! I shall not be accused now of succumbing to the general faint-heartedness. I wanted to crush G. in order to make sure that I was strong – alas, I am not as strong as I thought ... My heart does not prove as equal to the task as my brain! [64]

If the struggle within Tristan resembles the struggle between Méphis and Maréquita, it is because under the guise of the difference created by their sexual identities, these two characters actually represent two sides of Tristan's own nature. The struggle between them owes its intensity to the fact of the essential similarity of these two characters, which is much more profound than their differences, and the ultimate reason why their union must result in death.

The evidence of the closeness of these characters to Tristan's character can be found first of all in their names. Both Méphis and Maréquita are names that have as their first syllable the personal pronoun 'mes' and 'ma', which refers to the first person. The letter 'm' of course is the letter that introduces Tristan's family name, Moscoso. If these similarities seem coincidental, then we can go one step further and see in the second syllable of each name a reference to place: 'aréquita' closely resembles Aréquipa, the Moscoso patriarchal family seat, the site of one of Tristan's experiences of betrayal. And the second syllable of Méphis resembles an anagram of 'Paris', also a place where betrayal had occurred, but which also represented for Tristan freedom, 'the only city in the world that I have ever loved'.[65]

In fact, the two points of view on the role of women, the essential point of difference between the two characters, replicate very closely the points of view Tristan found predominant in each place. Maréquita personifies the typical French woman. Trained by the Catholic Church like her sisters in Aréquipa, she shares the limited perspective on life that they held, namely that love should be all-absorbing, the only career to which a woman should devote herself, and that it should be consummated under legal auspices only. Like them, she admits of physical contact only in marriage. She believes in woman's intuition and, above all, she needs societal approval ('I cannot live with the thought that the world scorns me'). (*Méphis* II, p. 208) It is this that makes her passive, and makes her constrain her natural instincts. Méphis criticizes this perspective, saying, 'It is not sufficient.' (*Méphis* II, p. 98) Méphis insists that woman's devotion and sacrifice results in 'the ill-advised sacrifices of women [which] add to the woes of society.' (*Méphis* II, p. 100) It is this that Méphis, the representative of the new law, attacks: 'Woman at the present time can only weep, pray, and sacrifice herself.' (*Méphis* II, p. 94)

As we have already seen, the resemblances between Tristan and her characters Méphis and Maréquita are numerous. These connections seem to increase. All three share a disenchantment with love, resulting from a very early traumatic experience. Méphis, like his creator, '... abandoned any hope of ever finding a woman worthy of him, capable of understanding his lofty social concepts and to be fired with a holy enthusiasm to second him in his endeavours to rehabilitate society'. (*Méphis* II, pp. 25–6)

Indeed, for Tristan this statement could apply to people of both sexes. Like his author, Méphis began to view the opposite sex 'as someone of whom he'd make use as long as he judged doing so useful to his projects'. (*Méphis* II, p. 26) Her description of Escudero in *Pérégrinations*, and the temptation to reinforce her power with him at her side, sounds strangely like Méphis' project: 'It seemed to him that her love would make him stronger.' (*Pérégrinations* II, p. 28) Like Tristan, Méphis was attempting to restrain his passionate nature, but he took pleasure in exercising his power over others, dominating them 'par le regard'.

His attempt to exploit Maréquita becomes all the more suspect because she also resembles Tristan so closely. She too is described as a 'belle andalouse'. Her guardian fears that 'his grand-daughter like her mother would be the victim of some seducer or other from the high nobility'. (*Méphis* II, p. 38) Both Tristan and Maréquita are of Spanish origin. Both are orphans. Both discover that their husbands are tyrants who want to prostitute them. Both flee and travel, changing their names and lying about their marital status. Both choose to live in Paris.

Maréquita (like Méphis and Tristan) frequents the world of artists. Perhaps the most striking similarity is this slip: '... the wound in her heart was still too painful to let tender feelings disturb it again.' (*Méphis* II, p. 84) Tristan's fresh bullet wound is surreptitiously evoked here.

If Méphis and Maréquita resemble their creator, they also resemble one another. Tristan seems to sense this: 'Méphis identified so well with Maréquita ... that it seemed to him he had never been away from her since childhood.' (*Méphis* II, pp. 35–6) Indeed, their 'irrepressible need to take possession of the other' seems to be the wish for the two split sides of Tristan's being, the male and the female parts, to unite. Or perhaps it expresses the ultimate narcissistic wish for fusion with the mirror image, with the self.

There is however a struggle between the two, a struggle for power over each other. The two represent different doctrines of the role of woman: Maréquita favours the 'passive role of self-denial' taught by the Church, and Méphis believes it is woman's role 'to inspire man', to be 'the new woman'. (*Méphis* II, pp. 91–2) Méphis seems to fore-shadow his defeat in the struggle between the two ideologies when he finds himself mastered by Maréquita: 'all possibility of resistance was frozen in him and he obeyed as a slave obeys his master.' (*Méphis* II, p. 31) (In this sense, Tristan wanted to show how contemporary women destroyed not only themselves but the progressive men who sought to improve their lot.)

Thus Maréquita and Méphis are united in many ways, and obviously the similarities are more than coincidental. They have shared parallel experiences: unrequited love, exploitative relationships, betrayal. Finally, they are linked even in death: 'The same bullet which had killed Méphis has pierced my heart. I cannot live without that man.' (*Méphis* II, p. 282) Both share a common project: to constitute themselves as a kind of elite by sacrificing themselves to a worthy cause. This sacrifice in both cases is questionable in the sense that it derives as much from hatred of an enemy as it does from love. Méphis advises Maréquita at his death that 'the only revenge I bequeath to you is to continue putting my projects into action.' (*Méphis* II, p. 267)

Within the circle of the identification between Méphis and Maréquita however is the negation of that identification: for Méphis also signi-fies, or reminds us, of the term 'mépris', whis is echoed throughout the book. Not only Méphis' overt criticism of Maréquita's ideology, but the very lifestyle in which he would engage her is full of the danger of 'mépris'. For Maréquita, this is fatal: 'I am only a feeble creature; I cannot bear to think that society despises me – contempt kills me!' (*Méphis* II, p. 208)

As she explains, for women the danger of contempt or scorn is enormous:

To a greater degree than men, woman needs esteem and respect. Her heart needs the goodwill of those around her, even though public opinion is so often of little value; and in our position, it would be impossible for me to win that public consideration without which woman falls from repute. (*Méphis* II, p. 163)

It is after all in woman's profound need for respect (the opposite of *mépris*) that Tristan locates Maréquita's fatal flaw. For Maréquita, Méphis and Tristan, the object of desire is mediated by the desire of the Other. What we witness in *Méphis* is the construction of an infinite number of 'désirs triangulaires'[66] that reverberate around the two parallel triangles of desire in which the two main characters are caught.

In his desire for Maréquita, Méphis is confronted with the opposing desire of Torepa, the representative of the aristocracy. Because Méphis really desires to be Torepa (an aristocrat) and Torepa Méphis (a proletarian), neither can attain Maréquita, because she is not what they are after. The other triangle consists of the opposing desires of Xavier and Maréquita for Méphis. Xavier represents the Church, and it is really that institution's acceptance that Maréquita desires. Thus, it is appropriate that these two 'villains' (Torepa and Xavier) should reappear at the end and together be responsible for the death of Maréquita and Méphis. The atmosphere reigning in the 'univers de la Médiation interne', accurately described by Girard, is the one that pervades the novel:

The contagion is so widespread, in the sphere of interior mediation, that any individual may become his neighbour's mediator without understanding the role he is playing ... He will be tempted to model himself on the model of his desire ... Two identical but opposite triangles are then superimposed on each other. Desire reverberates faster and faster between the two rivals ... We now have a mediator-subject and a subject-mediator, a model-disciple and a disciple-model. Each one imitates the other while asserting the priority and anteriority of his own desire. Each one sees in the other a terribly cruel persecutor. All the relationships are symmetrical; the two partners believe they are separated from each other by an unfathomable abyss but it is impossible to say about one of them anything that would not be true as well for the other. It is the sterile confrontation of opposites, becoming more and more deadly and futile as the two subjects draw nearer to each other and as their desire intensifies.[67]

'Le mal' is however perceived in a mystified way. The enemy, personified by Xavier, is clearly a target because of the fact that he represents the 'puissance occulte' that has been organizing itself as a political force at the same time as it has been destroying the lives of women from within. This drive for power, which Maréquita only vaguely comprehends, is attacked by a series of charges: 'The priest is without mercy! There is no hatred as implacable as his! ... I die victim of a priest ... Xavier, you are the devil incarnate in the guise of a priest, as I am the lamb incarnate in the guise of a proletarian.' (*Méphis* II, pp. 246, 267, 229)

The last charge is significant, for just as Xavier is not 'the devil under the guise of priest', neither is Méphis 'the lamb under the guise of proletarian'. This exaggerated and inaccurate polarization of characters exposes the paranoia within Tristan's perception of reality. Because of the deep desire and hatred she felt, she would continually try to integrate these two sides of herself, but finally the union would be fatal, as fatal as the desire itself: 'The conceited person tries to draw everything to himself, gathers everything in his self, but he never succeeds. He always suffers from a flight toward the other through whom he loses his essence.'[68]

This dynamic becomes clear when we observe the confused presentation of the titles of books ascribed to Méphis' pen. Although early in the novel he has declared himself to be working on a study of 'the moral and physical condition of the people in France', on his death Maréquita refers to the important text that he has left behind as, 'Woman's Education in the Future'. (*Méphis* II, pp. 226, 296) The confusion of causes to which Méphis has devoted himself indicates that the causes were perhaps only a pretext.

Another significant error is revealed in the various evaluations of the concept of egoism. It is described in both a positive and negative sense depending on to which character this quality is attributed. Is it evil, or is it the life force? First, it is defined favourably: 'The men in whom it [this noble impulse] controls egoism, are exceptional beings; there are very few of them in the history of nations!' (*Méphis* II, p. 290) Later Maréquita describes the lesson that her daughter, in whom all hope for the future has been placed, will learn: 'She will learn ... that egoism is the result of ignorance.' (*Méphis* II, p. 296) Later still, at the end of the novel in the chapter on Xavier, egoism is referred to in the following derogatory context: 'in this period of atheism, depravity, egoism and cynicism'.(*Méphis* II, p. 316) Tristan's difficulties in evaluating egoism are central to her problem of defining the mode of action her characters undertake and the evil that befalls them.

It seems likely that in this age, which witnessed the demise of the Romantic ego in favour of a much less dangerous 'bourgeois ego', there was confusion of terms of definition and above all perception of the self. Especially for women this perception was obfuscated by contemporary trends in education and by prejudice, and it is the final legacy of this contorted novel that it is based on 'méprise', (again, close in sound to Méphis) or the mistake: the mistake lies in the confusion over the forces of history and of sex roles. Tristan herself recognized the difficulty of the project to set oneself up 'defending the oppressed'. (*Méphis* II, p. 293) Because she was engaged in recuperating women's lost power and importance, Maréquita thought this could only be achieved through martyrization: 'her successes will be bought with the blood of martyrs.' (*Méphis* II, p. 294) In essence Tristan herself was to carry out the project ascribed to the daughter of Méphis and Maréquita in her effort to organize the working classes.

In the novel, the project for social change is realized only through the destruction of certain myths about the power and function of love. The critique of contemporary women is undercut by the attraction of the mythic, all-powerful woman, based on the Saint-Simonian credo. In tandem, this conflicted view was designed to produce martyrs, but it was not really designed to produce social change. Still, it offered an image of the superior woman, one that imbued Tristan with the courage to struggle for change even under the aegis of martyrdom.

Tristan accurately perceived the enormity of the shadow of the *Prolétaire* and its protrusion across history for the rest of the century: 'the awesome voice of the proletarian', 'the gigantic shadow of the proletarian' (*Méphis* II, pp. 293, 281) would make itself felt more powerfully than would the shadow of one single woman. Her own prediction would come true in part: 'During the 20 years preceding my daughter's coming of age, many voices will be heard speaking on behalf of the proletarian, and once that time has passed, Méphis' writings will get an enthusiastic reception.' (*Méphis* II, p. 299)

On Tristan's premature death, the task left to the daughter of Maréquita and Méphis would also be left in some sense to Tristan's daughter, but ironically Aline, taken under the wing of George Sand, would soon dream of little more than marrying.

Although certainly not a 'great' novel, *Méphis* offers us a privileged view of the labyrinthine struggle of a woman against her private and public demons in a society characterized by the Romantic malaise during the years of the July Monarchy.

5
The Discovery of a Mission:
Promenades dans Londres

From Aesthete to Rebel

In 1839, on her fourth visit to England, Tristan saw the devastating effects of class society even more clearly. She determined to document them in her next book, *Promenades dans Londres* (1840). It marks an important change in Tristan's perception of society and of the role she began to shape for herself.

Her hope of bringing change through art now seemed illusory: 'Good heavens, what is art compared to humanity! Nothing, absolutely nothing!' (*Promenades*, p. 153) By deciding to drop the veil of art in order to confront social reality more directly, Tristan was not renouncing her desire to be an 'être d'élite'. Instead, like her character Méphis, she vowed to use her talents to study the evil effects of modern society and abandoned artistic creation. If in *Méphis* she seemed to endorse the view that 'art alone has allowed man to be ranked with the Gods' (*Méphis* I, p.32), now it appeared to her that social critique was more vital at this historical juncture and perhaps more responsive to her own needs and hopes.

Indeed, *Promenades* is situated at a critical point of transition in the development of Tristan's political and aesthetic theories. Like her character Méphis, she decided to reject the notion of merely painting the 'Femme-Guide, l'Avenir'; she was already beginning to envision herself as the 'Woman-guide', and to imagine creating 'the future'. She later admitted this desire in a very contradictory manner in the notes from her journal on *Le Tour de France*, published posthumously: 'I have *unintentionally* become the Woman-Guide as I had imagined her' (emphasis added). *(Tour de France*, p. 71) Her decision to renounce art in favour of politics was based primarily on her reaction to the human suffering she witnessed in England, the country that was supposed to represent the showcase of progress.

Promenades was the most well-received book Tristan ever wrote. In spite of the fact that she revealed a side of England that anglophile France preferred not to see, she must have impressed her compatriots with the strength of her description. In this book, Tristan eliminated autobiographical elements entirely. Only in her mode of expression and organization of material did her personal preoccupations intrude on this narrative. She made no pretence of adhering to the principles of logical development or chronological order, as she had in her earlier books. Rejecting the aesthetic codes of the novel and of the memoir, in *Promenades* Tristan presented in miniature elements of both genres as she strove to document and describe the social effects of progress. Just as in *Pérégrinations*, where the 'travel' elements were overshadowed by deeper concerns, Tristan's fragmented presentation offers evidence that leads to unavoidable conclusions.

Promenades is a disorderly, hybrid work, riven by a need to take account of history and the shocking effects of industrial capitalism on human beings. In it, Tristan deals with material outside the traditional boundaries of travel literature and of upper-class female experience: prisons, madhouses, whorehouses, slums. In all these places, and in the amusement parks of the rich, she finds evidence of the effects of the new economic system, and implicitly anticipates Marx's theory that 'The mode of production in material life conditions the general process of social, political and intellectual life.'[1]

Not only the dire social situation led Tristan to repudiate art at this juncture. She had come to believe that society itself needed to be transformed before true art could be created. 'Nowadays it would take nothing less than a social revolution for drama to be reborn.' (*Promenades*, p.275) In this statement she is groping toward an understanding of the dialectical interaction between history and art. Her logic was that because social classes were frozen poles apart from one another in English society, audiences were increasingly homogeneous. As a result, authors found their material increasingly restricted. In her view, in order to create real art one would first have to create the conditions which would permit it to flourish.

Although *Promenades dans Londres* was supposed to exist outside the realm of art, it actually proved to be a more important work of art than *Méphis*. Perhaps this was so because in breaking with the social definition of woman, Tristan broke also with the traditional conception of art. For a middle-class woman to be an artist in the 1830s, it was necessary that she rid herself of the blinders imposed by class and sex. In Tristan's case, this meant a rupture with a class experience rooted in nostalgia and with her own traumatic experience of being a woman. The tension involved in this rupture, and the concomitant freedom it permitted from traditional artistic considerations, allowed 'art' to enter the confines of this wilfully non-arty book in unusual ways.

Tristan's *Promenades* did this first of all by posing the question of whether art was a luxury society could afford at this historical juncture and also by postulating a new reality for writers to study, the effects of the industrial revolution and bourgeois marriage. By asking these questions, Tristan was pondering the problem of the relationship between art and social reality, and coming closer than ever to the dictum Marx later formulated in his theses on Feuerbach: 'Philosophers have only *interpreted* the world in various ways; the point, however, is to *change* it.'[2]

Tristan's Diverse Audiences

The pattern of an author's personal and historical concerns is often indicated by the way in which these interests undermine a chosen literary form. Especially in the structure of a work created by an unsuccessful artist, the intrusion of these concerns enables us to gauge the dominant preoccupations of a period.

In *Promenades*, a book announced by the publisher as a travel book, Tristan's confusion about her own status and that of her audience and her uncertainty about the book's purpose and its destination resulted in a hybrid work full of unresolved paradoxes. Her ambivalence toward her own role and her subject matter is revealed by certain omissions and excesses: by a lack of connection, by the separation of troublesome material into its component parts, by the sudden surge of inappropriate material charged with excessive energy and by the eruption of powerful metaphors reminiscent of certain descriptions in *Méphis*.

All these deviations from the dominant metonymic pattern are evidence of evasion. Who is the author, or rather, what does she want? And for whom is she writing? Close analysis of the following passage from the third edition of *Promenades*, which she addressed directly to the workers, reveals her confusion:

> The privileged classes are frightened, they are terror stricken, they threaten, the ground shakes. The poet's songs must be put aside for happier days, for this is not the proper time to *enjoy* reading novels, poems, fables or dramas. The *useful*, first, the useful. Now, it is imperative for *the workers to learn the causes of their sufferings and find the means to eliminate them*. (*Promenades*, p. xiv)

The first sentence of this passage is characterized by its fragmentation. Through the lack of connectives, causality has been suppressed. The reason for this suppression is perhaps to be found in the unclear reference of the pronoun 'they' at the end of the first sentence: 'ils menacent' ('they threaten'). Who is the subject here? Certainly not 'the privileged', although grammatically it ought to be. We must search several sentences back in the preceding paragraph to find the correct subject: 'les peuples'. The lack of clarity is not without significance, especially since this passage appears in the 'Dédicace aux classes ouvrières' that introduces the 'édition populaire' of *Promenades dans Londres* (1842). If this material was addressed to workers, why were they referred to as 'ils' and 'les peuples', in the third-person form and not addressed directly in the second-person, using 'vous'?

The second sentence is also elliptical: 'The poet's songs must be set aside for happier days, for this is not the proper time to enjoy reading novels.' *Who* should put aside this pleasure is unclear. At the end of the passage, however, Tristan tells us that it is urgent that 'the workers should be educated'. If the workers have to be educated, then it is unlikely that the injunction in the first sentence is addressed to them. Would they read Shakespeare, or novels? Even if they could read and had the money to purchase books, would they ever have the leisure time to do so? This series of questions arises because of the confusion about the subject of the second sentence. Why aren't the workers addressed directly as 'you'? Why is this inappropriate advice seemingly addressed to them? This confusion over the identity of the subject obscures the fact that clearly it was Tristan herself who was meant to receive this advice: it was she who had to leave aside these pleasures, the typical pleasures of a lady of leisure. What this injunction really implied was that Tristan would have to cast aside her conventional self-image in order to instruct the people. But to reject being a member of the privileged class was all the more difficult since she was only so in fantasy.

Perhaps that is why the real subject of this sentence, Tristan, had to be omitted. For neither of the two social spaces was ever clearly her rightful one, the one to which she belonged. How to reject that which she had glimpsed but never possessed? In reality, as we have seen, although she had for the most part of her life been poor, she never considered herself as such and never identified her class status with that of the poor. Indeed, through the arts, she had tried to recuperate the lost status of nobility. Nothing represented this confusion more accurately than the contradictory class status of Jean Labarre, alias John Lysberry, alias Méphis, the proletarian banker.

Moreover, if this injunction was really addressed to herself, there was still another error, or omission. In this passage Tristan was really commanding herself to cease a certain kind of writing, as well as reading: she must reject the frivolous characteristics that her age associated with and demanded of art. In so doing she was implicitly rejecting her identification with a certain image of the recipient of such art – upper-class women. That her sexual identity and her class predilections should have allied her with the 'beau' rather than the 'utile' is clear. So, to reject the 'beau' was to renounce the image of herself as the pretty, doll-like creature, 'la belle andalouse'. (Her attraction to this description, frequently made of her by contemporaries, was indicated by the myriad and contradictory representations of 'la belle andalouse' in the portraits of Maréquita and Clotilde in *Méphis*.)

Although Tristan later denounced her own beauty ('I have the misfortune of being a beautiful woman'), still when she described her search for the ideal portrait of herself, she said it ought to include both elements, that of the beauty and the social outcast, 'The Andalusian-born woman condemned by society'.[3] How to integrate into one person the aristocratic beauty and the pariah? *Méphis* illustrated the enormous problem this posed for Tristan. In that novel she chose to resolve it by dividing the contradictory tendencies into separate characters. But in real life, resolution was possible only if she could transform herself into a 'femme forte' and 'femme guide', a synthesis that would mean suppressing the other aspects of her character. (Perhaps that is why both Maréquita and Méphis had to die; each represented only one side of her character).

And yet with *Promenades* Tristan did succeed in revolting against the upper class (the 'beaux arts' establishment) and in surprising the working class (via the press) – the two external manifestations of her internal struggle.

To understand why Tristan had to reject the upper-class 'beaux arts' partisans, we need only glance at a statement made by a figure representative of that milieu, Hortense Allart de Méritens, and to observe her appraisal of Tristan's book as written in a letter to Saint-Beuve, one of the major critics of the period: 'Mme Tristan has sent me her *Promenades dans Londres* … It is a cry of compassion, of indignation on behalf of the English people. As it is wanting in good taste and refinement, you will not want to read it.'[4]

In this same letter, Allart, a prominent 'femmes de lettres' of the period and a moderate feminist, went on to reveal her class allegiance by criticizing *Promenades* on the grounds of its style, and by warning Saint-Beuve that he would find it unreadable. Allart rejected the 'social' content of *Promenades* on the basis of its style. Her hypocritical message was rendered more devastating by the fact that it closed with a request that revealed that for Tristan, at this juncture, the support of women was important: 'Tell me if she has sent a few copies to Marie [Mme d'Agout, or Daniel Stern], for she applies to women for selling them.'[5] With attitudes such as those revealed in Allart's letter, it is unlikely that Tristan got the support she needed.

Tristan indicated her distress at the reactions of contemporary women in a letter:

If you don't feel all this, Women, abstain from making a judgement about the works of a woman who feels on her heart the chains that weigh so heavily on one-half of humanity. Stay comfortably snuggled in your sofa – to pray and invent your Gods, and let her fight for you.[6]

Another commentary from Allart, this 'failed literary woman', whose liaisons with Chateaubriand and then Sainte-Beuve showed what close 'bedfellows' conservative and liberal Romanticism were, indicates the dominant view of women among upper-class intellectual women, the group Tristan must have felt closest to: '... women as a whole are child-bearers and child-rearers, as men as a whole are farmers and artisans ... if all women were free and treated fairly, there would be but a few among them who would, with men, get well-deserved positions and honours.'[7]

Indeed, *Promenades* shocked the upper classes (and their women) because it presented the part of society they preferred not to see. Their well-being was based on this blindness. Hence, their rejection had to be couched in the proper context of 'goût' and 'délicatesse'.

The difficulty of Tristan's position can be gauged by the response of the working-class press to it: approving of Tristan's courageous investigation, these journalists were shocked to see such material coming from a woman. 'Mme Tristan's boldness, if unexpected in a woman is nonetheless useful,'[8] said the *Revue du progrès*, edited by Blanc. Vinçard, editor of the newly formed *Ruche populaire*, edited entirely by workers, also praised Tristan, recommending that his subscribers read her book in spite of the author's sex: [He admired] '... the fervent enthusiasm which inspires the author on behalf of the working class, and the author, my friends, is a woman.'[9]

The distance that separated these two publics and their demands was enormous. To please the upper-class 'beaux arts' establishment, Tristan would have had to renounce the very characteristics of her writing that attracted the other public, the working-class press. To please the latter, she would have had to renounce her gender!

T. J. Clark's distinction between two terms, the 'audience' and the 'public', is useful here. For him, the 'audience' is simply the mass of social classes in a given place and time; the 'public' is a more select group, 'created by the private representations that are made of it in the discourse of the critic'.[10] (In our study, this discourse is illustrated by the representative voices of Allart de Méritens, Blanc, and Vinçard.) Clark believes that this discourse exercises tremendous influence on the artist. Even if he or she rejects it, its impact can be felt in places where the voice of the unconscious surges: it 'determines the structure of private discourse; it is the key to what cannot be said.'[11]

In writing *Promenades*, Tristan was not following the rules of either public nor those of her class or sex, yet she was conscious of all their demands. Her life had become a struggle against the status quo, however, and her writing expressed this clash between psychological and historical dimensions: reminders of her identity as 'la fille andalouse', of her brush with 'real' femininity as conceived by her society, were evoked continually by her striking beauty. Remnants of her brief encounter with wealth in Peru and the upper-class preferences and mannerisms taught her by her mother and mirrored in the dominant cultural ideal haunted her, and demanded articulation. So *Promenades* is a hybrid work, charged with the tension of these unresolved conflicts of class and sex as they clashed with the traditional expectations of the author's various 'publics'.

Tristan, the Reluctant Travel Writer

The confusion between the identity of the subject and object of Tristan's discourse is one of the major areas in which this unresolved tension emerges. The two terms are linked historically, and the real nature of their internal connection is revealed in another passage from the same 'Dédicace aux classes ouvrières', in which it is even more clear that Tristan is not directly addressing the workers, to whom she again refers as 'they':

> Ah! ... if the English workers would imitate the noble resolve of their brothers in Lyons. Alas! for a good many years the English worker has gone hungry! ... Hunger, that implacable Fury has undermined his strength, and today, the unfortunate people, worn out, exhausted, fall to the ground and die! Yes, they die without a word of complaint; they no longer have the strength to complain ... But the responsibility for their deaths will fall on those who assassinate them so ruthlessly! (*Promenades*, p. vi)

Here, only indirectly through the pronoun 'ceux' ('those who') does that other public, the rich, enter the discourse. We can see that they would not be pleased by the tone of this book. It was to them that *Promenades* was addressed: it was an indictment of them. Yet later in this passage, Tristan displays a certain sympathy for the upper classes, for they also suffer and are dehumanized by this kind of society. Besides, Tristan regarded herself as one of them.

The use of inappropriate juxtapositions and equivocal correlations also reveals the tension between the various publics and the various voices within herself that Tristan was trying to serve. One striking example is the choice of the book's title, *Promenades dans Londres*. If we compare our idea of what kind of book the title promises with the actual text, we discover, as Tristan's contemporaries must have, that the title is inappropriate. 'Promenades' is a banal word commonly used to describe a haphazard, casual activity that only the rich can afford. It is a word we associate with the Andalousian Lady, and seems to promise a travel book for tourists – but Tristan's study can hardly be characterized as an undirected walk. Her more serious purpose is clear: 'I have attempted to prepare the way for those who truly wish to serve the cause of the English people.' (*Promenades*, p. v) As it turns out, the word 'promenades' is rarely employed in the text. It occurs only once and refers to the activity of 'procuring' as engaged in by prostitutes. (*Promenades*, pp. 114–5) Thus the alter ego of the Andalousian Lady, that is, the prostitute (revealed in the unmasking of Clotilde in *Méphis*) returns. It seems as if the prostitutes' 'promenade' is the only kind of walking that can be carried out in London; for as Tristan later points out, walking as a social activity, or as a means of maintaining human relationships, is nearly impossible there. The city is too large, its streets too labyrinthine. Only the prostitutes, who have deciphered its new and strange face, engage in walking, for they know that if one is to survive in the new society all activity has to be geared to money-making.

Tristan herself had to survive, and she was having trouble with her publisher, Ladvocat.[12] Thus, in choosing *Promenades dans Londres* as her title in the hope of selling her book, she may have wilfully engendered some of the confusion about which public she wanted to please. Sections appealing to the working-class public bump up unexpectedly against those destined for the moneyed audience, jarring the unsuspecting reader. In this sense, one can view the book as an unconscious manifestation of the class struggle, and this dynamic seems well-described by Engel's notion that 'neither thoughts nor language in themselves form a realm of their own ... they are only manifestations of actual life.'[13]

The popular edition of *Promenades dans Londres* published in 1842 bore the added title 'ou l'aristocratie et les prolétaires anglaises'. In this later edition, the focus was much clearer. Tristan eliminated some of the material she considered extraneous, choosing innocuous material that would have been of interest to the reader of travel literature – the rich, the leisured person.

In every edition of this book, however, the reader must make the difficult transition from the seemingly innocuous title *Promenades* to the demonic heading of the first chapter, 'La ville monstre' without much help. Once past this gate, we know we have entered a world charged with meaning, a world distant from the one usually perceived by the tourist in his 'promenades', although that world slips in from time to time.

Tristan approached the object of her study in the best tradition of Hegel, with whose writings and method she was probably unfamiliar. In the tangible she saw the intangible; in the reality she observed, she saw all that was wanting. Her vision was therefore saturated with the power of negative thinking. In the Hegelian mode of seeing, 'Every fact is more than a mere fact; it is a negation and restriction of real possibilities.'[14] For Tristan, the 'dialectic of negativity' as Marx called it[15] seemed to come naturally. It was simply her way of perceiving the world. Perhaps her status as a foreigner allowed her to peer beneath the veil of ideology, thus strengthening this tendency, as did the contradictions of class and sex. She began to recognize the means by which the ruling class perpetuated domination. Three institutions with which Méphis and Maréquita wrestled, '*the schools, the Church*, and the *press*', she now declared to be 'the *accomplice* of the oppressors'. (*Promenades*, 1842, p. vi) She recognized that together with hunger, these were the means by which the status quo was maintained.

The reader who entered this text expecting pleasurable travel information would be very surprised. On the first page, he would discover that the 'grandeur' of London 'calls immediately to mind both the oppression ... and the commercial superiority of England!'. The presentation of these contradictory aspects of English society was extraordinary in this kind of book, but Tristan went further, emphasizing the negative aspect of the dialectic she perceived and infusing it with a strong Enlightenment dose of optimistic fatality:

> But the wealth, a result of the successful use of force and ruse, is ephemeral; it cannot endure without reversing the universal laws by which, when the time has come, the slave will break his chains, enslaved people will shake off the yoke, and knowledge useful to man will be disseminated so that ignorance may also be set free. (*Promenades*, p. 1)

Yet at this point Tristan's humanism was still vague: she had still to experience the actual conditions of industrial slavery before she could define her philosophic concepts in terms of social and economic realities.

Because she brought the intention to 'negate the negation' with her in her reading of reality, Tristan anticipated the critical method of Marx and Engels and its concrete application to social change. In the course of *Promenades*, she discovered the actual conditions which lay beneath the abstract concepts of the revolution. In this too she anticipated Marx and Engels. In discovering both sides of the dialectic, she uncovered the contradiction that would produce the necessity for revolution. For if 'Twenty-six million human beings are brought up as slaves' despite the fact that it is they who 'create all the wealth', then one could predict

with some certainty that they would become the agents of their own
liberation, as Tristan did: 'Resistance to oppression is not only man's
natural right, but what is more, when the people are oppressed, insurrection becomes a sacred duty.' (*Promenades*, 1842, p. v)

Tristan cemented her view of the class struggle in this text in a way
that presaged the *Communist Manifesto*. Before Marx, she accurately perceived and described the basis for revolution in the class struggle:

> ... but the great struggle, the one which is destined to transform the
> social order, is that which opposes on one side property owners and
> capitalists who control everything, wealth, political power, and for
> whose benefit the country is governed, and on the other, the
> workers of city and countryside who have nothing, neither land, nor
> capital, nor political power, who pay, however, two-thirds of the
> taxes, furnish recruits for the army and the navy, and whom the rich,
> as they see fit, keep on the verge of starvation to make them work
> for lower wages. (*Promenades*, p. 58)

Class Conflict within Tristan herself

But in the opening chapters of *Promenades*, Tristan's limited perception
of the working class is obvious. She refers to upper-class experience as
if it represented all human experience:

> Ordinary errands involve distances of five or six miles; so that if one
> has several things to do, one is likely to cover fifteen or twenty miles
> a day; it is easy to imagine the time lost in this manner; on the
> average half the day is spent walking the streets of London ... The
> Londoner, when he comes home in the evening, exhausted from the
> day's errands, is not likely to be cheerful, witty, nor inclined to cul-
> tivate the pleasures of conversation, music, or dancing. (*Prome-
> nades*, pp. 4–5)

This passage indicates the extent to which Tristan was still unfamiliar
with the real work world. For working people did not exhaust themselves nor amuse themselves in 'errands'. Therefore, the category she
described as 'le Londonnien' was not representative of all Londoners,
only of the rich. Clearly this passage reflects the image Tristan had of
herself and of her reader, as people who engage in the 'plaisirs de la
conversation, de la musique ou de la danse'. Here again, as in the earlier
passage where she denounced reading for pleasure rather than instruction, Tristan revealed her class sympathies through her choice of
cultural preferences.

Tristan must have recognized the oversight implied in her description of the universal Londoner. In order to complete the picture, she carelessly threw in another term to illustrate the other kind of physical exhaustion caused by labour: 'the farmer, when he comes home, after twelve hours of hard work'. (*Promenades*, p.v) She obviously chose this example from her Rousseauist stock of images. It reveals the limits of her comprehension of the situation she encountered in London. Her concepts were not yet adequate to describe the industrial society that had produced London's diverse classes. This brief and somewhat illogical introduction to the fate of the inhabitants of 'la ville monstre' strikes one mostly by what it omits and surprises one by the disparate items it includes.

Tristan's book offers an example of the limits of class consciousness and paradoxically an insightful vision of future conflict. This is not surprising, since it is one of the first accounts of the huge social transition then taking place in England. It is marred by the psychological and ideological impediments that blocked a full disclosure of the society's ills, compounded by the anticipation of how such a revelation would be received, especially by the rich. For instead of presenting the rich with the glorious aspect of triumph, Tristan was determined to reveal the devastating misery industrialization caused.

Of course, the foreign visitor was supposed to be enthralled by the spectacle of the wealth and power of England and not to look beneath it; the visitor was to be a tourist, and not a muckraker. To perceive without blinders the sector of society that was supposed to be invisible, that the rich preferred not to see or be shown, was to embarrass and scold the upper class: it reminded them that their well-being was not shared by all, but that it depended on the labour and penury of others. In electing to expose this social truth, Tristan risked ostracism from this class and its writers.

Tristan's desire to explore the reality of the working class was problematical, as we have seen. When she finally identified with it, she infused it with a powerful, positive image that made its martyrization all the more admirable: 'The workers, who have lifted England's fortune to such heights, are the pariahs of English society.' (*Promenades*, p. 62) Only then could she attribute to them the term of 'praise' that she had reserved for herself, women and artists: pariah. And, yet, instinctively, she was also repulsed by this class, for they represent the 'ugly'. When she walked in the slum of St Giles, she had to remind herself that these people were human beings, that she must observe the disgusting spectacle before her no matter how repulsive.

Here again, Tristan's attack on the perpetrators of this social evil can be read as a project of vengeance against the class she had come to regard as murderers: 'But the responsibility for their deaths [that of the workers] will fall on those [the upper classes] who assassinate them so ruthlessly!'. (*Promenades*, 1842, p. vii) She wrote this to make the upper-class aware of the effects of their well-being, and to make them uncomfortable. In so doing, she renounced her nostalgic membership in that class by refusing to observe its code of *politesse*.

Yet, on certain occasions, such as her visit to St Giles, Tristan's profound identification with the upper class was revealed in the things she felt she could say. In describing her strong antipathy to the sight and smells usually associated with work and with poverty, her deep repugnance for the poor emerged. The fact is that Tristan felt more comfortable with her idea of the working class than with the reality of their lives. '… I've never seen such bestial, ugly faces … '[16]

This passage from the uncensored pages of the journal she kept during her tour of France in 1844 suggests how profoundly she was affected by her class preference. Only her faith in the future transformation of these people (through her efforts) prevented her from another more instinctive reaction to the knowledge of them she had acquired on her tour: 'If I did not believe in a good, just, powerful, providential God, I would this very instant, become an outlaw and burn and destroy this human race that I loathe!'[17]

Obviously her perception of class reality was to be deeply coloured by her own psychic jousts with the 'high' society that had refused her admittance. Her identification with and compassion for the working class was inextricably bound to her quest for vengeance against her own wished-for class. It is likely that her unconscious repugnance for the working class delayed their appearance in the text, for the task she had set herself was in some respects an unpleasant one. And yet, her *exposé* performed a vital service to her contemporaries and probably left its mark on Engels and Marx, who knew her work.

Historically, her ambivalence was reinforced by the fact that France still had not developed a proletariat of its own, and that her approach to the reality she perceived in England was based on the only model she knew, the one from the continent. In England the economic effects of industrialism were more obvious and the class struggle more advanced. For in the 1830s, as Edouard Dolléans points out, there was still an enormous difference between the two countries:

Between 1830 and 1836 the two countries have developed at an unequal pace; capitalism has advanced much further in Great Britain than in France. In Great Britain … the Industrial Revolution has had its full impact. In France on the contrary, the Industrial Revolution is just beginning to take effect. France remains a nation of artisans and cottage workers. The industrial proletariat is relatively unimportant and almost exclusively limited to the textile industries.[18]

Thus he explains that while in England economic factors were primarily responsible for the development of working-class consciousness, in France, psychological factors based on the disillusioning experience of the July Revolution played an important role in creating a class consciousness antecedent to the actual development of such a class. We have to keep this historical comparison in mind to understand Tristan's depiction of the situation of workers in France as idyllic in contrast to those in England. She was able to mythologize the lot of the French worker in part because she was unfamiliar with it (her work experience could be classified 'artisanale') but also because capitalism at home was at an earlier stage of development. In a sense, Tristan had to go to London to discover the truth about France's future.

The psychological and historical factors we have analysed above delayed her discovery of England's economic significance. The capital city itself, its climate, its French colony, the Chartists and the Parliament, all these areas had to be examined before Tristan got inside a factory and actually saw the worker at work. Her long journey represents the allegory of the development of class-consciousness in a middle or upper-class person. First, he or she must study the areas of reality most closely associated with his or her own class. Only after the basis for Tristan's own class hatred was established could she depict the suffocating and murderous qualities of upper-class society and the pernicious effects of their comfortable existence, and then assign responsibility.

Bourgeois Vampirism

In the preface to *Promenades* Tristan announces the plight of workers to be the subject of her study, and this subject is the absent presence that haunts the first 90 pages of the book. The worker is first introduced as an abstract idea, the slave who must break his chains. He next appears indistinguishable amidst the crowds of London, 'the waves of people silently pouring out in the long dark streets', in the city in which the foreigner or stranger is 'overwhelmed by the sheer weight of such vastness and is humbled at the thought of his own insignificance'. (*Promenades*, p. 2) In these early pages the connection between theory and reality has not been drawn, there is only the contrast of size, of the reduced dimension of the human being next to the works he has created (in passages that give a vague premonition of Marx's notion of alienation).

The author saves for last the items most foreign to her experience. In her catalogues of the enormous hulks of architecture, it is only after the docks, ships, and churches, that industrialism rears its head: 'These buildings strangely deformed by the mists; these monumental smokestacks which belch their black smoke into the sky and reveal the existence of the great factories ... ' (*Promenades*, pp. 2–3) Even the manner of the description indicates a holding off: the great factories have been reserved the last space, and yet they are of primary importance.

But if the city and its myriad inventions aroused in her a desire to 'devote herself to the study of men of every class' (ibid.), it was first of all the impossibility of such a study that struck her. Where could such a study be conducted in this maze-like city, in which even the most basic of human relations, that of the family, seemed impossible? In these early chapters, the dehumanizing qualities of the industrial city impressed Tristan but the causality was still unclear. To us now it seems clear that the Romantic malaise originated in the paradox that the joyous discovery of the individual and his worth occurred just at the moment when social and economic structures were beginning to submerge that individual. But pioneer chroniclers like Tristan needed 'supernatural elements' to explain the confusing phenomena they perceived around them. How to describe this reality except by 'the bridges which one is tempted to believe were cast up by giants', or 'la vision fantastique'; these are the only terms she can use to describe 'the confusion of images and sensations'. (*Promenades*, pp. 2–3) In these passages, the Romantic writer enhances the drama represented by the new industrial society.

In describing the geographical division of the city according to classes, Tristan demonstrated her understanding of class relations and their effects. Engels would make use of this means of introducing class distinctions in his *Condition of the Working Class in England*[19] written five years later, but Tristan's statement is one of the most powerful:

> The contrast found in the three parts of the city is the same that civilization presents in all great capitals: but it is more pronounced in London than anywhere else. On the one hand, there is the busy population of the city whose only motive is desire for profit, on the other there is the haughty, disdainful aristocracy who come to London, each year, to escape from boredom and make an unbridled display of wealth, or to revel in their own superiority in contrast to the poverty of the people ... And finally in the suburbs, there are the masses of workers, so thin, so pale ... the swarms of prostitutes with shameless gait and wanton glances ... the troops of children, who, like birds of prey, come out each evening from their holes, and fall upon the city, where they plunder without fear ... (*Promenades*, p. 7)

Note that the negative term was again saved for last. Thus it is that the proletariat briefly rears its ugly head, in the guise of thieves and prostitutes, in the first chapter of *Promenades*, 'La Ville monstre'. The reader is still confused, as is the writer. Which is the 'monstre', the city, or, as the rich believed, the proletariat? From Tristan's description of the latter, her own view seemed to be ambivalent. Until she was willing to leave behind the comfortable ambiance of her own class and confront the reality of working-class life, she would not understand class relations. What she could already perceive was the atmosphere produced by this new urban civilization, and its effect on human life. The image of the future offered by London was not comforting. It dehumanized rich and poor alike, she observed:

> In London, everything breathes gloom, it is in the air; it enters by every pore. Ah, nothing is so lugubrious as the aspect of the city on a day of fog, of rain or fierce cold! ... On those days, London is awesome! One imagines oneself wandering in the necropolis of the world, one breathes its sepulchral air, the light is wan, the cold is damp; and the long rows of identical houses with their small dark windows, and their black iron-work are like two rows of tombs which stretch to infinity and among which cadavers stroll awaiting the hour of their burial. (*Promenades*, p. 10)

In this charged, romantic description, the cause of London's malaise remains obscure. Is only the weather to blame for London's inhospitability, for its inhumanity? London was indeed a necropolis, but causes other than the weather were to blame. Yet, in this nightmare vision, all the class divisions are once again subsumed under the rubric of 'sadness'. Note that the factories have been omitted from this catalogue. The author again conveniently dodges the original purpose of her quest by returning to the perspective of the upper-class London inhabitant.

In these early chapters of *Promenades*, then, each time we brush up against the brutal reality of working-class life, the force of that image is dissipated by a return to the universal. Enormous resistance to this material characterized the author as she set out to explore this unknown territory. Tristan understood the idea of revolution only in abstract terms; she still had not confronted the real conditions of working-class life, nor her own class's responsibility for them. Universality, delays and a lack of connection between theory and reality resulted from her evasion, so that the force of the book has to be discovered later, after reading it, by a reorganization of its parts.

For what Tristan was ultimately avoiding was the horrible knowledge that once she had placed the blame, she too might be implicated in it. In the text she never fully recognizes her complicity, but it is implicit in one of the last descriptions she makes of the class situation, one in which the two classes confront one another, and responsibility is finally assigned. This passage is to be found in her journal *Le Tour de France* on the occasion of her visit to St Etienne, made approximately five months before she died. Here again, as in the first chapter of *Promenades*, Tristan depicts class warfare in terms of geography. But in

the earlier work, she presents the physical characteristics of the proletariat, and only vaguely describes the houses of the upper classes. The
later description, based on much more intimate knowledge and entirely
outside the tourist's ken, is more detailed and concrete:

> [The houses] are even dirtier, sadder and gloomier [than in Lyons].
> Those inhabited by the workers are filthy, a few new ones are not
> bad – they all belong to ironmongers, manufacturers of metal strips
> and armament. Perched here and there on the hills around the town
> are some nice houses which belong to the manufacturers. (*Tour de
> France*, p. 133)

Had it ended at this point, this passage might have seemed rather
innocuous, a simple contrast in living conditions. But Tristan decided
to interpret the significance of these houses in terms of the class
struggle. In what follows, the houses of the rich take on an active role,
for Tristan found in them the visible signs of a certain form of vampirism that lay at the heart of capitalism. This phenomenon seemed
horrific to those who examined it carefully:

> When I see those houses I experience a most disagreeable impres-
> sion which I cannot control – as I immediately think about what
> they were bought with, I see in every stone a part of a human
> being. And this mass of stones in the distance represents for me a
> mass of men, women, children, moaning and dying under their
> burden! (*Tour de France*, p. 133)

Again the passage could have stopped here, the author contemplating
from afar. But, in another section she intensifies the effect of the
causality just described and in doing so explains what she has been
evading:

> At times, the thought and the image it creates is so vivid in my mind
> that walking by those houses I can hear groans, sobs, curses! Oh, how
> it hurts me! I go by hurriedly, and I move away from those horrible
> places where my enslaved brothers' flesh has been turned into
> stone, handsome furniture, crystal, bronze, gold – silk, delicate
> batiste – beautiful flowers. All that luxury bought with the tears, the
> blood, the life of my unfortunate brothers! All that luxury repels me!
> I could not bear living in the midst of it. Oh, no! I should go mad.
> (*Tour de France*, p. 133)

No longer is her perception only visual: now it is visceral. As the
author comes closer to the evidence of this exploitation in the houses
of the rich and the poor, she hears the suffering and the curses of the

expropriated. Quickly she withdraws, to conceptualize from afar. But what she perceives from a distance is no more comforting. Her reaction intensifies from 'Oh, how it hurts me!' to a final rejection of the horrific vision of the society that it represents and the class for whose well-being this form of vampirism is necessary. Her final rejection is very painful: 'Oh, no! I should go mad.'

This admission follows the catalogue of valuable objects whose presence depends on the negation of the humanity of the working class, 'stones, handsome furniture, crystal, bronze, gold – silk, delicate batiste – beautiful flowers'. Both passages reveal the psychic cost of Tristan's political position. To take this stance was to accept her own class's responsibility for the act of expropriation of the other class; and implicitly it involved a rejection of a whole mode of being which Tristan had long ago learned to cherish. The personal cost of this final cutting of the umbilical cord is represented by the inappropriate inclusion of *belles fleurs* among the catalogue of valuable objects literally extracted out of the worker's body. Hardly objects whose exchange value is comparable with the other items mentioned in the list, *belles fleurs* immediately remind us of her name, Flora, and of her only job, as a colourist. It gives us a clue to Tristan's deep ambivalence and represents her unconscious belief in her own complicity, and therefore her guilt. But the reference also signifies her deeply repressed desire to be included in that house, the symbol of her class.

Social Change and the New Novel

Knowledge of the psychic and historical context of this vision enables us to see how closely art is linked to resistance and/or receptivity to social change. In rendering her apprehension of the new social order, Tristan produced a formulation that could be of use to both writers and philosophers. Tristan went beyond Balzac's perception of the demonic quality of accumulation to take stock of the nature of its actual constitution. This process, begun in *Promenades*, widened the parameters of realism.

Historical change was closing up the available modes of representation. After the July Monarchy, writers would have to decide to devote themselves to the shape of their sentences, to hewing out art-objects which might escape the reality of the vampirism that characterized capitalism, or to try to make the scientific assessment of the effects of the new economic order the subject matter of their literature.

Tristan's work marks the transition between the literary modes of Romanticism and Realism leading to Naturalism. For what she did was to begin the systematic study of the 'ugly'. Discovered by the Romantics, who were fascinated by the taboo nature of this area of reality that rested outside traditionally acceptable aesthetic codes, the 'ugly' was at first relished for its 'local colour' or gothic appeal. Soon it entered Realistic novels, charged with an often unexplainable demonic energy. Tristan's was a pioneer effort in the attempt to understand the 'ugly' in general economic terms: to conceive of its function in class society, she elaborated a more complete conception of reality.

Because she came to see the historical dynamic that created this category of the 'ugly', she viewed it as neither accidental nor permanent. The story of its creation became for her the centre of narration. Thus she also designated a new focus for literature in which the story of expropriation could be seen from the other side – a focus and a subject matter which Naturalism could exploit. In so doing, she uncovered a causality and indicated a method appropriate to the study of this dynamic consistent with the positivist trend developing in France at the time. In the preface to *Promenades*, she announces the procedure she followed:

> Faced with reality, I was able to form a true judgement of things. My book is a book of facts, of observations collected with all the accuracy of which I am capable; I have refrained as far as it was in my power from flights of enthusiasm or indignation. (*Promenades*, p. vi)

Even though she could not follow her own prescription consistently, and sometimes allowed herself to be carried away by her disgust with the dehumanization she saw, Tristan valued this 'scientific' method so highly that she rejected 'art' in order to employ it. And yet the writer who officially renounces literature sometimes produces work that contains the seeds of a new approach to literature. Tristan discovered this approach and this material because of the interaction of her own experience of class and sex with the historical development that these two terms were undergoing during the period of the July Monarchy.

We would not insist that her experiment 'outside' literature 'caused' the development of Naturalism, because we do not believe in the abstract dynamic of literary parthenogenesis by which forms of literature beget new forms of literature. Still, we must take account of the connections between her experiment, social change and the development of literature. Writers after her would be greatly influenced by the documentary material uncovered by Tristan and others like her who sought to explain the glaring historical contradictions produced by capitalism, because they were themselves affected by those very historical contradictions. Thus her work is a harbinger of the Naturalist trend. Whether writers decided to evade or to understand the new interpretations of reality first made explicit in *Promenades dans Londres*, they would have to pay attention to them because of historical circumstances.

Tristan anticipates Marx and Engels

As Tristan shifted away from art and directed her gaze toward social reality, her work took on another important dimension, that of political and historical analysis. If at the beginning her approach seemed closer to that of journalism, soon enough she began to peer more deeply beneath the surface to discover the dynamic process at its base. Her contribution in this domain is still largely unmeasured.

Although scholars have begun to assess the importance of the socialist milieu Marx encountered when he arrived in Paris, few have studied closely the contribution Tristan's work made to his intellectual development at this crucial point. Although she was an autodidact like Engels, she was less familiar with the German philosophical tradition. Nonetheless, she was perceptive enough to uncover the concrete basis for Marx's theoretical assumptions and to describe her findings in terms similar to those Marx and Engels later employed. Especially in her description of the economic foundation of English society in *Promenades*, her prescience becomes apparent. For *Promenades* is a hybrid text that deserves a place not only in literary history but also in the history of socialism.

Over the course of the last century, historians have sought to establish the sources for Engels' *The Condition of the Working Class in England*, published in 1845. Few have speculated on the influence that Tristan's *Promenades* may have had on his work. While it is beyond the limits of this study to document the full extent of Engels' dependency on *Promenades*, we have made an effort to indicate points of convergence between the two texts. Similarities to formulations made by Marx beginning in 1844 will also be taken into account in order to begin to explore Tristan's historic importance: hers was one of the first truly socialist appraisals of the effects of industrial capitalism.

Although it is not necessary to prove that Marx and Engels were familiar with Tristan's work to show the way in which her writings anticipated theirs, the evidence points to direct influence. It was in late autumn 1843 that Marx arrived in Paris and began to make the crucial transition from vague Hegelian humanism to scientific socialism. In Paris,

He was now at the heart of socialist thought and action ... Marx was breathing a socialist atmosphere and even living in the same house as Germain Maürer, one of the leaders of the League of the Just ... It is not surprising that his surroundings made a swift impact on Marx.[20]

Engels had left for Manchester and his father's factory, but he was in contact with Marx, whose acquaintance he had made just before leaving Germany: the articles Engels wrote for English newspapers on the theoretical developments on the Continent were based on the information Marx and others were sending him. On his way home, in late summer 1844, Engels stopped in Paris for ten days and the first collaboration between the two was initiated with the project of *The Holy Family*, for which Engels wrote a brief essay attacking Bruno Bauer and defending Flora Tristan.[21] It is interesting that it should be Engels, who had just returned from England, who cited Tristan, and not Marx, whose residence in Paris would have given him more opportunity to become familiar with her work. But it should be remembered that Marx kept Engels informed of events in Paris. Moreover, Tristan's *Promenades* was being sold in London, and Engels could easily have purchased a copy there. Direct evidence of influence is especially difficult to prove in this case, as we shall see.

Marx's description of his level of development on his arrival in Paris is telling: 'In the year 1842–43, as editor of the *Rheinische Zeitung*, I first found myself in the embarrassing position of having to discuss what is known as "material interests".'[22] Tristan, on the other hand, was holding meetings with workers at her flat at rue du Bac to discuss her little book *Union ouvrière* and to plan the implementation of her idea for a workers' international. Among the workers at these meetings were several Germans, including Germain Maürer and Arnold Ruge, the two countrymen with whom Marx was in closest contact during this period. (It was in order to collaborate with Ruge on the *Deutsch-Französiche Jahrbucher* that Marx originally came to Paris. Ruge has left a record of his impressions of the evenings he spent at Tristan's in his *Zwei Jahre in Paris*.)[23]

The whole question of how the Germans should relate to the French socialists was a major point of discussion among these men. In a letter Ruge wrote to Marx while the former was off in Germany for a few weeks, he warned that it would be better to avoid most of them. However, Ruge advised: 'We must alert women, La [George] Sand and La Tristan. They are more radical than Louis Blanc and Lamartine.'[24]

Actually, there was no need to alert Tristan: she was aware of the problematical nature of French socialism. Nonetheless, this note proves that not only was Marx well aware of Tristan's existence, but that his closest collaborator held her in high esteem.

At this juncture, in 1843, *Promenades* was going into its third 'popular' edition, which included the 'Dedication to the Working Classes', and *Union ouvrière* had just appeared. In these books Marx and Engels would have found material useful to them at this point in their development. For it is clear that as one socialist historian has put it:

·... as paradoxical as it may seem, it is because the originality and the realism of the Idea (Tristan's) did in no way escape his notice that Marx carefully avoided either establishing personal relations with Flora Tristan, or giving her, in his work, a special place or mention ... By appropriating the Pariah's message Marx was cleansing it of any mystical residue.[25]

Although she did not name the processes of capitalism, whose effects *Promenades* condemned, Tristan defined them: alienation, reification, the division of labour, the 'cash nexus', the class struggle – these concepts are implicit in the material she chose to present and in her mode of presentation.

Her demystification of the nature of the class struggle was accompanied by her discovery of the real nature of objects. She perceived in them, beneath the demonic qualities that some Romantic novelists such as Balzac had revealed, the concrete source of those qualities: exploited wage-labour.

In the passage cited above from *Le Tour de France* on the houses of the rich, a premature and unnamed depiction of the process of alienation is apparent: for what does that passage describe if not the following phenomenon, formulated by Marx in *The Economic and Philosophical Manuscripts of 1844*: 'It is true that labour produces wonderful things for the rich – but for the worker it produces privation. It produces palaces – but for the worker, hovels. It produces beauty – but for the worker, deformity.'[26]

Indeed Tristan's description had included this dimension, this contrast between the rich and the poor, and had rendered the process by which the rich absorbed the entire being of the worker. Marx would describe it this way: '... the more the worker spends himself, the more powerful becomes the alien world of objects which he creates over and against himself, the poorer he himself – his inner world – becomes, the less belongs to him as his own.'[27]

What did the houses of the rich in St Etienne represent, if not a manifestation of the externalization of the human loss experienced by the worker and of the simultaneous gain made by the owners of production? Marx would have formulated the figurative depiction of the process Tristan described in more theoretical terms: 'The *alienation* of the worker in his product means not only that his labour becomes an object, an *external* existence, but that it exists *outside him* ... and that it becomes a power on its own confronting him.'[28]

It was Tristan's perception of vampirism that affected her so deeply. Engels later expressed the idea in the following way: 'As though you rendered the proletarians a service in first sucking out their very life-blood and then practising your self-complacent, Pharisaic philanthropy upon them'.[29]

As we have seen, Tristan, like many of her fellow socialists, was more comfortable with ideas: she therefore studied what Marx would later call the 'superstructure'.[30] First she attended a meeting of Chartists and of the English Parliament before venturing to confront the actual situation of the industrial worker. She was struck by the energetic, idealistic individuals she encountered at the Chartists' meeting, and by contrast by the absolute nullity of human intelligence represented by the members of Parliament. Earlier, in her 'Dédicace aux classes ouvriers', she condemned the liberal wing of the Chartist movement by asserting that although political change was important, since the government only governed on behalf of the rich, it was more important to change the whole system: 'It is with the social order, the foundation of the structure that you must be concerned and not with politics which is a deceptive power.' (*Promenades*, 1842, p. x) Marx and Engels would certainly agree with this statement; they also called for a much more profound social change than that attainable by law.

It was in the chapter 'Factory Workers' that Tristan was able to draw her conclusion that 'So, men's lives can be bought.' (*Promenades*, p. 107) The concrete aspects of this statement were to be found in the new work process devised by capitalist manufacture – the division of labour. This method brought great progress to manufacturing but, for Tristan, this progress came at an incalculable human cost. For the division of labour 'has destroyed intelligence and reduced men to mere cogs in the machines'. (*Promenades*, p. 94) Her critique, like Marx's, sought to do away with the dehumanizing effects of this aspect of modern industry: like him, she envisaged the possibility of giving the worker diverse tasks so that 'he would not be overwhelmed by his own insignificance'. (Ibid.) Until such a change could be made 'the working woman is sacrificed to the thing', and workers transformed into 'the working human machines'.[31]

Engels also noted the brutalizing effects of the division of labour in his *Condition of the Working Class in England*. The writings of both Engels and Marx through the 1840s are saturated with this notion that the worker has become 'an appendage of the machine',[32] as they finally put it in the *Communist Manifesto*.

In describing her first encounter with a steam engine, Tristan shows how thin the line separating literature from social theory can be. Containing elements of the grotesque, this section evokes Zola's *Germinal*: it too is charged with a kind of Romantic demonic quality. In such passages, the old world confronts the new for the first time:

> Its enormous polished iron bars go up and down 40 or 50 times a minute and impart a backward and forward motion to the tongue of the monster which seems to suck in everything in order to swallow it up, the awesome groans it utters, the rapid turning of the enormous

wheel which emerges from the abyss to plunge right back into it, never revealing more than half of its circumference, fill one's soul with terror. In the presence of the monster one sees nothing else, one hears nothing but its breathing. (*Promenades*, p. 100)

'Upon recovering from your stupefaction, your terror, you look around for man; you can barely see him, reduced to the size of an ant by the dimensions of all that surrounds him.' (Ibid.) Here the diminution of man, hinted at in the early passages of *Promenades*, is finally concrete. Not only does he seem negligible in terms of his size compared with the force of the huge machine, but also, Tristan observes, so few men are necessary 'to do such enormous work'. (*Promenades*, p. 102) Will the machine age make man obsolete? she seems to speculate.

Tristan also visited a gas-works. Here again a demonic vision of the complete subjugation of the person is rendered, first in terms of a graphic description of the machine itself, and then by means of an account of its effect on the workers:

The furnace room is on the second floor, beneath it is the cellar destined to receive the coke; the stokers, armed with long iron pokers, opened the furnaces and pulled out the coke which fell in flaming torrents into the cellar. Nothing could be more awesome, more majestic than these mouths vomiting flames! Nothing could be more magical than that cellar suddenly illuminated by the burning coals which were rushing down like a waterfall cascading from the heights, and like them, engulfed in the abyss! Nothing could be more terrifying than the sight of the stokers, drenched with perspiration as if they had just come out of the water, and illuminated from both sides by those dreadful sheets of fire whose tongues of flame seem to be darting out to devour them. Oh, no, it would be impossible to see a more awesome spectacle! (*Promenades*, p. 105)

Romantic language and rhetorical sentence structure combine here to evoke a horrific vision of a landscape which is not the work of God, but of man, and whose power seems all the more terrifying. The terminology seems to come straight out of Chateaubriand: 'torrents', 'cascading', 'abyss'. The artifacts of the Romantic vision of nature are presented here not to illustrate the power and beauty of God, but to re-create the terror evoked by the works of man. The men who work these huge ovens are indistinguishable, unindividualized. (As Marx would say, they have surrendered their individuality to 'species beings',[33] that is, they exist only as a class, in terms of the common economic service they perform.) In the process of extinguishing the coke fire, they seem to be transformed: '... the stokers had turned black from head to toe, and the poor wretches, whom one might have taken for devils, merged into this infernal chaos.' (*Promenades*, p.106)

But these 'devils' were human after all. Tristan discovered that when they left, all asweat for their lodgings next door. They were practically nude, owning no clothes to protect them from the wind or the cold. The foreman, abjuring all responsibility for this insalubrious situation, blamed it on the workers' stupidity. Smugly he observed, '"That is how the men become consumptive. By going from hot to cold without taking any precaution".' (*Promenades*, p. 107) Tristan, thoroughly disgusted by his inhumane remark and by the irresponsibility of the manufacturers themselves, carefully pointed out that horses were treated better. But then, she understood the reason. The manufacturer must pay for a horse, 'while the nation furnishes him with men for nothing!' (*Promenades*, p. 106)

She declared this process to be nothing less than murder, by which 'Factory and manufacture owners, may, with impunity, dispose of the youth, of the vigour of hundreds of men, buy their existence, and sacrifice it in order to make money.' (*Promenades*, p. 107) Engels would also charge English society with murder: '... it has created for the workers an environment in which they cannot remain healthy or enjoy a normal expectation of life ... it brings them to an early grave.'[34]

What Tristan observed in this supposedly progressive country was the most complete degradation of human life that one could possibly imagine. Indeed, it seemed to her that the lot of slaves must have been better. The proletarian has no security at all, whereas, 'the slave is *sure of his bread as long as he lives*, and of being taken care of when he is ill.' (*Promenades*, p. 98) Engels made a similar comparison to show now that the worker was free from his master, 'no one guarantees him a subsistence.'[35] 'The serf's livelihood was guaranteed ... The modern free worker has no similar guarantee because he is only certain of a place in society when the middle classes require his services.'[36]

Tristan certainly did not mean to recommend slavery, but she did want to demystify the idealistic promise of capitalism. Therefore she devoted a part of the chapter '*Ouvriers des manufactures*' to explaining that slavery had been abolished in Jamaica not because of the altruism of the English, but because the alternative was more profitable for them. The change had robbed the Jamaican and made him practically destitute – free, but a slave of wages (in short, another proletarian). Ironically, this change had been carried out in the name of freedom: '... they also expect that the proletarians whom they thoroughly fleece, whom they squeeze dry in every possible way, whose bread they begrudge, they expect, cruel irony! that those slaves bent under their burden, will believe themselves free!' (*Promenades*, p. 222)

Engels similarly pointed out that: 'slavery of the working classes is hypocritically and cunningly disguised from themselves and the public.'[37] In fact, 'the worker *appears* to be free because he is not sold outright.'[38] This pretension covered up the fact that the new system was much more advantageous to the middle classes than the system of slavery. Engels observed that there is a potential for change concealed beneath this hypocrisy: 'the society which accepts this hypocritically camouflaged form of servitude does at least pay lip-service to the idea of liberty.'[39]

Although she did not name the process 'reification', Tristan perceived the deterioration of human relations under capitalism. In earlier times, more humane relationships existed between boss and worker. Now, 'no bond exists between the worker and the English master. If the latter has no work to offer, the worker dies of hunger.'

Or, as Engels would put it, 'there is no human tie between manufacturers and workers – only an economic link.'[40]

Another aspect of the dehumanization inherent in the new mode of work was to be found in the contrast of the workplace as she remembered it in France with the one she observed in England. In the former, she recalled that songs and laughter were heard, but in England, 'The master wants no reminder of the world to distract for a single minute his workers from their task; ... a deathlike silence reigns.' (*Promenades*, p. 97) Profit and efficiency required that the worker completely suppress his humanity in this process. Marx described it in similar terms – the humanity of the worker was denied: '... in his work, therefore, he does not affirm himself but denies himself ... does not develop freely his physical and mental energy but mortifies his body and ruins his mind ... what is human becomes animal.'[41]

For what had happened was that the cash 'nexus'[42] as Marx and Engels called it had replaced the ties which originally bound humans to one another. Earlier than they, Tristan described it this way:

Since in our societies all passions can be satisfied with money, since there are no obstacles nor any resistance that money cannot overcome; since it takes the place of talent, honour, integrity, and in a word since with it one can do anything, people balk at nothing in order to procure it. (*Promenades*, p. 151)

Engels' description of this process in the *Condition of the Working Class in England* resembled Tristan's very closely: 'Every single human quality is grossly debased by selfish greed and love of gain.'[43]

Tristan did not, however, advocate a return to feudal times. She recognized, as Marx and Engels would after her, that indeed technology could be used to benefit humanity: 'I soon realized the enormous improvement which one day would result from these scientific discoveries; brute force would be eliminated, physical labour would be per-

formed in less time, and man would have more leisure time to culti-
vate his mind.' (*Promenades*, p. 101) Marx would also point this out later
but, in the mid-1840s, Engels' main concern was the one Tristan had
mentioned only in passing, that 'Every improvement in machinery leads
to unemployment, and the greater the technical improvement, the
greater the unemployment.' (*Promenades*, p. 151)

Tristan observed that the humanization of work could not occur until
the workers appropriated technology and made it serve everyone:
'But for these great benefits to materialize a social revolution is necessary. It will come to pass – for God has not revealed those admirable
inventions to man in order to reduce him to being the helots of some
manufacturer or landowner.' (*Promenades*, p. 101) According to her, the
only way that this change could take place so that the workers could
work for their own benefit would be if the workers themselves became
'viewed as exploiters by those who owe their wealth to privilege'.
(*Promenades*, p. 64) Thus as early as 1840 she was calling for expropriation and, in effect, revolution. Later, Engels predicted similarly that
the only way the workers would regain their humanity would be by
'attacking the interests of the middle classes who live by exploiting the
workers'.[44]

In her 'Dédicace aux classes ouvrières' (of the 1842 edition of *Promenades*), Tristan gives an example of the international scope of her vision.
She determines to offer 'a great lesson that all the workers in the
world' could not refuse to ponder, by revealing the fact that this
nation of 26 million was being pressured, tortured and starved by 'a
handful of privileged people', and that resistance to oppression was 'not
only man's natural right, but what's more, when the people are
oppressed insurrection is a sacred duty'. (*Promenades*, 1842, I, p. vi) Five
years later, Engels also recognized the international character of his
audience. He addressed the working class as 'members of the great and
universal family of Mankind'.[45] Later in the text he would also call on
the workers to revolt against their oppression.[46]

Tristan's Legacy to Engels

We should not be surprised that there are so many points of connection between Tristan's book and Engels'. *Promenades* had gone through
four editions by the time he arrived in England; it was available in
England and in France, and it is unlikely that Engels in his determination to gather all that had been written on the subject would have
overlooked this book by a French socialist whose plan to organize the
first international workers' union had just been announced in her book
Union ouvrière.

As we have seen, Engels' *Condition of the Working Class in England* shared much common ground with Tristan's work. Not only are there overt structural resemblances, such as the use of the 'Dedication to the Working Classes', using the geographic division of the city to illustrate the class struggle, and overt conceptual and ideological similarities, but both bathe in the Hegelian mode of perception, viewing phenomena in terms of their negative content and their potential realization. Steven Marcus has described Engels' project as an attempt to make workers aware of '[t]heir loss of a semblance of humanity' in order that they might 'actively desire it'.[47] This description would fit *Promenades* as well.

Both Tristan and Engels were essentially outsiders to the working-class experience, observers who had to suppress their middle-class habits and preferences if they were to bear full witness to the horror of the industrial proletariat. Engels was much more frank about his class renunciation: 'I forsook the company and the dinner-parties, the port-wine and champagne of the middle-classes ... I am both glad and proud of having done so.'[48] But then his ties to this class were much firmer than Tristan's. By contrast, her renunciation was weaker: 'I refused to be dazzled by appearances; I have not been deluded by the rich and glittering décor of the English stage.' (*Promenades*, p. vi)

Indeed Engels, the son of a prosperous textile manufacturer, pronounced his intentions brashly, without disguise: 'From the first page to the last, I was writing a bill of indictment against the English bourgeoisie.'[49] Earlier than he, Tristan was engaged in essentially the same project, but never announced it in such an overt manner. Interestingly enough, neither ever completely transformed his or her lifestyle in order to join the working class. However, Tristan did *alter* her lifestyle in order to carry out her project, to serve the working classes, whereas Engels would live 'something like a double life throughout a major part of his career'.[50] For the greater part of his life he would live as 'a permanent lifetime member of the bourgeoisie',[51] as a manufacturer – an identity he found unbearable. Tristan on the other hand would die prematurely on the roads of France trying to realize her idea of the union of workers. Paradoxically, in this way she seemed to reaffirm her class identity.

To some extent, both of their projects, motivated by their ambivalent feelings toward their class, would be mediated by their association with the working class. Like Tristan, Engels would also present this class 'warts and all'.[52] Unlike Engels, Tristan would be unable to repress a certain sympathy for the rich, even as she chastised them. The intricacies of their respective representations of the class struggle were intimately tied to their own class experience. That it played an important role in mediating even the presentation of the subject matter of both books is clear. Marcus' prescription for a fruitful reading of

Engels' text applies equally to Tristan's. He finds the same kind of separation we find in Tristan's text reminiscent of 'displacement' in
dreams; the reader has to jump 300 pages to find the passage that com-
pletes a thought presented earlier, to find that which in his words
'renders explicit what was latent'[53] in the earlier passage.

Both Tristan and Engels felt hindered by the limited language at
their disposal to describe the realities they were witnessing. It is as if,
once they moved outside of their class experience, they had to learn
a new language, or create one capable of measuring the new phenomenon. Marcus ascribes the absence of figurative language in
Engels' text to the fact that 'the unprecedented magnitude of the event
is its own intensifier',[54] that 'language ... collapse[s] before such realities.'[55] This is what both authors would have us believe, but in fact
it is only the middle-class rhetoric and learned modes of perception
that give way before the new and horrifying reality. In this sense both
encountered the crisis that writers would soon experience: in their
attempts to write pure literature, could they continue to use realistic
techniques to represent the quality of this discomforting reality?
Should they instead choose to see the causality beneath it? Or, would
they seek refuge from it in the study of language and the artistic
form itself? The limits of expression that both Engels and Tristan experienced represent a harbinger of this literary crisis.

Moreover both were foreigners. Both sought to describe their foreign
experience in their own tongue, and this enhanced the strangeness and
limited quality of their expression. Engels bragged of his foreign status,
brandishing it as still another fact with which he could incriminate the
English middle classes: 'They have left it to a foreigner to inform the
civilized world of the degrading situation you have to live in.'[56] This
was a gross overstatement. Not only had Tristan provided such information in her book five years earlier, but six months after the publication of *Promenades* another book whose title even more closely
approximates Engels' was published: Buret's *De la misère des classes
laborieuses en France et Angleterre* (Nov. 1840). Tristan listed this book
in the bibliography of the second edition of *Promenades*, and remarked
in her preface that perhaps Buret's book would convince the French
public that she had not exaggerated or 'slandered England'. (*Promenades*,
p. xix)

She sent the sceptical reader to study Buret for further evidence of
the situation she had observed, and cited him herself in the later
editions where appropriate. (Marx would make use of Buret's findings
to support the theories he was developing, in the papers that comprise
The Economic and Philosophical Manuscripts[57] written during the period
March through August, 1844 and thus finished at just about the time
of Engels' stopover in Paris on his return from England.)

Although Engels may not have agreed with Buret's reformist stance, he surely must have known of the French economist's book. Like his own, it was fully documented. According to Michelle Perrot, Buret 'remained on the fringe of socialism', but exhibited 'pre-Marxist tendencies'.[58] Why did Engels neglect to mention Buret's study? He did not conceal his admiration for the French socialists; in his chapter on 'Labour Movements' he points out that: 'English Socialists will have to learn something from the example of their French comrades, so that they can ultimately make further progress themselves. Meanwhile, it is not to be expected that the French socialists will be standing still.'[59] Even here he echoes Tristan's view.

It is beyond the limits of this study to conduct a full-scale search for Engels' sources.[60] We have made this short digression in order to point out that just as Engels suppressed any mention of Buret, he may well have also concealed his use of Tristan. As for Engels' claim that he was the first foreigner to undertake such a study, neither he nor Buret could claim such a significant historical role.

Engels differed from Tristan in still another respect. Although he was also an autodidact, or perhaps because of it, he did not base his study primarily on what he observed, as had Tristan. He described his writing process this way in a letter to Marx: 'I am up to my ears in English newspapers and books from which I am putting together my book on the condition of the English proletarians.'[61] This approach constituted one of the essential differences between Tristan's study and Engels'. She presented facts as she experienced them, adding documentation when appropriate. Her book was composed primarily of the presentation of what she observed and her interpretation of reality. In this, she showed herself to be more closely tied to the research habits of France than to those of England, whose methods Engels exploited so extensively. (According to Perrot, in France the precise scientific examination of the workers' world did not really develop until the second half of the nineteenth century.)[62] Engels, on the other hand, anchored the impression of his encounters in a mass of documentary material that nearly obscured his findings. And yet he did not cite Tristan.

It is necessary to deal with psychological as well as sociological factors when taking account of Engels' probable omission (and Marx's later on) of any trace of documentary attribution and of any recognition of Tristan's precedent-setting work. In Engels' case, recent scholarship has already pointed out that Engels had a problem in regard to attribution: even when he named his sources he 'garbled' his citations, rarely quoting them accurately. The editors of one of the major editions of *The Condition of the Working Class in England* emphasize the significance and extent of this distortion by including a special appendix (V), entitled: 'Examples of Engels's Methods of Quoting', 'to illustrate the way in which Engels' quotations sometimes represent only very garbled and abridged versions of the originals'.[63] This wealth of erroneous documentation would seem to expose two contrary wishes: on the one side it would constitute a rejection of his need to depend on others, and on the other a need to appear professional.

It is clear from his ambivalent steps toward official German university training that this was a problematical area for him. Going into his father's business in England constituted the final rejection of any possibility of his attaining a real academic background. All through his life he felt the need to show he was speaking with authority, to show that he could perform just as well as a properly trained person could; and on the other hand to show that he could do without such training – an impossible double bind. This is best illustrated in a letter to Ruge, who had mistakenly addressed Engels as 'Doctor': 'Incidentally I am not a doctor and can never become one; I am only a businessman.'[64]

That it might have been especially problematical for him to give recognition to a woman's achievements is indicated by the oddly self-indulgent patronizing with which Engels viewed the death of his closest companion, Mary Burns. He wrote Marx of the event in the following terms: 'I cannot tell you how I feel ... The poor girl loved me with her whole heart ... I feel that with her I buried the last of my youth.'[65] The self-referential nature of these remarks has already been pointed out by Marcus. Indeed, they seem to imply a denial of all autonomy to this woman, even in that most autonomous of acts, death, and to indicate to what extent the life and works of women were for Engels (and men like him) only relative to themselves.

To realize how representative Engels' remarks and the attitude they revealed are, one cannot do better than to compare them to the statement made on a similar occasion by his contemporary Guizot, the arch-representative of the French bourgeoisie, who stood for everything Engels hated. On the death of his first wife, Pauline, he wrote to a friend: 'You know what it means for the honest worker who has done his day's work to return home to find his wife and his children, to sit by his fire, to find peace and quiet in this private and congenial existence where man no longer reflects on anything but *himself, his loved ones, his happiness* [my emphasis].'[66]

Throughout the nineteenth century men like Engels viewed women chiefly in relation to the men with whom these women were associated.[67] Similarly, when Engels did refer to Tristan's work, he perceived it within the context of a man's work: the only mention of Tristan in the entire Marx-Engels *oeuvre* occurred in the critique of Bruno in Bauer's review of her *Union ouvrière*. Hidden away amidst the 28 pages that Engels hurriedly wrote for 'The Holy Family', on his ten-day stop in Paris in August, 1844, these few pages bear the only official witness to the existence and importance of Tristan. He briefly alludes to the historical significance of Tristan's findings and interpretation, her discovery that 'The worker makes everything, produces everything, and yet he has neither rights nor property, he has nothing.'[68]

Is Engels, in these pages written on his way home from England even before he had started to put together *The Condition of the Working Class in England*, unconsciously paying his debt to Tristan in this defence of her? What is extraordinary about these few pages is the very overt contradictions in them. For, after attacking Bauer's charge that Tristan's work represents 'le dogmatisme féminin,' Engels goes on to define the 'real' 'dogmatisme féminin' which he associated with Hegelian abstract thinking. In the process, he has recourse to an image which involves the denigration of women. It is perhaps significant that in this defence of Tristan he should evoke an image which demeaned all women; that one of the few references to the work of a specific woman in the *oeuvre* of Engels and Marx should call up the following comparison: 'It [the Critique] is and remains an old woman: one can recognize in her the Hegelian philosophy, that jaded widow who paints and decks out her wizened body, reduced to the most ignoble abstraction, and wanders all over Germany, in search of an admirer.'[69]

Instead of examining 'cette grande thèse', which he attributed to Tristan, and for which she had so unjustly been treated 'like the rabble',[70] Engels, presumably taking for granted his audience's familiarity with the work in question, simply used it for his attack on Hegelianism. Nonetheless, these few pages are significant because they prove that Engels was well aware of theoretical advances on the continent, and in particular of Tristan's *Union ouvrière*, if not also her *Promenades dans Londres*. (Bauer's review had appeared in the *Allegemeine Literatur-Zeitung* during 1843.)

The Woman Question

If there was one subject in *Promenades* or in the society it depicted that did not seem to interest Engels much, it was the subject of women. Although he took careful account of the deleterious effects of industrial labour on women in his book, he was not really concerned with the specific nature of their alienation in their role as wife or prostitute. If anything, Engels showed a complete lack of awareness of this problem. The position he defended in *The Condition of the Working Class in England* might have constituted a dossier for the advocacy of the protective legislation that developed through the later nineteenth century and was based on the pseudo-scientific definition of woman as invalid. This concern extended beyond the physical to the moral dangers of women's 'exposure' at the work place. Such a view sought to protect the woman, ostensibly, by keeping her safely at home.

Because of Engels' role in the development of socialism, it is important to examine his early position on women to see the striking
contrast between it and Tristan's. This disparity helps to explain in part
why the latter's efforts to link feminism and socialism were ill-fated and
have been obscured. Engels' position on the question of working
women was surprisingly reactionary. The problem it posed for him is
obvious from the illogical way in which he presents it. Like many men
of his age, he equated feminine sexual status with motherhood. Thus
he viewed all women as mothers and accused them of effectively
killing their children by leaving home to go to work. 'The *Manchester
Guardian* is continually reporting cases of children who die from
burns. It is, moreover, self-evident that the total death rate for small
children is increased by the fact that their mothers go out to work.'[71]

Yet he had just finished bemoaning the fact that men were losing
their jobs due to the availability of female labour, pointing out 'to what
extent the adult males have been displaced in the factories'[72] by
women. Conceivably these 'fathers' could care for their children.
However, this 'reversal of normal social relationships'[73] upset Engels.
He never bothered to accuse the unemployed men of negligence or
murder of their children. For Engels did not consider men to be primarily 'fathers'. So, somewhat illogically, he blamed women: 'It is
inevitable that if a married woman works in a factory, family life is
inevitably destroyed and in the present state of society, which is based
upon family life, its dissolution has the most demoralising consequences both for parents and children.'[74]

Obviously, in 1845, Engels believed and supported what he and Marx
would call 'the bourgeois claptrap about the family' in the *Communist
Manifesto* five years hence.[75] If anything, here he defended the very
structure he later condemns in *The Origin of the Family, Private Property
and the State* (1884) where he charged in very Tristan-like terms: 'The
modern individual family is founded on the open or concealed domestic
slavery of the wife.' Instead he endorses that 'slavery' in his early
book:

> Very often the fact that a married woman is working does not lead
> to the complete disruption of the home but to a reversal of the
> normal division of labour within the family. The wife is the bread-
> winner while her husband stays at home to look after the children
> and to do the cleaning and the cooking. This happens very frequently
> indeed. In Manchester alone there are many hundreds of men who
> are condemned to perform household duties. One may well imagine
> the righteous indignation of the workers at being virtually turned
> into eunuchs.[76]

This extraordinary passage should be dragged out of its present obscurity to expose the original point of convergence of shared ideology of all men of that period, the point at which socialists and conservatives converged in their thinking. It is clear that Engels used the term 'workers' to refer to only one sex, the male, and that their maleness was based on the sexual division of labour. In fact, he contemplated the class struggle at this point as a manifestation of manliness, and therefore implicitly as a liberation for men only: '... it is natural, therefore, that it is when he is taking action against his oppressors that the English worker is seen at his best. It is then that he appears to the fullest advantage – manly, noble and attractive.'[77]

To be fair, later in his discussion of this problem of the reversal of roles, he does speculate that, perhaps it '... can be due to some radical error in the original relationship between men and women. If the rule of the wife over her husband – a natural consequence of the factory system – is unnatural, then the former rule of the husband over the wife must also have been unnatural.'[78] Rather than explore this interesting possibility, he passes it by quickly and jumps to an area in which he is more secure, that of defining the real bond holding together the family: 'not family affection, but private interest lurking under the false concept of family property.'[79] (This idea would be further developed in the *Communist Manifesto*, where the disappearance of the bourgeois family would be predicted.[80])

In *The Condition of the Working Class in England*, Engels accepted the contemporary thesis that competition for jobs from women was intolerable, although he concealed it beneath the rationalization that factory work was especially harmful to women. In further arguing this case, he reveals an excessive, almost prurient interest which became common in the late nineteenth century in treatises on the threats industrialism posed to women's sexual organs, and therefore to their primary role as propagators of the race. Not only does he state the fear that her pelvis would be deformed by work,[81] but he also voices the concern about the effect of heat on women in the factory. He likens the workplace to a 'tropical climate', and implicitly compares young girls to fruit, worrying that they will physically mature too early. He cites an authority on the problems of early and excessive breast development.[82]

To consign women to the home, however, was not to assure their physical well-being. Parent-Duchâtelet, in one of the first studies of prostitution, *De la Prostitution dans la Ville de Paris* (1837), found in fact that prostitutes were often healthier than housewives: 'Despite so much excess and so many causes of diseases, they are healthier than the ordinary women who have children and work in their homes.'[83]

Perhaps beneath this 'concern' for the well-being of the race, there lay a deeper fear: that women's sexuality was about to break out of its traditional chains. This fear has always been expressed in the way Engels puts it, disguised as a concern about 'the favourable development of female virtues'.[84] It is noteworthy that neither he nor other male researchers worried as much about the effect of the close, crowded heterosexually-mixed workplace on males. Indeed, with the growth of industrialism, there was a surge in the illegitimacy rate.[85] That, together with what Engels regarded as the dangerous 'reversal of all roles in the family' (accurate only from a middle-class view: workers' wives had always worked beside their men) would be perceived by many as a threat to the new conjugal family unit with its division of labour based on sexual lines – the type of family structure that 'fit' best with the needs of capitalism.

Moreover, sexual freedom was closely related to another kind of freedom that women could attain by working in the urban centre: economic independence. At this early stage, Engels does not confront this question forthrightly. Instead, he reports evidence of a case where young working girls refused the authority of their father, and left home.[86] Engels does not comment on this story, but leaves it as a testimony to his fears. Evelyne Sullerot observes the way in which these two fears, of sexual freedom and of economic independence, have been used to oppress women: '... it is in the name of the dangers of sexual freedom that economic independence through work has been grudgingly given to her, and most of the time denied ... Sexual and economic factors have always been closely intermingled where women are concerned ...'[87] Taken together, these fears and the protective legislation they bolstered produced a situation in which, 'as industrialization advanced ... , fewer married women worked.'[88]

Although he does not overtly endorse the exclusion of women from work, Engels' position is clearly indicated by the way he presents it. First he gives the professional opinion on the matter, and then he offers examples to bolster that view, one he obviously shares: 'I cannot help on these and other grounds, especially for the better preservation of infant life, expressing my hope that a period may arrive when married women shall be rarely employed in a factory.'[89]

Nearly 50 years later in a text that feminists still quote, Engels takes precisely the opposite position: 'To emancipate women and make her the equal of the man is and remains an impossibility so long as the woman is shut out from socially productive labour and restricted to private domestic labour.'[90]

But throughout most of the latter half of the nineteenth century, his writings reinforced the schism between socialism and feminism, and helped to foster the very family structure he would later attack. His views in *Condition of the Working Class in England* promulgate a concept of the family as the 'véritable unité sociale',[91] one to which the individual's needs (and especially woman's) must be sacrificed, a thesis quite similar to that propounded by Balzac, the ideologue of aristocracy in the 'Avant-propos' of his *Comédie Humaine*.

Ironically, this position supported the very bourgeois edifice Engels hoped to destroy. For the nuclear family would be the pillar of industrial capitalism, permitting it to obtain a mobile, urban work force. Lorenz von Stein, whose book *Der Socializmus und Kommunismus das heutigen Frankreich* (1842) introduced Marx (and probably Engels) to the new social situation in France, describes the significance of the change in family structure that he witnessed this way: 'It is comparable only to the dramatic event when the son leaves his father's home to set up his own household. The whole class of labourers took this step wherever machines were introduced.'[92]

Interestingly enough, in contrast to Guizot's idealized description of the worker who returns home to the comfort provided by his wife and the ambiance she has created – a description that more accurately fit the bourgeoisie of which he was a member – Von Stein's representation proves that the bourgeois family model had not yet filtered down to the working classes: 'When his work was finished nobody cared for him. He got paid in cash and was able to spend it as he liked. He had to set up his own household. No matter how modest it was, it made him self-reliant and independent of any individual control. Only labour was his master.'[93]

This optimistic view of the new freedom of the worker offered the ideological rationalization for the system. Only the wife was necessary to complete the formula and make certain that the worker's freedom could be controlled. Indeed Tristan perceived the dangerously conservative force women would come to represent: 'I maintain that the emancipation of the workers is impossible so long as women remain in their present state of degradation. They stop all progress.'[94]

To the extent to which social theorists supported this traditional view of the family, they supported the capitalist system that it upheld. Tristan must also be counted among those who supported this family unit, but her life bore witness to the contradictions implicit in it and the hardships its contemporary form signified for women. As such, her description of the oppression of woman in the family may well have laid the basis for the change in direction Engels' theories on women took in *The German Ideology* (1845–1846) and his later works.

Women as Property

For it was Tristan who pointed out before Engels and Marx that in a society whose motto is 'Nothing is free, everything has a price' (*Promenades*, p. 292), it is above all women who become objects of exchange. In *Promenades*, she focused on the way in which capitalism negated the specific humanity of women as well as that of men: if industrialists reduced the working man to a mere machine, it was man in general who treated woman 'as his thing, as a piece of furniture, for his personal use only, and which must always be at hand'. (*Promenades*, p. 309)

This 'state of nonentity to which men reduce their wives' was possible only because of the property arrangement, 'the unequal distribution of wealth!'. (*Promenades*, pp. 312, 110) In effect, it had totally dispossessed women and presented them with few alternatives: 'What kind of moral standards can be expected of *a woman who is not her own woman, who owns nothing*, and who has, all her life, been trained to escape chance through the use of deceit, and to avoid restriction through seduction?' (*Promenades*, p. 111) [emphasis added]

Woman had been taught only one skill, 'the art of pleasing', and it was her only means of providing for herself. If she chose to work honourably in the few occupations open to her, she would barely receive a living wage, despite the fact that often her labour was more productive than that of men. Tristan pointed out this double standard of remuneration in *Union ouvrière*, written just after *Promenades*. 'It should be noted that in all the trades in which both men and women are employed the daily wage of woman is half as much as that of man.'[95]

In *Promenades*, Tristan concentrated on the two situations in which women found themselves most often, as prostitute and housewife. In both cases, women were alienated in an even more basic sense than men: they were alienated from their own bodies. In dealing with these two options, Tristan was anticipating the course the institution of sexism would take in the second half of the nineteenth century. On the one hand, Proudhon would offer women the famous alternative: be either 'housekeepers or whores'.[96] On the other, socialists meeting at the first International in 1866 would proclaim, 'Better a baby-making machine than an industrial machine'.[97]

As early as the 1840s, Tristan decried the narrowing of options available to women. She perceived that just at the moment that socialists were dedicating themselves to the realization of the unfulfilled promise of 1789, and trying to create a society in which all men were equal, a society whose sole concern would be to develop 'all the faculties of the individual for the benefit of the general welfare', another system of slavery was being instituted – that of women. In *Union ouvrière*, Tristan therefore calls on men to 'free the last slaves' and envisages the time when for women 'their '89 [i.e. the French Revolution] will ring'.[98]

She recognized, however, that at the moment women were either instruments for men's pleasure or 'reduced to being baby-making machines'. (*Promenades*, p. 313) How could this be changed? Tristan calls for a recognition that the category 'women' should not be subsumed under the family. 'She should be recognized as a social being', Tristan asserts. (The full implications of this demand are still not visible today: it is the cry of feminists around the world.) But in a society which recognized woman as 'the property of the husband', only a transformation of the nature of property arrangements would change the status of 'the last slaves'.[99]

Tristan's public stance on the question of property was contradictory. In *Union ouvrière*, she addresses herself in part to the bourgeois class of which she considered herself a member, and promises that property will be respected. However, in *Promenades* her condemnation of it is implicit:

> Ah! those capitalists, those landowners who have enriched themselves so greatly by giving the worker a bit of bread for their 14 hours of work, are a long way from compensating for all the evils and disorders caused by the accumulation of wealth in their hands through the use they make of their fortunes. (*Promenades*, p. 113)

Still, this idea was not formulated into a call for the abolition of property until much later, in her notes for 21 September, 1844, in *Le Tour de France*, just two months before her premature death. There she was presented with a temptation: she found a small, pretty wristwatch in her hotel room; should she keep it? The account of this tortured decision made her finally enunciate her repressed theory of revolution:

> How is it that I who swore to destroy all property – by despoiling and killing the owners if there was no other way of eliminating them ... was not able to steal that little watch? ... I am naturally inclined to attack thieves, to fight them to the bitter end – to death – but I am also inclined to resist the temptation to steal even from thieves. (*Tour de France*, p. 265)

Out of this realization came a decision: '... that all property is theft – of land, capital, women, men, children, family – of ideas ... A terrible curse must be called down on property! Within ten years the worst insult will be: "You are a property owner". The motto of the first revolution must be: "No more property, of any kind".'[100]

Although Tristan does not go this far in *Promenades*, she clarifies the contradictions inherent in woman's situation. Women of her age were still dominated by the regressive *Code Napoléon* and by the spirit of its creator who had declared: 'Woman is our property; we are not hers, because she gives us children ... and man does not give her any. She is therefore his property as the fruit tree is that of the gardener.' In legal terms, this property arrangement was the basis of the French marital system which rendered woman equal to children: 'The woman's and the child's wages are given over to the father through the sanction of the law; they are considered as income from a personal estate.'[101]

In elaborating her theory of the present condition of enslavement of women, in calling upon 'Travailleurs et Travailleuses', Tristan was thus covertly attacking this system of property. The common attitude toward such a project of affranchisement of women was expressed in Michelet's reaction to the word 'ouvrière': '... blasphemous, sordid word, that no epoch before the age of steel understood'.[102]

That Engels shared this view at the time he wrote his *Condition of the Working Class in England* is clear from close analysis of his argument. But it is blatantly apparent in the way he chose to open his 'Dedication to the Working Classes of Great Britain', written in English. He addresses this group, which consisted of both sexes, as 'Working Men!'. This makes his solicitude to women's welfare in the text all the more suspect. Given his views, expressed by omissions such as these, it is not surprising that he neglected to mention Tristan. She committed the double sin of being a woman and a feminist.

Her case for women must however have had its effect, for in Marx and Engels' *The German Ideology*, published one year later, they present a different analysis of property, one which implicitly includes Tristan's findings. Property's 'first form ... lies in the family, where wife and children are the slaves of the husband'.[103] By 1848 in *The Communist Manifesto*, this perspective had developed into a call reminiscent of Tristan's for the abolition of the status of women 'as a mere instrument of production'.[104] (But it was not to be developed much further until later, in Engels' *Origin of the Family*.)

How profound Engels' real antipathy to feminism and women's rights continued to be is shown by the attitude he revealed in the 1863 letter to Mary Burns, quoted above. The prevalence of this attitude explains why the feminist branch of his and Marx's theory remained dwarfed and saturated with the universal and philosophical interpretation associated with their Hegelian past, which Engels branded as 'dogmatisme féminin', while the rest of their theory was developed concretely within the method of historical materialism. In adopting Fourier's conception of the position of woman as 'an index of general social advance', they made it a symbol – as such it retained 'universal importance at the cost of depriving it of its specific substance'. And when the subject of woman did enter their work later, it was subsumed under the heading of the family, itself viewed entirely in relation to property.[105]

Although several socialist historians have pointed to *Union ouvrière* as the probable origin of Marx and Engels' call for an international union of workers, no one has studied the likelihood that their inclusion of this minimal feminist plank in the *Manifesto*, and even in its first formulation in *The German Ideology*, may also be attributed to Tristan's influence. If their co-optation of her idea of uniting the working classes was to be forgotten, and it has been on the whole, it is much less surprising that their taking over her views on women should be obscured. Yet, what other source for these ideas could they have had? Tristan was literally the only vocal feminist in the 1840s. Her articulation of feminism and of the disastrous effects of the master–slave relationship went beyond Fourier's – besides, he was dead, and his disciples had more or less dropped the controversial issue, although Considérant continued to support Tristan. The entire problem of 'What to do with women?' is inextricably bound up in the conception of the Marxist project, and Tristan's influence on it has to be taken into account.

Indeed, Tristan seemed to think that feminism's revolutionary potential had already begun to be felt in the growing number of women's assassinations of their husbands. She tells her readers to confirm this fact by reading *La Gazette des Tribunaux*, whose pages contained a daily account of crimes. In these acts Tristan took pride, for they 'show that the exasperation of the slave is at its peak'.[106] Tristan revealed her own values in describing her reaction to the crimes committed by Mme Lafarge, one of the famous women criminals of the period, a woman who had stolen diamonds and killed her husband. Of these acts, Tristan declared somewhat strangely, 'I believe she is guilty of theft – which is much worse than murder!'[107] This statement shows how far her views had developed since *Promenades dans Londres*, where she contented herself with the neutral statement 'We know that the indissolubility of marriage has put the knife or poison in the hands of the spouses.' (*Promenades*, p. 151) That she continued to view theft as a more serious crime than murder shows how profound her class allegiance was. To liberate her sex, both the problem of the family and that of property would have to be resolved.

Tristan and Women

The complexity of Tristan's view of women was revealed in part by the contradictory and highly charged way in which she represented women in *Méphis*, as we have seen. The question of her own sexuality and her sexual identification, that of her relationship to her mother Marie Thérèse Laisney and to her daughter Aline – all of these aspects affected her perception of women as well as the pressure exerted on her by contemporary standards of the ideal woman.

In the structure of *Promenades*, Tristan unsuccessfully tried to separate these issues. The order of the chapters follows no logical pattern, and therefore reveals very clearly Tristan's mode of perception and 'vision du monde'. One of the most telling aspects is the way in which she separates the two classes of women she depicts by nearly 200 pages. Moreover, by her choice of the title 'Femmes anglaises', she seems to attribute womanhood and English nationality only to one class of women, the upper class. 'Honest' working women are practically omitted from the book. The fate of English women seemed to be summed up for her in the formation of the two groups: married women of leisure or 'filles publiques'.

The omission of working women from the text can be understood in part from Tristan's lack of knowledge of their lives, and yet that is an insufficient explanation. She explored English society from top to bottom, yet she was particularly fascinated by women in prisons, madhouses, and whorehouses, often shocking her middle-class readers, as in the following commentary: 'The details she gives are interesting, but one would prefer not to have them furnished by a woman whose eyes should not see certain things, whose lips should not say certain things.'[108]

And yet she avoided the study of the women she supposedly respected the most, working women, although later she bragged, 'I have made workers of my two children.'[109] This omission was to be a characteristic of *Union ouvrière* also. The discussion of the actual condition of working women was to be relegated to a footnote in that text. It is as if Tristan had decided to confine herself, as in *Méphis*, to the only condition of womanhood she knew and to the one which interested her most. Unfortunately it was one that demeaned women more than any other, for it was based on the exchange of woman's body.

The chapter on 'Filles publiques' followed the chapter on 'Ouvriers des manufactures', which focused entirely on men. Indirectly, Tristan seemed to imply that these were the major occupations in which the two sexes of the working class were engaged: for the males, factory work, and for the females, prostitution.

In the chapter on the 'Femmes anglaises', she deals with upper-class women only. Echoing sentiments similar to those of Mary Wollstonecraft, this chapter features long extracts from *Vindication of the Rights of Woman*. Much less interesting than the chapter on prostitutes, 'Femmes anglaises' is twice as long. It must have been easier to write, since the experience depicted in it could be presented without fear of betraying any 'improper' attitudes. Her description of the husband's total control of his wife anticipated Marx and Engels' analysis of the family. Tristan's indictment of women authors in this chapter echoes her earlier indictment of George Sand in *Pérégrinations*. Tristan gives what seems to be an accurate appraisal of the situation of feminism in England in 1840, where the Chartist movement and socialism seemed to have absorbed a great deal of radical energy and where even women writers had been integrated into the new social structure:

A good many of those ladies write for magazines ... But it is very distressing to me to see that no one has taken up the cause of freedom for women, that freedom without which all others are so ephemeral, and for which women writers especially should fight. (*Promenades*, p. 316)

Self-justification is implicit in this critique of women authors, but it is also an accurate appraisal of the situation of feminism in England in 1840. Perhaps because women of her own class who had the leisure and education to fight against their 'nullity' chose not to do so, indeed seemed to glorify in it, Tristan turned her attention to an even more shocking spectacle of human degradation caused by the class structure of society: prostitution.

The way in which Tristan describes her presence at the whorehouses is most revealing. In depicting this milieu, she betrays a part of herself that she usually kept well-concealed. As in the representations of sexuality in *Méphis*, these scenes also present a contradictory face: they are linked only by a recurring word, 'mépris' (contempt). The repetition of this word in several contexts indicates that the phenomena and the identities connected with it were not as disparate as Tristan would have liked them to seem.

The word appears first in the opening sentence of the chapter 'Filles publiques' where the narrator informs us, 'Never have I been able to see a prostitute without being moved by a feeling of *compassion* for our societies ... without experiencing *contempt* for their organization and hatred for their rulers.' (*Promenades*, p. 109) [emphasis added] I have underlined the word 'compassion' because this feeling seems misplaced, or displaced. Should it be directed toward society rather than toward prostitutes? Moreover, the word 'contempt' also seems displaced: should it refer to the prostitutes? Can the author switch from compassion to scorn so easily? Or does the scorn apply in reality to the prostitutes? The narrator admits that she cannot understand 'la fille publique':

... surrendering her very self! annihilating both her will and her feelings; surrendering her body to brutality and suffering – and her soul to contempt! The prostitute is an unfathomable mystery for me ... physical tortures constantly repeated, death of her soul at every moment ... *and self-contempt*. (*Promenades*, p. 110)

This passage seems to imply that the prostitute had a free choice and that the choice she made bewildered Tristan, although the author clearly understands the logical economic basis of prostitution. Of the two occurrences of 'mépris', the first is unattributable: 'au mépris de qui?' (contempt from whom?). Later in the statement the 'mépris' is assigned: 'de soi-même' (of oneself). Does Tristan endorse either kind (or both kinds) of 'mépris'? That remains unclear. In any case, it is clearly is the word which she most closely associated with prostitution.

Directly after this passage Tristan provides a description of the social and economic factors that caused prostitution, exculpating the prostitute herself in the process. The word 'contempt' occurs still once more here, but this time the narrator has curiously removed herself and also the prostitute from the picture: 'Respectable women feel contempt for those unfortunate women, a harsh, cold and cruel contempt.' (*Promenades*, p. 124) Yet this is where Tristan ought to have been, among the 'femmes honnêtes', especially according to the tone of her opening remarks. She seems to have intentionally separated herself from these virtuous women; and after her preliminary indictment of prostitutes, she launches into an attack on men that allows her to conclude: 'Blame this monstrosity on your social order, and let women be exonerated!'. (*Promenades*, p. 111) The order of her charges against men seems to indicate a revealing priority, as the moral precedes the economic:

> Indeed, if you had not made of chastity a virtue required of woman and not of man, woman would not be spurned by society for having yielded to her heart, and a young girl who has been seduced, betrayed and abandoned would not be reduced to prostitution. (*Promenades*, p. 111)

Only after this attack on the double standard of morality does Tristan shift to the economic sphere: 'Indeed, if you allowed woman to receive the same education, practise the same trades and professions as man, she would not fall into poverty more frequently than man.' (Ibid.)

Last of all, she examines the realm of marriage: 'Indeed, if you did not force woman to submit to the abuses of paternal despotism, and the indissolubility of marriage, she would never forced to submit to oppression and infamy!' (Ibid.) (Tristan, we should remember, was the victim the 'pouvoir maternel' [the rule of her mother], which had consigned her to Chazal and condemned her for leaving him.)

Later, she affirms her belief that until women were emancipated, 'Prostitution will always be on the increase', describing it as one of the only options open to women, when they are excluded from nearly all professions, 'when their children have no father to give them bread'. (*Promenades*, pp. 112, 152) These statements justifying prostitution seem to contradict the initial presentation of it. The horror with which Tristan reacted to the 'finishes' where the prostitutes were first inebriated, then forced to vomit, after which all sorts of alcoholic beverages were thrown at them until they were reduced to 'a bundle of rubbish', together with her determination 'to see everything' despite her repugnance, make it seem as if indeed Tristan might have herself experienced some form of prostitution, as her husband publicly charged. (*Promenades*, pp. 120, 117) Even if only in fantasy, the whole notion of it seems to have exercised a profound fascination.

Her preoccupation with prostitution and rape was clear in *Méphis*: the first seems to recur in the novel with over-determined frequency. Chazal's charge of prostitution was returned by Tristan, who charged that it was he who wanted to prostitute her. There is no clear proof on either side, but in her petition calling for divorce, Tristan admitted the nature and extent of the material difficulties she had faced: 'I have been sorely tried, gentlemen, by the sufferings caused by the indissolubility of marriage. Forced, although penniless, to leave my husband, I have had, when still very young, to provide alone, through my work, for myself and my children.'[110] How she did this has always remained obscure. It is almost as if Tristan were punishing herself by forcing herself to see the 'spectacle' of the debasement of her sex in these 'finishes', as she had in the various scenes in which woman was 'de-faite' (undone) in *Méphis*.

Curiously enough, her visit to the whorehouse seemed to be a cathartic event for Tristan, by which she cleansed herself of all association with this 'materialistic life of the senses' that she insisted she found so 'repulsive'. (*Promenades*, p. 123) It allowed her to establish for herself the identity of the 'femme honnête' (respectable woman) who would find the spectacle disgusting: 'The pen recoils from describing the disorders, the depravity.' (Ibid.) And, once she had clearly assumed this identity, she could proclaim forcefully the physical repugnance she felt:

> The sight of the satanic debauchery is revolting and frightening; and its atmosphere nauseating; the air is heavy with foul vapours, the smells of meat, drink, tobacco, and others even more fetid ... they catch in your throat, your temples throb, you are seized with dizziness. (*Promenades*, p. 120)

Her transcription of the horror of the disappropriation of the self, or of the loss of the self (which she calls 'materialism') betrays a rejection of all sensuality and sexuality – a renunciation all the stronger because of the force of the desire being repressed. The intensity of this renunciation is represented by the transference to the realm of food and drink of a description that ostensibly deals with sexual activity. Her stance as the 'femme honnête' who rejects this debauchery permits Tristan to appear undisguised (whereas in the much less troublesome *lieu* of the Houses of Parliament she had appeared dressed as a male). Here her feminine clothes offer a protective device, distancing her from the men; yet, as an observer, she is (supposedly!) permitted to seem disinterested and somehow superior. All the while, she can indulge her fancy of watching 'la femme dé-faite' ('woman un-done'): 'I saw in that *finish* four or five superb women, the most impressive was an extraordinarily beautiful Irish woman ... My eyes filled with tears.' (Ibid.) Before the evening was over this beauty came to resemble a heap of garbage, so sullied was she by the 'finish'.

Tristan seemed to take a particular interest in this spectacle of the debasement of her sex, in watching woman 'done and un-done'. It is a repetition, in essence, of the story of Clotilde. Tristan includes another such description in *Promenades* – of a woman being tied in a sack and thrown into the street. No one cared and she nearly suffocated. Of course, all these stories represent in part the actual condition of women during the period, but Tristan's preoccupation with them seems excessive nonetheless, and her repetition of this primal event is significant. Tristan's account of the upper-class women on Ascot Heath includes another reenactment of this event and reveals its attraction for her: 'All those lovely ladies with their pink, blue, yellow or green silk dresses eating enormous pieces of ham ... drinking copious quantities of wine ... were for me a spectacle as curious as it was novel.' (*Promenades*, p. 247) At the end of the day these same women reappear: 'It was truly a pity to see those ladies who, in the morning were so neatly and so elegantly turned out, coming home covered with dust, dirty and completely unrecognizable.' (*Promenades*, p. 250)

In *Promenades*, the only individual woman who appears outside of this process is already 'undone', and is branded as a prisoner. Also a spectacle, this young woman prisoner in Newgate who has stolen to feed her young is idealized: 'She was a mother who had felt the horrible hunger pains tearing at her children's bellies ... Such a creature could not be a prostitute or a professional thief.' (*Promenades*, p. 160) At last, here in prison, the blame for woman's undoing can be placed: now Tristan can enjoy the spectacle of women suffering. Here she does not have to pretend to be disgusted, for with this woman's martyrdom she can stigmatize society. The contradictions in Tristan's responses are too complicated to be worked out simply. That she should glorify motherhood here, after having spent so much energy avoiding its responsibilities (George Sand would attack her on this basis), seems hypocritical.

Within *Promenades dans Londres*, the profound nature of Tristan's contradictory response to specific women, her interest in the sight of them suffering, is emphasized by a curious omission. Although she is constantly in the company of men friends throughout her sojourn in London, on her visit to Bethlehem, the insane asylum, she is accompanied by Mrs Wheeler, 'the only socialist woman I met in London'. (*Promenades*, p. 253) At last, it would seem, she had encountered a woman whom she could respect, whose ideas she shared. Indeed, Mrs

Wheeler should have been of great interest to Tristan, for she was not only a socialist but a feminist. With William Thompson, she had in 1825 written a feminist tract entitled *Appeal of one Half of the Human Race, Women, against the Pretensions of the Other Half, Men, to Retain Them in Political, and thence Civil and Domestic Slavery*.[111] Yet, according to *Promenades*, Tristan seemed to be unfamiliar with the book (she had mentioned only Wollstonecraft as her precursor) and with Mrs Wheeler's feminism, which is never discussed. Moreover the appearance of this first sympathetic woman is completely overshadowed by another event that illustrates the complex nature of Tristan's interest in women, indeed, her avoidance of all rapprochement to them, and her adherence to a personal myth of messianism.

This preference is betrayed by the emphasis Tristan places on her encounter with an inmate of Bethlehem, an encounter that she viewed as providential and that completely obscured Anna Wheeler's presence. In Bethlehem, she and Wheeler meet a 'fou' whose ideas, Tristan thinks, resemble those of Jesus, Saint-Simon, and Fourier. This inmate is a Frenchman who happens to be named Chabrier. For a moment, Tristan believes him to be the amorous captain with whom she had sailed to Peru. However, she represents him quite differently from her original portrayal in *Pérégrinations* as 'the man who had loved me with such delicacy and such devotion!'. (*Promenades*, p. 256) Her interpretation of this encounter transforms it into a messianic call: 'It seemed to me that God had inspired me with the idea of coming to London to save the poor man.' (Ibid.) But as she looks at this Chabrier, she discovers her mirror image: he also considers himself to be the messiah.

This meditation on messianism is however brusquely interrupted. All of a sudden he begins to curse Mrs Wheeler, to accuse her of embodying 'la matière' and of being responsible for his assassination. He throws himself at her, and Mrs Wheeler quickly withdraws in fear. One would have thought that after this spectacle Tristan would also have withdrawn from the cell in solidarity with Mrs Wheeler if not in fear. But she stays on, and listens to the madman's evocation of 'la loi nouvelle', taking him completely seriously as he calls for the end to all servitude, of poor to rich, of woman to man: ' "Oh!" he cried, "woman is the image of the Virgin on earth! and men do not know her! they humiliate her, they drag her through the dirt!" ' (*Promenades*, p. 261) (Indeed, this is exactly what he had done to Mrs Wheeler minutes earlier.)

This obvious contradiction between the man's actions and his words did not occur to Tristan, nor is Mrs Wheeler mentioned ever again in the text. Instead, Tristan declares her sympathy for Chabrier's ideas: 'I found in him much exaltation, but I could not discern the characteristics of insanity ... There was no doubt hatred for his persecutors;

but his discourse was logical and I could easily understand the reasoning that inspired it.' (*Promenades*, pp. 261–2)

Indeed, Tristan identified more closely with this self-proclaimed messiah than with Mrs Wheeler. Disregarding the dangerous and illogical way in which he had treated her companion, Tristan focused on the idea which attracted her. This choice indicates the tendency she was to heed, and prepares us for the consolidation of Tristan's own project: to immolate herself and become the messiah. She had in the course of her *Promenades* found an object worthy of her attention, the unrealizable goal worthy of her sacrifice. In this project, to be elaborated in her next book, *Union ouvrière* (1843), women would be once more 'un-done', dragged in the mud, so to speak, in the course of Tristan's rescue operation for all mankind. In the process, Tristan's own martyrization would glorify 'la femme', especially 'la femme guide', the role she would assume.

6
The Consolidation of a Project: *Union Ouvrière* and *Le Tour de France*

Of all Tristan's books, *Union ouvrière* was the most overtly political. She dismissed all notion of description in this work, and instead prescribed a solution to the problems of the working class and women. She sought to make them conscious of their collective interest, and to inform them of the power they could wield if they were unified. Although her plan may seem limited to us now, it struck her contemporaries as quite daring, for it was international in scope, socialist in purpose and included *both* sexes. In brief, she called for the following:

> Unity is strength. Unity. Brothers, let us unite. Human, social, political unity. Equality between men and women. Riches for all, men and women. Realization of equality, freedom and justice. Right to work. Right to education for all men and women. Organization of work, talent, capital.[1]

The historical importance of what Tristan tried to accomplish cannot be underestimated. Historians of socialism as diverse as Lorenz von Stein, writing in 1851, and G.D.H. Cole, in 1962, have attested to it. Von Stein, her contemporary, described her significance this way:

> Her style is clear and lucid, although she lacked any knowledge of economics; but she showed an awareness, more than any of the other like-minded authors, that the working class is an entity and that in order to improve conditions it must recognize itself as such and strive to achieve a solidarity which would help it to move towards a common goal.[2]

Cole, the great historian of socialist thought, declared Tristan's plan to be 'the first published project of a world-wide Workers' International'.[3] Although he found certain aspects (such as her idea of building workers' palaces in every town) 'chimerical', and he pointed

163

out that her acquaintance with business was 'nil', nonetheless he decided: 'She has a right to a place in this record because, so far as I have been able to discover, she was the first person to put forward a definite plan for an all-inclusive Proletarian International.'[4]

Despite these testimonials to her importance, Tristan's place in socialist history has been neglected. She herself recognized that her sex might disqualify her ideas from serious consideration. In 1843, when she was writing, the workers were still loosely organized into 'compagnonnages', or 'devoirs', traditional associations dating back to the Middle Ages that grouped workers of similar skill and engaged them in futile rivalry and meaningless rituals. Tristan sent a copy of her book to each *compagnonnage*; and in the letter that accompanied it she pleaded for a fair reading:

> I entreat you, gentlemen, to be impartial in reading my little book. Do not be blinded by a foolish and fatal prejudice. Let not the fact that I am a *woman* be a reason for you to reject my work. Remember that love, intelligence, strength *have no particular sex*. In reading the *Union ouvrière*, be only concerned with studying the value of its ideas … What I want, what I am striving for, is to serve effectively the largest and the most useful class. (*Union ouvrière*, p. vi)

Of course her gender did affect both the production and the reception of her Idea. In part it was responsible for the failure of her dream that 'each worker might have the *Union ouvrière* (Workers' Union) in the bottom of his hat'. (*Union ouvrière*, p. vii) The factors that prevented her from completing her mission were many. Her premature death at the age of 41, of exhaustion and typhoid fever while on her tour of France was of course the fatal one, but as we have seen, the complex social, historic and economic pressures against which her plan had to work – and the intricate psychological needs which determined the formulation of her plan – ensured its failure, at least in her lifetime.

Tristan's premonition of her tragic destiny was clear even in the text of *Union ouvrière*, and in the exalted and disillusioned passages of *Le Tour de France*, the journal that she kept as she travelled through the provinces attempting to organize the union.

> … if I am left to carry such a heavy burden alone, however great my faith and goodwill may be, I will fall exhausted by its weight … But what distresses me is that I look everywhere for workers, bourgeois, women, capable of carrying on my mission, once I am gone. I find no one anywhere. They all think the task is too arduous! (*Union ouvrière*, p. vii; *Tour de France*, p. 100)

While the loneliness she felt was very real, and her disappointment at not finding comrades fit to carry on the work after her historically plausible, still it seems as if Tristan was in part responsible for the loneliness, as we have seen. As in *Pérégrinations* and *Méphis*, here again she began her mission by eliminating potential allies in the name of 'truth'. By the time the first edition of *Union ouvrière* was published, on June 1, 1843, Tristan had already severed relations with most of the leaders of the working-class press in Paris or they had broken with her. It is important to study the origins of this critical schism: once again Tristan was constructing an elaborate image of herself and of her mission, one that inevitably clashed with those who sought to work with her.

In part her gender and the increasing rivalry among the apostles of the working class were responsible for this state of affairs, but the prefatory material in *Union ouvrière*, the notes she has left in her journal (*Tour de France*) and the letters that have been found tell another story of the origin of this rupture. They record an account of the schism that developed and permit us to understand Tristan's own character and the way in which she perceived her relationship to the working class. These documents also allow us to draw an incisive portrait of the state of bourgeois and working-class consciousness at this important moment in the development of France and of socialism.

Why was it that when Tristan left for her tour of France, only one newspaper supported her, that of the Fourierists? In part, the rupture originated in Tristan's high-handed attitude toward her ideological predecessors, the theoreticians from the working class. She admits certain of their works influenced her writing:

> It is while reading *Le Livre du Compagnonnage* by M. Agricol Perdiguier (a cabinet maker), the little brochure by M. Pierre Moreau (a locksmith), *The Plan to Regenerate the Compagnonnage*, by M. Gosset, master blacksmith, that my mind was struck, illuminated by the great idea of the *universal union of working men and women*. (*Union ouvrière*, p.11)

She finishes, however, by disparaging the work of her contemporaries, thus making her own contribution seem more original and more important: '... none was likely to bring any real and positive improvement in the moral and material condition of the working class.'(*Union ouvrière*, p. 11)

Actually, Tristan's disparagement was excessive. Although it was true that in the main Perdiguier and Gosset had attempted reform of the old *compagnonnages*, as she charges, the idea of eradicating sectarianism and establishing one large union was already implicit in Perdiguier's book. He called for the following: 'Unite ... Whatever your trade, your "Devoir" ... learn that it is in our interest to stop fighting each other and to establish sincere and fraternal relations among ourselves.'[5]

Therefore it was natural that Perdiguier, who had publicized and criticized the war raging between the various *devoirs* before she had, resented her treatment of him. So ignorant of psychology was Tristan that she approached him for help after denouncing him. He declared:

> ... you have not been fair toward the working-class authors who tried to destroy the prejudices and hatreds of the *compagnonnage* associations ... you are wanting in fairness from the very first, you offend, you crush those who have been helpful to you and who may still be helpful to you.[6]

Tristan's reply further exacerbated the situation. Instead of recognizing the justice in his remark, she denounced his pride. Blaming it on the way in which he was being courted by the *literati* of their time (especially George Sand), she questioned his loyalty to his class:

> ... instead of being struck by the *idea*, you see nothing but the idea, you, worker, you who claim to be *serving* the working class, you only see in my work the *lack of praise* ... Perdiguier, do you know what ruined you? It is *flattery*. Well, Brother, I, for one, will not flatter you.[7]

Her remark was partly correct. However, Tristan need not have flattered him but neither need she have denounced the utility of his work so glibly. In refusing to understand this, Tristan assumed the position of the *être de vérité* and further ensured her isolation. She declared that she could be of greater service to the working class than he. Even after this bitter exchange, Tristan had the nerve to ask him for a contribution 'after she treated me so badly in her letters and in her comments',[8] as he told George Sand. Doggedly, she persisted in trying to make use of him. She asked him to help sell her *Union ouvrière,* and requested his aid in spreading her Idea. Needless to say, Perdiguier refused.

In view of the poor relations she had with Perdiguier, it is all the more surprising that she should have ignored another working-class theoretician, Pierre Moreau, when she visited his home town of Auxerre. From her letters we see that she was on good terms with him. He had supported her from the start as best he could, both morally and materially. He had never attacked her for stealing his ideas, although well he might have, since Tristan had learned much from his work. His only mention of her possible debt was oblique: ' ... I do not have to tell you (my book speaks for me), we are in agreement on many points.'[9] Indeed, Moreau's ideas and actions were closer to Tristan's than those of the others. He had begun to organize workers outside of the *com-*

pagnonnages into 'sociétés de l'Union', and it was this group Tristan visited on her stop in Auxerre. It is all the more surprising therefore that she omitted his book, *De la réforme des abus*, from her list of sources for *Union ouvrière*, and that she omitted all mention of him in her journal notes on her visit to Auxerre, despite the fact that she was constantly seeking contacts in each place. Here was a man to whom she needed no introduction, with whom she shared many ideas and methods, and yet he was completely overlooked. Again in this omission (as in the too-brief mention of the feminist-socialist Mrs Wheeler in *Promenades*) we see a certain 'will' to be isolated, to be the only one espousing such ideas, a will that could only lead to failure and martyrdom. Why else should she have continued to solicit Perdiguier and ignore Moreau?

Tristan's behaviour towards these two individuals was more or less replicated in her actions toward the two working-class groups with which she made contact in Paris. Her own stance toward them is apparent in her journal description of the meeting-place and the way she was received. The place was obviously repulsive to her, out of her ordinary *neighbourhood*:

> It is in the rue Jean Aubert, a small muddy and filthy street ... in a miserable house, a narrow, dark alley, a dangerous death-trap of a staircase ... We walked into a rather clean room ... They kept me waiting, although I had told them I was bringing salvation to the working class. (*Tour de France*, pp. 11–12)

In this description the exalted character of the would-be apostle stands out. She presents her class position unabashedly for all to see by describing her subscription for the *Union ouvrière* in the following way: 'writing my name at the top of the list; having my daughter, my servant, my water-carrier sign'.[10] Thus she entered this other world of the working class with her own class superiority intact.

The pose of superiority intruded very early on in her relationship with the two groups. Although she had ostensibly approached them for suggestions and criticism of her plan, when these were forthcoming she showed extreme insensitivity and disdain. One of the major aspects criticized by the workers' groups in Paris was her depiction of the harshness of working-class women, and of the excessive drinking of working-class men. The group that published *La Ruche populaire*, one of the first workers' newspapers, tried to explain to her that in a book destined for the working class it was not necessary to repeat these common bourgeois images of the worker, that they were insulting to the working class and ' ... would give an excuse to the bourgeois class to renew its attacks on the working class.'[11]

These leaders of the working class spoke with the best intentions, in the hope 'that the Idea would not die before it has been put into effect'.[12] Instead of heeding their advice, Tristan justified her critical presentation on the grounds of honesty, as she had done in her exchange with Perdiguier. They too, it seemed, wanted to be flattered. Instead, no matter how painful it was, she would tell the truth. Not only were they 'sick' but 'you want me to heal you without looking at your wounds.' It was obvious from her imagery that she had assumed a patronising position toward them. They recognized Tristan as the stranger, the bourgeois rather than the saviour: 'Among ourselves we can admit our faults, but we cannot tolerate that strangers should come and lecture us – we must on the contrary conceal our flaws from the bourgeois.'[13]

They withdrew their support. She lamented the fact that she, 'who had promised to bring salvation to the working class' (*Tour de France*, p. 12), was not understood. When it became clear to her that they wanted to make some changes in her text, she broke off relations and sought to disband the committee. She was reminded that 'you came to us for advice.' They complained that although she did not find that 'we would all blindly applaud your work', she had no right to try to dissolve a committee that she had not formed. Her interpretation of the rupture indicates the posture she took: 'The letter reveals the nature of the worker: he is not allowed to form a committee so he forms a committee. It is always the same problem, *vanity* ... [N]o matter, I think I have already helped them to make progress.'[14]

In each case, rather than consider the criticism and its validity, Tristan attacked the person who enunciated it: in this way she confirmed her own superiority while reinforcing her image of the dire ignorance and lack of comprehension of those she would save. Since she insisted on publicly degrading the worker, she seemed to augment the difficulty of her task and by implication the grandeur of the sacrifice she was to make. With such a stance it was not surprising that by the time she left Paris she had only the bourgeois journal the *Phalange* backing her.

The Fourierists recognized their influence on her, evidenced by her promulgation of 'palaces'. As Joseph Reynier declared: '... in your palaces you have the old people, the children, and the sick do [that which] ... we want everyone to do in the *phalanstery*.'[15]

Tristan made no attempt to hide this debt: 'One should consult Fourier's works. The part dealing with the education of children has some very good things in it. Setting aside *his system*, one would only take from him *what could be applied* ....'.[16]

Determined to proceed on her own, she must have known too well that without allies the realization of her dream was unlikely. 'I am outside every clique',[17] Tristan proudly announced, the solitude of her quest making it even more heroic. This assured the uniqueness of her project but fatally limited the support she could get from others. Dissociation from all groups was a stance she had proclaimed for a long time. In *Promenades*, it had taken the form of a specific declaration: 'I am neither Saint-Simonian, Fourierist or Owenite'.[18]

In April 1844 on the eve of her tour of France, she described her predicament in a letter to Considérant with prescience, and with a certain pride:

> Imagine, my friend, that I am leaving, *alone* with *no support*, no money to pay the journalists of the provincial towns who could do some *publicity*; I have almost *everyone against me*. Men, because I demand the *emancipation* of *women*; *property owners*, because I demand the emancipation of *workers*. [19]

One of the few exceptions to this rule was, indeed, Victor Considérant, who publicized her idea by printing a chapter of *Union ouvrière* in *La Phalange* on 29 and 31 March, 1843. Although he believed her idea to be utopian, he said 'the existence of the idea is good'.[20] She asked him to go one step further, to write an article about her project 'in order to win ... the goodwill of *all the phalansterians*'.[21] In fact, Tristan cared little for their support. She had another plan. Like her character Méphis, she conceived of converting others to her own cause and of gaining control of a newspaper to propagate her Idea:

> I believe that inserting my chapter in the *Phalange* is going to be a momentous event for that newspaper – because it will then find itself involved and forced to follow in that direction. What I find amusing is the surprise of the subscribers, bourgeois, property owners, who are accustomed to reading articles favouring the rich, their eyes must have popped out of their heads when they saw how I treat property owners! (*Tour de France*, pp. 24–5)

Her interpretation of her influence on Considérant's ideological position is telling (and as it turned out, incorrect):

> Considérant finally realizes that he can do nothing with the rich, that he has gone ahead for eleven years without moving one inch, he is finally becoming impatient, and according to what I predicted to him seven years ago, he is at last willing to rely on the only real strength which exists in society – the strength of the largest group. It took my article to convince him of that. In his heart he approves of the way I speak, but he would never dare speak that way. (*Tour de France*, p. 24)

In 1837, in a letter to the editor of *La Phalange*, she described her ideological position: 'I am not a phalansterian, but the extreme *tolerance* that I exercise allows me to take in each system what seems good and useful to me.'[22] This was to be Tristan's method: she would take from each system what she found useful and reject the rest. Indeed, Tristan is to be admired for her independence of mind and her determination to realize her ideal despite all obstacles. Her critique of contemporary ideas had a certain validity. One of her key criteria for the composition of her own ideas would be that they must be practical, 'exécutable', unlike those of so many utopians around her.

As we have seen, back in 1836 Tristan had accurately denounced the major tendency of the utopian socialists to obscure their ideas in a veil of mysticism. But clarity was not forthcoming, and much later, on her tour of France, Tristan encountered many examples of the ill-effects of the Fourier doctrine. In Lyons she met a young priest and said of him: 'reading Fourier has perhaps been irremediably damaging to him. He has become "doctrinaire" '. By this she meant that he had become dogmatic and supported Fourier's system without any consideration of its relationship to reality. She found it 'disheartening ... that those men of goodwill can do nothing to improve society'.[23] In essence, Tristan was right.

As she travelled through the provinces of France, Tristan developed her own social critique in the margins of her attack on the Fourierists. She became more revolutionary as she observed their entire nullity as a social force:

> Fourierists are wonderful! I find them amusing. They are as bourgeois as the best of the bourgeois, these courageous men are afraid to come and see me. They are afraid to compromise themselves. Ah, my gallant Fourierists, you can do and say anything, or see anyone you wish, the authorities are not afraid of you and they are quite right! (*Tour de France*, pp. 97–100)

As she came to understand the Fourierists she realized that they were little more than 'bourgeois defending capital: property was the Ark of the Covenant. It cannot be touched!'. (*Tour de France*, p. 98) This was the reason they were not dangerous: they supported the principle of the capitalist system. And yet at the outset of her book *Union ouvrière* Tristan had also given similar assurances – that she wanted to guard the present order, and preserve property relations.[24] Was she more honest in the pages of her journal, or did her encounters on her journey across France make her more revolutionary? It is difficult to know, but we can say for sure that by the time she wrote her journal her revolutionary intentions were clear.

In any case, Tristan's denial in *Union ouvrière* of any revolutionary intentions is not very convincing. Despite her forthright assurances within the plan of the *Union* itself, her definition of the relationship of each class to property already implies a 'class struggle', although she calls for none overtly. In describing the contrast between the rights and goods granted to the worker, who has no property but his 'arms' and is accorded neither 'the right to work' nor 'the right to live,' and those of the other class, which owns everything ('those who operate the governmental machine are landowners and capitalists'), Tristan designates property as the base of the system. Peace seemed unlikely, since the rich 'will never agree to grant such rights to the working class'.[25] Mustn't the working class then *take* these rights by themselves? What could be clearer? Even if she had more reformist ideas at the outset of her project, these ideas contained the seeds of a more radical position.

Her encounter with actual conditions led her to formulate this position. In her journal Tristan refuted the basic Fourierist tenet: 'To rely upon the bourgeoisie'. She proclaimed this 'a madness that should be left to the Fourierists'.[26] Before long, she articulated this position publicly. In a letter of August 1844 to the workers of Toulon, she called for the working class's complete independence from the bourgeoisie. She warned them that the working class must be the agent of its own liberation, and implicitly recognized that social change might not be achieved peacefully, given that class interests were basically opposed.

> You have not understood that in order to organize yourselves, workers, you must *exclude all the bourgeois* ... The *great proletarian party* must *first* be built in order to destroy all masters and all slaves – because *to love one another* we must *first* all be equal ... Are not all the bourgeois, by their *position,* against the union of workers![27]

This letter, written several weeks before she died, shows how clearly Tristan understood the class relations of her time.

Implicit as this comprehension was in her idea of constituting the working class as a class, she chose to conceal this truly revolutionary aspect of her project. For, to her dismay, she soon discovered how ignorant the workers could be. They seemed 'stupid to the extent of not understanding what organizing the working class means'.[28] Instead of understanding 'the serious and important questions of social economy',[29] they were mostly taken with her proposal to use their contributions to construct a *palais* in each town to serve them as an old-age home and educational centre. Here, as Tristan finally confronted the working class, she seemed more disturbed by the limitations of their vision, and less intent upon patronizing them.

Moreover, the freedom of movement so vital to her organizing effort depended on her being seen as a peaceful utopian. Even on her first trial visit (to Bordeaux), she became aware of police surveillance. Throughout her journal, Tristan anxiously noted their watchful presence. It became more threatening until finally, in Lyons, they entered her hotel room and seized her papers. On another occasion, they disbanded one of her meetings. The police treated her as an *agent provocateur*. In view of the repressive nature of the regime, it would have been in Tristan's best interests to conceal the radical dimensions of her tour.[30]

Although Tristan's perception of the true interests of the working class sharpened on her tour, even in the 'Dédicace aux classes ouvrières' of *Promenades* she had already recognized the limits of 'political' change: 'It is with the social order, the foundation of the structure that you should be concerned, and not with politics, which is a deceptive power ... Politics itself deals only with special interests between States and those of certain privileged classes.'[31]

As she pointed out in her journal, one of the unpublicized goals of the tour was to teach the working class that they could *not* depend on the bourgeoisie. While in Lyons, Tristan conceived of a way of achieving this:

> I shall apply to them [the bourgeois] for the first Palace, I wager not one of them will answer, but it will be a good lesson for the people, it is imperative that the people should rely only on themselves, if they trust the bourgeois with their interests, they are lost. (*Tour de France*, p. 79)

Tristan accurately observed that one of the gravest dangers facing the working class was that they would be tempted to imitate the upper classes, to appropriate riches for themselves in order to become oppressors in their turn. Perhaps here she recognized in them a structure of desire similar to her own. Painfully she observed that material improvement often resulted in a dangerous shift in ideological focus: 'Every time a worker becomes a bourgeois financially and shares interests with the bourgeois, you can be sure he turns out to be even more of a scoundrel than the worst bourgeois.'[32]

Because she found the class interests of these two groups so opposite, she found her position as a pacifist impossible: 'I could not say the same things to the masters and to the workers.'[33]

Tristan at War: With Herself and with George Sand

To some extent, the success of Tristan's plan was sabotaged not only because the working class was not ready for it, but also because of the aegis of psychological trauma under which it was conceived, that is as a means of heroic escape from the labyrinth of her own personal problems. *Union ouvrière* can be viewed in this sense as the final consolidation of the martyrist project that Tristan had been formulating from the outset of her career to resolve the paradox of her divided self.

As we have seen, two extremes were always at war within Tristan: her actual class status versus her nostalgic class preference, the 'have-not' versus the 'have'. Marx's description of the different experience of each class explains the severe nature of the division within her:

> The propertied class and the proletarian class present the same human alienation. But the former feels comfortable in its alienation, it finds its confirmation in it, it recognizes in the alienation of the self its *own power*, and possesses in itself the appearance of human existence; the latter feels *annihilated* in that alienation, sees in it its own powerlessness and the reality of an inhuman existence. [emphasis added][34]

The words Marx used to oppose the two classes and their states of being, *aise* (ease) and *anéantie* (exhausted), reflect the diverse moods in which Tristan most often found herself and were the very words she used to describe her alternate conditions. She was rarely 'at her ease'. For her, ease represented a kind of death, a 'sleep full of sensual pleasure'.[35] She constantly sought activity that would leave her 'exhausted'. The sexual overtones of this struggle represent still another aspect of her divided self.

The strength of the identification between the two aspects of herself is revealed in part through a comparison of Tristan's own view of the working class with that held by the bourgeois she detested so much. As Tristan got closer to the workers, she seemed to share the bourgeois view of them:

> The workers are *scum*[36] ... How many things I have learned during these two weeks among the workers. They are disgusting up close! Some are stupid, others are vulgar, rude ... but who will serve those poor people, so brutish, so ignorant, so vain, and so disagreeable ... at close quarters! A good many compare the people to animals, but animals, even the wild ones, would be infinitely less disagreeable to deal with. (*Tour de France*, pp. 15, 17, 28)

The working class evoked complex and diverse reactions in Tristan. On the one hand, they were repulsive physically and intellectually. The extent to which she found them disgusting was the extent to which her actions seemed noble, for it enhanced her sacrifice and made concrete her martyrization. On the other hand, she viewed them with pity ('those hapless people') and referred to them as 'poor workers'.[37] This augmented the value of her decision to serve them. By transforming herself into their saviour and their martyr, she could redeem her own worth. Clearly, she sought this redemption for herself also in her project. By elevating them, by performing such a noble task, she could achieve respectability. The words she used to describe her hope make this evident: '... isolated, you count for nothing ... But as soon as the Workers' Union is established the working class will become respectable and powerful.'[38]

Yet paradoxically she was caught in a double bind. For if she viewed her own class as murderers, she could only achieve respectability by denigrating it, and thus a part of herself. That this project was over-determined is indicated by the way in which she described her relationship to it. Whether or not her services were wanted she intended to impose them: 'Poor worker, I shall serve you in spite of yourself ... Against their will I shall force them to escape that appalling poverty.'[39]

Without doubt, Tristan was moved to her sacrifice by humanitarian, idealistic motives. But on a deeper level, in statements like these Tristan revealed the personal nature of her mission. By uniting the working class, providing for the needs of children, the sick, the old, evoking the kindness in women and rehabilitating their role in the family, Tristan was able to engage in wish-fulfilment, to reconstitute her own lost family paradise. In her plan for the Palace, with its male defender to represent the interests of the working class, she resurrected the lost aristocratic dream of kindness and protection that her Peruvian family denied her and that the cash 'nexus' had replaced, as Marx would later perceive.

On the other hand, perhaps she knew that her dream was unrealizable, just as her recovery of her elusive class status and her idyllic family circle was also impossible. Still, such visions provided the perfect vehicle for Tristan's masochistic needs.[40] The ideal of the unity and salvation of the working class would lead her on, make her suffer, and finally die, even while the object of her attention sympathized with her plight. But this masochistic vehicle would 'never disappoint her by yielding to her passionate declaration of love',[41] with the exception of the young Eléonore Blanc, the Lyons *blanchisseuse*, who took up Tristan's apostasy after her death.

She took pleasure in suffering for the working class: her wounds justified her cause and proved her devotion to it. This was more pleasing perhaps than actual sexual relationships, because no one could complain of an excess of her devotion and yet she still deserved pity for her suffering. The pleasure of suffering increased her feeling of personal righteousness and eased any guilt she may have felt because of her own wish for power. But although her wounds proved the justice of her cause, she (like Rousseau) ended up the prisoner of the image she had created of herself, the victim of her own legend.

Indeed, Tristan shared with many artists and writers of her time the illusion of the self as martyr or saviour. It fit well with the needs of the burgeoning capitalist state. It gave artists and women the illusion of wielding power in a society that had relegated them to the decorative sphere. By choosing to analyse the class structure instead of individual representatives of the new order, by choosing to represent the interests of all women and all lower-class people instead of her own, Tristan lifted herself out of the realm of personal confrontation that had proved so traumatic for her. Rather than allow her affection to be rejected, to be 'one of those cold, calculating beings for whom a great passion has the appearance of madness',[42] she chose to focus it on a *class* whose needs would ensure the grateful reception of her efforts. By becoming the defender of truth, justice and virtue, Tristan removed herself from the dangerous world of petty human emotions, provided a solution to her personal problems, and postulated a social remedy as well.

The greatness of Tristan's perception and achievements should be in no way diminished by this analysis. The complex nature of her *oeuvre* and of her commitment cannot be denied. To understand her failure, however, it is necessary to study the complex origins of the motivation that led her consciously to construct an image of herself and of her mission that proved to be fatal to its success.

She determined to take on the task of the 'salvation' of others who suffered as unjustly as she did. This 'rescue' involved her own martyrization, but paradoxically at times it seemed as if the reverse were the case. Women and the working class as a whole were martyred (in her imagination and through her representation of them) for Tristan's own salvation. At certain moments this process is blatantly clear. The nobility of her efforts was secured in proportion to their debasement.

> ... I am beginning to get accustomed to the idea that the people of our time are destined to die in degradation. But a new people will be reborn ... The Christian people have died today in degradation, and Flora Tristan, the first 'new' woman, will bring them back to life. (*Tour de France*, p. 139)

The over-determined nature of the project is also apparent in the prefatory material that introduces *Union ouvrière*. By elaborately recounting the difficulty she encountered in trying to get the book published, Tristan underlined her dedication to the cause and, at the same time, proved to the working class that she was one of their few real friends. Again she took the opportunity (as she had in the preface to *Pérégrinations*) to flaunt her honesty and devotion, and publicly to denounce those who had complicated her already difficult task. In the preface to the first edition, Tristan published her exchange with M. Pagnerre, who, although he was considered to be the only publisher friendly to socialist causes, refused her book.[43] She presents her view of his refusal and of her determination to publish the book by means of voluntary donations in a melodramatic light that imbues the project and its initiator with an air of messianic zeal.

The second edition is prefaced with letters of praise from well-known socialists and writers including Considérant, Sue and others, and with Tristan's discussion of the reception of the first edition. She had been disappointed by the workers' lack of comprehension.[44] One wonders if she ought to have included her criticism of their ignorance in a book designed for workers. But of course it also underlined the difficulty of her task, her truthfulness and her dedication.

Perhaps the most telling section is the list of all those who had contributed to her book's publication, with an exact account of their donations. This constitutes in some sense an accumulation of the collective praise of the illustrious names of her generation. At the same time, by revealing the size of their donations and reminding her readers to observe carefully which names were missing, Tristan was able to punish those who did not support her entirely. These lists constitute valuable registers of the political sentiment of the period, even as they expose Tristan's paradoxical sense of megalomania and deprivation. Although she did not publish the list of those who refused her, by signalling their omission she sought to punish and embarrass them publicly.

One aspect of the martyrist project is that it must be doomed to failure. Tristan correctly recognized that the people were not ready for her Idea:

> I can no longer conceal from myself the fact that the time has not yet come for them [the workers] to move – since they do not even understand their situation. No one understands, no one even addresses the question! How many disappointments and sufferings I am preparing for myself. It is evident that it will take at least seven or eight years for all the ideas in my book to be popularized and disseminated among the people. (*Tour de France*, pp. 14–16, 67)

She predicted that she would fall ill and die, and even fantasized about her epitaph: 'She spoke to the deaf.'[45]

Yet martyrdom was a project she could not resist. She felt herself dominated by a force stronger than herself: '... it seemed to me that a will other than my own was ordering me to act.' Perhaps the delicious feeling of isolation, of martyrdom, was what attracted her to her task: 'I worked *alone* and felt almost certain that I would generally be badly received.'[46]

Like other women of her time, Tristan had to learn to sublimate her energies into acceptable channels: '... women, you who are usually consumed with the need to love, to act, to live; you who seek everywhere a goal for that ardent, ceaseless activity of your soul which inspires and destroys you, torments you, and kills you'.[47]

Tristan did not make the connection between her plight and that of all women, except indirectly. In her letter to women that followed the plan for the *Union ouvriére*, however, she formulated her own problem as well as theirs. Tristan described her own plight in much the same way in *Tour de France*, only this time even more explicitly:

> I get so impatient at being inactive, it affects me so strongly that for the last 10 days I have been ill with a fever every night. All the efforts I make to calm myself are useless. I try to occupy my mind in every possible way ... Such is my nature, when I am under the influence of an idea, it takes hold of me with such violence. (*Tour de France*, p. 19)

The acts of renunciation and redirection of energy were ones that required violence. In fact, they elicited from Tristan a description whose language is reminiscent of the description of the painting that Méphis' rival Louis had painted, over which the duel was fought. Again, a conquest, a repression of a powerful part of herself is visible: '... to calm my rebellious flesh takes an enormous effort and several days. Ah, miserable flesh! so like a spirited, untamed horse!'[48] But she could not 'maîtriser sa violence', the violence of that love she found in herself. Her solution was sublimation, turning it toward a project by which it could be 'annihilated': 'to make my brothers live in unity – altogether forgetting my being, barely feeling it anymore'.[49] Tristan accurately described the origin of the Romantics' chosen form of sublimation: '...in the incoherent and divided milieu in which we live, passionate temperaments being unable to give full play to their passions, inevitably fall under the influence of an idea.'[50]

In her agitation, Tristan differed very much from her more illustrious contemporary, George Sand, who at this very moment (1843) found herself extremely dissatisfied also, but only with the dull and boring life she found herself leading. In a letter to her friend Delacroix (one of those who had refused to contribute to Tristan's cause), Sand described her plight in these terms:

> We are the ones who have cause to complain, we live such a monotonous and bourgeois life ... And we carry our yoke with the patience of our oxen ... It is not great mental strength that sustains

me as you seem to think. It is a great weariness with all personal sat-
isfactions ... In short, I exist no longer ... My ideal no longer
belongs in my real life. It belongs to another world, another century
... In the meantime I write novels because it takes me out of
myself.[51]

From this statement we can see the chasm that separates these two
contemporaries. Somehow, for each, redirection of energy was necessary, but in one case this repression led to a comfortable, almost
boring bourgeois existence, while in the other case it led to the arduous
task of saving the working class, and, in the process, to self-sacrifice.
For Tristan the most difficult chore of all would have been to submit
to 'what is'. (*Tour de France*, p. 67)

In her frequent refusal unjustly to praise the working class, Tristan
was implicitly attacking George Sand and others for whom such
flattery had become a common and facile way of dealing with their own
class guilt. Sand defended her optimistic portrayal of the working
class this way: 'I was accused of flattering the people and of attempting to make them look better. Well, why not? ... I feel like portraying
them the way I wish they were, the way I believe they ought to be.[52]
It should not be forgotten, however, that Sand's project of changing
the world was totally different from Tristan's: '... I was still endeavouring
to solve that insoluble problem: the means to reconcile the happiness
and dignity of the people oppressed by that very society, without
changing the society itself.'[53]

The social change Tristan sought was much more profound. Still,
the Paris working-class press was probably right in demanding that she
expurgate the passages which denigrated the working class. And it does
seem as if Tristan was especially excessive in her description of the brutality of women, as Cécile Dufour, vice secretary of the *Ruche populaire*,
insisted.[54]

Tristan's Radical Contribution and Her Limitations

Despite the personal nature of the project, Flora Tristan's attempt was
important and courageous. She was one of the first actually to try to
significantly change the situation of the working class *and women*. While
her methods for changing the world were several, her proposals derived
from one initial discovery: the need to unite the working class. Tristan's
originality lay in this idea and in her international perspective. She conceived of an International before Marx did, because she recognized the
universal nature of the workers' plight. Moreover, she insisted that
women also be represented in this union.

Although her discourse was couched at times in mystical terms, her religion was that of humanitarianism. She denounced the present form of religion, and analysed the way in which it was used to oppress people. She recognized the manner in which the bourgeois and the Church worked hand in hand to maintain the *status quo*.

> There is an outrageous understanding between the priests and the bourgeoisie! The bourgeois, he who is well-to-do, shamelessly says to the priests: 'I agree to giving you alms, to going to your shop ... but on the condition that you will see to it that the people, my beasts of burden and source of profit, remain ignorant, brutish and resigned to the condition I have imposed on them.' And the priest, who is now but a mere store clerk, agrees to deliver his goods, foul poison! ... The first enemy, the one who leads society, weakens it, kills it, is the priest-church business – the second is the bourgeoisie; the government, that is to say, the king and the administration are but the slaves of priests and bourgeois. (*Tour de France*, p. 73)

For her it was axiomatic that organized religion was harmful: 'It is as evident as two plus two equal four that if religion harms the people, we must hasten its destruction in order to prevent it from doing harm.'[55]

Tristan seems to have been confused about the causes of the terrible conditions she witnessed. Engels' explanation illuminates why: 'The socialism of earlier days certainly criticized the existing capitalistic mode of production and its consequences. But it could not explain them and, therefore, could not get mastery of them. It could only simply reject them as bad.'[56] Such was partially the case in Tristan's analysis. She understood the basis of the evil to be property, but condemned it in moral terms only. 'An examination of the causes of the evil convinces us that there is but one single cause, it is property '... all evil results from competition ... There is no doubt about it, money is Satan incarnate.'[57] She did not systematize these causes into a theory based on the economic reorganization of society, but focused on several other causes, including ignorance and religion.

Tristan believed she discovered still another cause for the plight of the working class in its treatment of women. Therein she found an explanation for the terrible lives the workers led. Tristan hoped to ameliorate the situation of the worker and the children by converting woman into an 'agent of morality'. Invoking a conception of women not that far from the bourgeois one, Tristan was unwittingly working on behalf of the very capitalist system that she recognized was the cause of so much woe.

Above all, Tristan determined to become an almost epic 'Romantic' figure in order to resolve the social and economic problems of her society. She forged a myth of herself and of the role women should play in society. The abbé Constant, one of Tristan's closest friends, proclaimed his view of Tristan's project in *L'Émancipation de la femme, ou Testament de la paria*, published after her death. His description of Tristan seems to be accurate:

> Flora's personality became so impassioned in the struggle that even in her own mind she had become a myth, she believed herself to be the woman messiah; after having struggled so heroically, she longed to be transformed into a martyr, to soar heavenward on an angel's wings.[58]

Obviously such a myth served several functions. Myth is, to use Roger Garaudy's terms, 'a *relation to being*; it is also a *summons to making*.'[59] Indeed, Tristan's myth of her mission included both of these purposes, but underlying these overt uses of myth is the other function of myth, the one which lies behind the others. Lévi-Strauss' description applies here: 'The object of myth is to provide a logical model for the solution of a contradiction.'[60]

Motherhood – As Lived by Tristan and Sand

Throughout this study we have examined the contradictions of class and sex which ravaged Tristan's life. In the months of feverish exaltation which preceded her death, Tristan transformed these contradictions from the past into a myth of the future: she exchanged her status as the pariah, alone and powerless, for that of 'the first "new" woman'[61] and constructed for herself the mission of saving the world.

Of course, as we have seen, this was one of the archetypal myths of the Romantic period, and the specific mission of women was particularly akin to the theories developed by the Saint-Simonians in the early 1830s. Although Tristan lucidly rejected other aspects of their doctrine, declaring that 'their obsession is authority',[62] and appropriately attacking Enfantin's plan for the organization of work as too regimented and military in nature,[63] she was attracted, almost in spite of herself, to their search for the 'femme-messie'. At first she seemed to criticize this faithful waiting: 'He makes the same error as the Saint-Simonians, he waits. Waits for the advent of woman, he knows she is the one who will save the world, and he, the man, does nothing. That is the Saint-Simonians' weakness.'[64]

Then, however, she saw the advantage in it: 'This defect is the result of their faith ... Then, is it a defect?'[65] Much later she clarified this seeming ambivalence: in Lyons, she encountered a man who believed her to be the awaited 'femme-messie'. This was her reaction:

... My presence, the presence of a woman speaking to the proletarians is for him the coming of woman ... which he, the Saint-
Simonian is waiting for ... everyone else thinks he is insane. Those
who have been ahead of their times have always been regarded as
madmen ... In the future they will be regarded as superior men who
were the first to understand the coming of woman. All honour to
madmen! Among the 40 men assembled there only the madman
understands me. (*Tour de France*, p. 82)

Again, as in *Promenades*, Tristan had a privileged communication with
a madman. Despite all Tristan's protests about how much she hated
flattery, her journal notes indicate that only those people who recognized the 'femme-guide' in her were deemed worthy of her special attention and praise. Such a one was Eléonore Blanc, a poor laundry woman
from Lyons for whom Tristan felt 'a very special love', 'a new kind of
love, greater, more exalted than any other love'. Flora did not know
how to name this love, but it was much stronger than the one she felt
for her daughter Aline who was 'far from pleasing me'. Aline was
neither ready to make any sacrifices, nor willing to become a disciple.
Tristan compared the relationship between herself and Blanc to that
of Jesus and St John. The description of the magnetic power she exercised over Eléonore is another example of the power of Romantic
sublimation of the period.[66]

Tristan's conception of the superiority of women went much further
than that of the Saint-Simonians. She envisaged herself 'leading the great
European people', but there was *no* male figure next to her. All by herself,
the deed would be accomplished: 'In order to move that cold, selfish,
indifferent mass of people, the power of my words, of my countenance
is necessary.' The personal nature of this mission was so extreme that
at times Tristan seemed to welcome the martyrist project implicit in
the rescue she planned.[67]

As we have seen, this rescue project had dominated all her works
from the earliest plan to rescue single and foreign women in *La Nécessité de faire bon accueil*, to the project to rescue the corrupted upper classes
of Peru in *Les Pérégrinations d'une Paria*, to rescuing the working classes
in *Méphis* (not to mention all the other rescues operated within that
novel and in *Promenades*). Now finally the biggest project of all was to
be announced and planned: 'Society is evil, I want to change it, to regen-
erate it. I want to save this dying world.'[68] A worthy goal, but more likely
than not a self-destructive one. In order for Tristan's martyrdom to be
perfect, the task had to be almost impossible. This required that the
object of the rescue be debased, to make the task even more unpleasant and more difficult. We have seen earlier how she accomplished this
in her descriptions of the working class.

Tristan was fully conscious of her own image as a martyr: she viewed it proudly. For a woman to become a messiah, she would first have to be a martyr. It was the logical resolution of woman's quest for power in Tristan's society:

> To endure all this, one must have a predilection for martyrdom, fortunately I happen to possess it to a degree ... How strange, the more they hurt me, the more I love them. What a mystery! How can you love those who hurt you? Dear God, how many ways am I to be crucified! (*Tour de France*, pp. 154, 101, 142)

In effect, remarks like these are common in her journal for the tour. Tristan conceived of her suffering as greater than that of Jesus, with whom she often compared herself and believed her self-abnegation to be greater than that of St Thérèse.[69] Indeed, it must be said, she had set herself an impossible task, and as her health grew worse the delirious frenzy with which she pursued her project was necessarily augmented.

As we have noted earlier, it is probably accurate to view this rescue project in part as a rescue of the self. In the sense of class, it signified for Tristan a recovery of her lost status, through the acquisition of a magical, mystical nobility conferred on her by society's rejects, a kind of world turned topsy-turvy where at last real value would be recognized. Moreover, it represented a means by which Tristan could regain her virtue as a woman. For if society increasingly defined women's virtue in terms of their expression of the maternal instinct, then by her project she could become the ideal queen-mother, a sort of Mother-Goddess who could give life to all:

> I have lavished care and solicitude on them with such motherly love! When I could see one ready to receive spiritual life, my power would increase a hundredfold in order to give him a great, beautiful, splendid life. Oh, what great delight that travail, however painful it may have been, brought to my heart! To give spiritual life to your brother! It is to be God creating the universe. Oh, it is the purest joy! (*Tour de France*, p. 150)

In ascribing this image to herself, Tristan was taking the idealized version of the woman's role set up by the Saint-Simonians much further, eliminating the male figure as we have noted, and inaugurating a 'reign of women'.[70] In so doing, she was falling victim to the unrealistic hope that the world might be saved by love. It was a tempting idea, and since love had been, up to that point, the only power attributed to women, it was the only one they had at their disposal. It is easy to see how attractive a force love might be in contrast to the other forces Tristan saw operating around her, but it contained a fatal contradiction. Marguerite Thibert has accurately delineated this process of recovery on the part of women, even those who most loudly proclaimed their feminism:

> The regression of an idea which originally had been able to sustain a practically complete feminism, toward the quite incomplete feminism which indirectly came out of it, shows us the ambiguity of the position they adopted. To base the right to equality for woman on the fact that she may have received from God the gift of intuition, and that her reign may establish on earth the dominion of sentiment over reason, was to prepare the way for Proudhon's counter-thesis and legitimize beforehand the state of subordination in which, in the name of reason, the author of *La Justice* meant to keep women.[71]

The slippery ground on which Saint-Simonism had placed itself caused the distortion of feminist theories, not only among the more or less legitimate heirs of Saint-Simonian thought, but among pure Saint-Simonians as well. How easily this process degenerated into Proudhon's anti-feminism can be seen from the notes for a talk delivered by a Saint-Simonian, Charles Lambert ('the most faithful disciple of Enfantin'), to his friends, among them Maxime du Camp, in November 1853: 'Equality is the division of power between man and woman – man presides over the State, public interest, laws, doctrine – woman presides over the family, private interest, customs ... [W]oman loves man and conversely; that is equality.' Mme Thibert characterized this properly: 'That is the direction in which an orthodoxy too faithful to Enfantin's interpretations was to lead.'[72]

Today women are still being viewed as the repositories of 'life-protecting' characteristics,[73] and it is again becoming fashionable to argue that certain characteristics are innately female, although the more radical view remains that they are but a product of woman's exclusion from the marketplace. Despite the nineteenth century's attributions of this mystical force to women, still we must recognize in Tristan's call for women of her time to become the 'agents moralisateurs' a call for a rejection of the values of her society, and an attempt to transcend them. However, within the seams of her argument was the implicit recognition that if women did assume this role, their husbands would become not only better fathers but also better workers and thus the economic system would also be better served.[74]

Tristan believed the liberation of women to be the necessary pre-condition for that of men, but she never integrated this idea with the earlier economic argument. Tristan issued her call in this way: 'I demand rights for woman because I am convinced that *all the misfor-*

tunes in the world come from the neglect and contempt manifested so far toward the natural and inalienable rights of woman.'[75] In the sense we have described above, this argument has merit and it was original,[76] for at that time – as Daniel Stern (la Comtesse d'Agoult) had pointed out in her memoirs – marriages were still largely pecuniary arrangements and 'What seems to be the least provided for is precisely the household and the family.'[77] Since this was the situation, improved family arrangements might have seemed to promise progress. Besides, Tristan predicted correctly that unless she was made aware of her role, the working-class woman would be a regressive social force, driven entirely by her own 'pecuniary concerns'.[78] Unless women could be educated, they would continue to represent conservative notions.

In choosing to play the role of the *Mère*, Tristan fell prey to the double bind which Romantic ideology held for women: by glorifying the 'femme messie' in the abstract, it had begun, following the lead in Rousseau's *Émile*, to glorify the woman as mother in the practical realm. In real life, Tristan had violated this ideal and had committed the unpardonable sin of leaving her husband and her children. For this, she was to be attacked by her rival George Sand, who on Tristan's death took charge of her daughter Aline, denouncing Tristan's failure as a mother and revealing her own class and sex bias:

> Did her mother [i.e., Tristan] love her? Why were they separated? What mission can thus make one forget and send so far, in a milliner's shop, so charming and so lovely a creature. I would much rather we take charge of her future than raise a monument to her mother whom I have never liked despite her courage and conviction.[79]

Thus, in constructing an image of the ideal family,[80] in rehabilitating the 'brutal' working-class woman, and in setting herself up as the bountiful and benevolent Mother-Goddess, in some sense Tristan was recovering her lost status as a good woman and rescuing herself in her society's terms – even though probably no greater denunciation of the egoism of the family unit had ever been written, or for that matter lived, than her own: 'Family life seems abominable to me, and such immorality! To neglect humanity in order to take care ... of your son ... Those three little children alone consume more than do 30 children of workers.'[81] In her description of the bourgeois family, she perceived the evils of the nuclear family. And in her rejection of private happiness and particular loyalty to her own daughter, whose limitations were apparent to her, Tristan implicitly rejected for herself the very ideal family she had set up.

Hegel had argued for granting special consideration to 'world historical individuals' : 'The litany of private virtues of modesty, humility, love and charity must not be raised against them.'[82] Tristan might have invoked such protection against Sand's charges, but because Tristan was a woman in an age dominated by bourgeois values, she was doomed to be judged by these very values. An alternative judgement was passed on her by Jules Janin, the representative of the bourgeois Romantic ideology. Like Sand's it also imprisoned her – this time in the other half of the double bind that her age erected for women: 'The daughter of the Incas flees toward the sun ... She no longer had a position, a name, she no longer was a maiden, nor a married woman, nor a widow, she was something elusive, uncertain.'[83]

In life as in death, Tristan's portrait never turned out precisely as she had hoped. Two other historical judgements do her more justice. For despite the binds of class and sex in which she was caught and which prevented her from success in her lifetime, she left behind her a legacy. Sébastien Commissaire, a contemporary, sat in her working-class audience in Lyons. He heard and saw her, and declared that what she had accomplished was '... a step toward the amelioration of the workers' condition ... She had prepared the future by uniting the workers, and by making them understand the importance and benefit of solidarity.'[84]

More recently Agulhon, a historian of the workers' movement, has defined Tristan's success:

> Flora, in Toulon, not only succeeded in spreading ideas, firing enthusiasm, in helping to establish or enlarge organizations, she has awakened militants ... From the 2nd to the 9th of March, 1845, for the first time, all the workers of the arsenal went on strike for their demands. The importance of that event for the history of the workers' movement cannot be over-estimated.[85]

Clearly Agulhon finds Tristan's disciples among the 'originators' of that massive strike.

In terms of her efforts on behalf of the liberation of woman, we can see that even though she was trapped by the ideology of her time and her own bad conscience about having so totally rejected the role assigned her, she nevertheless called for woman to be recognized as a social individual, to be granted equal rights before the law, to receive equal education and pay, and to cease being 'a nice little doll and a slave destined to amuse and serve her master.'[86]

In her derogatory description of working-class women, she was perhaps excessive, revealing the extent to which she had come to hate women. Her mother had never been a model for her, and in describing the harshness of working-class women, she was in part describing her own upbringing.

Conclusion

Beyond Her Contemporaries

Even though Tristan sought to distance herself and her work from that of other utopian socialists, and indeed to write a critique of them, she was trapped, as they were, in the confused ideology of her time, bequeathed in part by Rousseau. On the whole, Tristan rejected the Rousseauist 'culte de moi' and submerged her concern for herself in her passion for social change. In this sense, she escaped from the privatism and self-absorption epitomized by her contemporary George Sand.

We have seen with what enormous difficulty Tristan rejected Rousseau's prescription for women to 'please men'. For Tristan was also a child of her time, and soaked up much of Rousseau, to the detriment of her developing social theory and praxis. Although she did not make the error of other Romantics in glorifying individual subjectivity, the purely private domain, she did, along with the others, share Rousseau's belief in the primacy and soundness of 'feeling'. In contrast, Hegel had pointed out that this is 'indeed the worst mode, a mode which he [man] has in common with animals ... In feeling, the mental content is the smallest possible.'[1] Hegel described it as an indefinite and subjective state, a retreat 'from the common soil of understanding'.[2] But it was the grounds on which the French utopian socialists based their call for association. Although Tristan and the others also appealed to self-interest and pragmatism, the basic incentive they used was drawn from the supposedly common fount of 'feeling'. The effect of their call was therefore weakened.

Perhaps a graver error was derived from the first: essentially the utopian socialists confused the historical process with that of nature. That is, they extended the nature metaphor to history and viewed its development as 'organic' change. Because they had no access to Hegel's theories (or chose not to use them), the French utopian socialists worked outside of the conceptual framework of the dialectical method; thus they could not distinguish between the 'quiet unfolding' of nature and historical development, which 'is not the harmless and

187

unopposed simple growth of organic life but hard, unwilling labour against itself'.[3] Indeed, they erred, as Marx would point out, because they believed in peaceful change within the current system, not recognizing that, as Hegel put it (more abstractly), 'the degradation, destruction, annihilation of the preceding mode of actuality'[4] might be necessary. In this area, Tristan was much closer to Hegel than her contemporaries, as we have seen.

Because the French utopians' vision was obscured by Rousseau's concept of nature and of morality, they relied upon 'irrelevant' forces,[5] as Hegel called them, and cherished the notion of a recovery of the good society that had belonged to the 'noble savage'. They easily came to view progress and 'civilization' as corrupt, and sought to return to a simpler societal organization, outside of the corrupt one in which they found themselves. Believing in the essential goodness of man, they conceived of ways of permitting this goodness to manifest itself. Although Tristan began with this perspective, she soon became aware of its limitations.

Indeed, Hegel made his own use of the 'nature' metaphor, but in a totally different fashion, one that stood the utopian socialists' optimistic faith in cooperation and consensus on its head. He argued that the 'life of a community of people brings a fruit to maturity, for their activity aims at actualizing its principle. But the fruit does not fall back into the womb of the people that have produced and ripened it. On the contrary, it turns into a bitter drink for the people. The people cannot abandon it, for they have an unquenchable thirst for it. Imbibing the drink is the drinker's destruction, yet at the same time gives rise to a new principle.'[6]

Here too Tristan was much closer to Hegel than any of her contemporaries. In her encounter with French society on her *tour de France*, Tristan came to understand this process. Unfortunately she died before she could implement the knowledge she had gained.

In this study, which we view as preliminary to an understanding of the July Monarchy and of the development of socialism, feminism and literature in nineteenth-century France, we have tried to find the origins of the essential structural and conceptual biases which oriented the work of Flora Tristan and which made it unacceptable to her contemporaries. We have attempted to illustrate, on the one hand, a method for studying the genesis of forgotten works of art, and on the other, we have sought to learn how to read such works as an index to the tastes and mentality of an age. Tristan's 'literary' production, and her life for that matter, offer us a valuable guide to the prescribed limits of literary and political activity during the July Monarchy. Although Tristan finally decided she felt she had to choose between aesthetics and social change, her life and work were irrevocably tied to both spheres, and what she created in one could not help but affect the other.

Notes and References

Chapter 1

All quoted material unattributed to another source is taken from: Flora Tristan y Moscoso, *Les Pérégrinations d'une paria (1833–1834)* 2 vols. (Paris: Arthus Bertrand, 1838).

1. See Ian Watt, *Rise of the Novel* (Berkeley: Univ. of California Press, 1959) p. 67, for discussion of the implications of Weber's thesis for the novel.
2. For elaboration of this view, see Edmond & Jules Goncourt, *La Femme au dix-huitième siècle* (Paris: Charpentier Cie., 1887) p. 375.
3. Chloderlos de Laclos, *Oeuvres complètes*, ed. Maurice Allem (Paris: Gallimard, 1951).
4. Paule-Marie Duhet, *Les Femmes et la Révolution, 1789–1794* (Paris: Juilliard, 1971) pp. 68–74.
5. Duhet, *Les Femmes*, p. 71.
6. Marc de Villiers, *Histoire des clubs des Femmes et des Légions d'Amazones, 1793–1848–1871*, (Paris: Plon, 1910) pp. 78–9.
7. Evelyne Sullerot, *Histoire et sociologie du travail féminin* (Paris: Gonthier, 1969) p. 77.
8. Crane Brinton, *French Revolutionary Legislation on Illegitimacy* (Cambridge, Mass.: Harvard Univ. Press, 1936) p. 79.
9. *Code Napoléon*, ed. H. M. J. Wattel (Leiden: Blankenburg, 1888.)
10. Sullerot traces this process in *Histoire*, pp. 21–86.
11. Gabriel Lepointe, 'La Femme au XIXè siècle en France', *Société Jean Bodin*, t.12, p. 508.
12. Angus McClaren, 'Medicine and Private Morality in France, 1800–1850', *Feminist Studies*, No. 2–3 (Spring 1975) p. 51.
13. Jules Michelet, *L'Amour* (Paris: Charpentier Cie., 1889) p. 52.
14. McClaren, 'Medicine', p. 45.
15. Jean-Jacques Rousseau, *Émile*, vol. 4, eds. Bernard Gagnebin and Marcel Raymond, *Oeuvres complètes* (Paris: Gallimard, 1969) pp. 256–7.
16. McClaren, 'Medicine', p. 45.
17. Sullerot, *Histoire*, p. 101.
18. Honoré de Balzac, *La Physiologie du mariage, pré-originale* (1826) ed. Maurice Bardeche (Paris: Droz, 1940) pp. 137, 106, 138, 143.

19. Honoré de Balzac, *Physiologie du mariage* (1830) ed. Maurice Regard (Paris: Garnier-Flammarion, 1968) p. 48.
20. Balzac (Bardèche 1826) pp. 145, 143.
21. Balzac (ed. Maurice Regard, 1830) p. 154.
22. Ibid., p. 155.
23. Rousseau, *Émile*, p. 446.
24. Balzac, *Physiologie* (1830) p. 242.
25. Rousseau, *Émile*, p. 768.
26. Germaine Necker, baronne de Staël, *De la littérature considérée dans ses rapports avec les institutions sociales*, v. 2, ed. Paul Van Tieghem, (Geneva: Droz, 1959) p. 342.
27. The quote Tristan used to open her novel *Méphis* (which she borrowed from Balzac's *Séraphita*) is telling: 'Our instinct is precisely that which makes us so perfect. That which you learn, you others, we ourselves feel.' [*Méphis* 1 (Paris: Ladvocat, 1838) p. 2]
28. *Gita May, De Jean-Jacques Rousseau à Mme Roland*, (Geneva: Droz, 1964) p. 38.
29. Jules Peuch, *La Vie et l'oeuvre de Flora Tristan* (Paris: Marcel Rivière, 1925) p. 9.
30. Jean Baelen, *La Vie de Flora Tristan* (Paris: Le Seuil, 1972) p. 13.
31. Flora Tristan, 'Lettres de Bolivar', *Le Voleur* (31 July 1838) pp. 91–2.
32. Norman O. Brown, *Life Against Death: The Psychoanalytical Meaning of History* (Middletown, Conn.; Wesleyan Univ. Press, 1959) pp. 266, 268.
33. Puech, *La Vie*, p. 69.
34. Ibid.

Chapter 2

All quoted material unattributed to another source is taken from: Mme. F. T., *Nécessité de faire bon accueil aux femmes étrangères* (Paris: Chez Delaunay, 1836).
1. Evelyne Sullerot, *Histoire de la presse féminine en France des origines à 1848* (Paris: Armand Colin, 1966) pp. 186–8.
2. *Le Citateur féminin* (1835), p. 325.
3. Puech, *La Vie*, p. 69.
4. Marguerite Thibert, *Le Féminisme dans le socialisme français de 1830 à 1850* (Paris: Marcel Giard, 1926) pp. 110–224, 228. This book is indispensable.
5. For further discussion of his real sexual identity see Marie-Louise Puech's 'Le Mystère de la *Gazette des Femmes*: la presse féministe sous Louis Phillipe', *La Grande Revue* (March 1935) (A la Bibliothèque Marguerite Durand).
6. *La Gazette des femmes* (1 Jan 1838) p. 10.
7. *Pérégrinations*, 1, p. xxvi.
8. *La Gazette des femmes* (1 Jan 1838) p. 11.

Chapter 3

All quoted material unattributed to another source is taken from *Les Pérégrinations d'une paria (1833–1834)*.

1. Puech, *La Vie*, pp. 69–70. This letter to Fourier (and others), quoted in Puech, are the source of quotations, pp. 27–8.
2. Ibid.
3. See Puech, *La Vie*, Chapter IV.
4. Honoré de Balzac, *Eugénie Grandet* (Paris: Garnier-Flammarion, 1969) p. 129.
5. In his *Mémoire à consulter pour M. Chazal*, contre Madame Chazal, procès de 1838 (Tribunal civil de 1ère instance de la Seine, 3è chambre, p. 5.)
6. Jules Janin, 'Madame Flora Tristan', *La Sylphide*, 1, no. 1 (5 Jan 1845) p. 84.
7. Lettre à Olympe, Août 1, 1839, dans *7 Lettres* présentées par André Breton, *Le Surrealisme même*, 3 (Automne, 1957) p. 8. Future references to these letters will appear in footnotes as: Breton, *7 Lettres*.
8. Simone Debout, 'La Geste de Flora Tristan', *Critique*, no. 308 (Jan 1973) p. 84.
9. Flora Tristan, *Méphis* 1, Paris: Ladvocat, 1838) p. 62.
10. Chazal, *Mémoire*, p. 54.
11. Wayne Booth, *The Rhetoric of Fiction* (Chicago: Univ. of Chicago Press, 1961) p. 153. 'I consider the "dramatized narrator" to be almost another "character" in the "story"' Tristan recounts.
12. Ibid., p. 152.

Chapter 4

All quoted material unattributed to another source is taken from: Flora Tristan, *Méphis*, 2 vols. (Paris: Ladvocat, 1838).

1. Flora Tristan, *L'Émancipation de la femme, ou le Testament de la paria*, ouvrage posthume, complété d'après ses notes et publié par A. Constant (Paris: La Vérité, 1846). The authenticity of this work is dubious. For further bibliographical information, see Puech, *La Vie*, p. 491.
2. Letter to Tristan from Constant (Lévi), quoted in *Eliphas Lévi, rénovateur de l'occultisme en France* by Paul Chacornac (Paris: Chacornac Frères, 1926) p. 33.
3. Ibid., p. 52.
4. Jean-Pierre Auget, *Les Grèves sous la Monarchie de Juillet, 1830–1847* (Geneva: Droz, 1954) p. 126.
5. Sébastien Charléty, *La Monarchie de Juillet, 1830–1848*, v. 5 of *Histoire de la France contemporaine depuis la Révolution jusqu'à la Paix de 1919*, ed. E. Lavisse, (Paris: Hachette, 1920–2) pp. 122–3.

6. Granier de Cassagnac, 'Fantasies; la femme libre', *Le Siècle* (28 January 1838).
7. Thibert, *Le Féminisme*, p. 247.
8. Wilhelm Reich, *Sex-Pol: Essays 1929–34*, ed. Lee Baxandall (New York: Random House, 1972) p. 42.
9. Marguerite Ikanyan, *The Idea of the Novel in France: The Critical Reaction, 1815–1848* (Geneva: Droz, 1961) p. 124.
10. Ibid., p. 120.
11. Ibid., p. 97.
12. Louis Reybaud, *Jérôme Paturôt à la recherche d'une position sociale*, 3rd ed. (Paris: Calmann-Lévy, 1879) p. 14.
13. Théophile Gautier, *Mademoiselle de Maupin*, ed. A. Boschot (Paris: Garnier, 1955) pp. 20, 23.
14. Benjamin Constant, 'De Madame de Staël et ses ouvrages', *Adolphe* (Paris: Garnier, 1963) p. 257.
15. René Girard, *Mensonge romantique et vérité romanesque* (Paris: Bernard Grasset, 1961) p. 193.
16. Quoted in 'La Déesse blanche', by Roger Laporte, *Critique*, XXXI, no. 333 (Feb 1975) p. 158.
17. Chazal, *Mémoire*, p. 8.
18. M. Jeanne Peterson, 'The Victorian Governess: Status Incongruence in Family and Society', in *Suffer and Be Still, Women in the Victorian Age*, ed. Martha Vicinus (Bloomington: Indiana Univ. Press, 1973) p. 10.
19. Ibid., p. 15.
20. For example, see Jules Janin, 'Madame Flora Tristan', in *La Sylphide*, p. 4.
21. *Les belles femmes de Paris et de la Province accompagnées de lettres aux belles femmes*, par M. de Balzac, le comte de Beauvoir, Théophile Gautier, Gérard de Nerval, Arsène Houssaye, et al. 2è série, 2è livraison (Paris, 1840).
22. S. Freud, 'Contributions to the Psychology of Love: The Taboo of Virginity' (1918), in *On Creativity and the Unconscious,* ed. Benjamin Nelson (New York: Harper & Row, 1965) p. 187.
23. Breton, *7 Lettres*, p. 10.
24. All quotes in this paragraph from Robert Darnton, *Mesmerism and the End of the Enlightenment in France* (New York: Schocken, 1970) pp. 146, 127, 126.
25. Puech, *La Vie*, pp. 52, 89.
26. Breton, *7 Lettres*, p. 6.
27. Ibid.
28. Flora Tristan, *Le Tour de France: état actuel de la classe ouvrière sous l'aspect moral, intellectuel, matériel*. Préf. de Michel Collinet, Notes de Jules Puech (Paris: Têtes de feuilles, 1973), p. 227. All subsequent references in these footnotes will appear as *TF*.
29. Michel Thévoz, 'Peinture et ideologie', in *Les Temps modernes*, no. 330 (Jan 1974) p. 1284.

30. A. Schnapper, 'Painting during the Revolution, 1789–99', in *The Age of Revolution* (exhibition catalogue) ed. Robert Rosenblum (New York, 1975) p. 107.

31. Arnold Hauser, *The Social History of Art*, v. 3, trans. S. Godman, (New York: Random House, 1951) p. 154.

32. Helen Gardner, *Art Through the Ages*, 5th ed., revised by H. de la Croix and R. G. Tansey (New York: Harcourt, Brace and World, 1970) p. 652.

33. Philippe Jullian, *Delacroix* (Paris: Albin-Michel, 1963) p. 75.

34. Flora Tristan, 'L'Atelier de Girodet', in *L'Artiste*, 28è livraison (1838) p. 413.

35. K. Marx and F. Engels, *La Sainte famille*, eds. N. Meunier and G. Bada, trans. Erna Cogniot (Paris: Editions sociales, 1972) p. 238.

36. Reich, *Sex-Pol*, p. 70.

37. Sigmund Freud, *The Interpretation of Dreams*, trans. James Strachey (New York: Avon, 1968) p. 362.

38. Nora E. Hudson, *Ultra-Royalism and the French Restoration* (Cambridge: Cambridge Univ. Press, 1936) p. 188.

39. Charléty, *La Monarchie*, p. 107.

40. Ibid., p. 106.

41. François Génin, *Les Jésuites et l'université* (Paris: Paulin, 1844) p. 3.

42. Ibid., p. 34.

43. Reich, *Sex-Pol*, p. 41.

44. Breton, *7 Lettres*, p. 7.

45. Girard, *Mensonge*, pp. 33, 60.

46. Chazal, *Mémoire*, p. 2.

47. Ibid.

48. Ibid., p. 3.

49. Charles Mauron, *Des métaphores obsédantes aux mythes personnels: introduction à la psychocritique* (Paris: Corti, 1964) p. 210.

50. Flora Tristan, *Union ouvrière*, 3ième ed (Paris: Editions d'histoire sociale, 1967). All subsequent references in these footnotes will appear as *Uo*.

51. S. Freud, 'The Poet and Day-Dreaming', in *On Creativity and the Unconscious*, pp. 47–8.

52. Reich, *Sex-Pol*, p. 26.

53. Juliet Mitchell, *Woman's Estate* (New York: Pantheon, 1972) p. 118.

54. D. O. Evans, *Le Roman social sous la Monarchie de Juillet* (Paris: Presses universitaires du France, 1934) p. 106.

55. Chazal, *Mémoire*, p. 71.

56. Ibid., pp. 5–6.

57. Sébastien Charléty, *Histoire du Saint-Simonisme* (Paris: Editions Gonthier, 1931) p. 111.

58. Edith Thomas, *Pauline Roland, socialisme et féminisme au XIXè siècle* (Paris: M. Rivière, 1956) p. 42.

59. Ibid., p. 65.

60. Ibid., p. 57.

61. Girard, *Mensonge*, p. 189.

62. Jean-Paul Sartre, *Being and Nothingness*, trans. Hazel F. Barnes (New York: N. Y. Philosophical Library 1956), p. 445.
63. Ibid., p. 447.
64. Breton, *7 Lettres*, p. 6
65. Pérégrinations, 1, p. xxxviii.
66. See Girard, *Mensonge*, p. 97, *passim*.
67. Ibid., p. 104.
68. Ibid., p. 69.

Chapter 5

All quoted material unattributed to another source is taken from: Flora Tristan, *Promenades dans Londres* (Paris: H.-L. Delloye, 1840).

1. K. Marx, 'Excerpts from Capital: A Critique of Political Economy', in *Marx and Engels, Basic Writings on Politics and Philosophy*, ed. Lewis S. Feuer (Garden City, N.Y.: Doubleday Anchor, 1959) p. 43. All subsequent references to this anthology will appear as 'Feuer'.
2. Ibid., p. 245.
3. Breton, *7 Lettres*, p. 6.
4. Puech, *La Vie*, p. 116.
5. Ibid.
6. 'Neuf lettres a ...' (Amsterdam: International Instituut voor Sociale Geschiendenis).
7. H. Allart de Meritens, *La Femme et la démocratie de nos temps* (Paris: Delaunay, 1836), p. 122.
8. Puech, *La Vie*, p. 114.
9. *La Ruche populaire* (August 1840), p. 8. See Puech, *La Vie*, p. 117.
10. T.J. Clark, *The Absolute Bourgeois: Artists and Politics in France, 1848–1851* (Greenwich, Conn.: New York Graphics Society, 1973) p. 12.
11. Ibid.
12. Puech, *La Vie*, p. 112.
13. K. Marx and F. Engels, *The German Ideology*, ed. C.J. Arthur (New York: International Publishers, 1973) p. 118.
14. Herbert Marcuse, *Reason and Revolution: Hegel and the Rise of Social Theory* (Boston: Beacon Press, 1960) p. 282.
15. K. Marx, *The Economic and Philosophic Manuscripts of 1844*, trans. M. Milligan, ed. Dirk J. Struik (New York: International Publishers, 1972) p. 177. All future references in these footnotes will appear as *EPMS*.
16. *TF*, p. 128.
17. Ibid. The remainder of her statement is significant in terms of her martyrist project: 'But since I believe in the existence of a good God, I will serve Him in serving humanity, *I will make myself an apostle and prophet and I will love that poor humanity even more when I find it ugly, unhappy, and suffering.*' [emphasis added]

18. Edouard Dolléans, *Histoire du mouvement ouvrier, 1830–1871*, v. 1 (Paris: Armand Colin, 1957) p. 32.
19. Friedrich Engels, *Condition of the Working Class in England*, trans. and ed. W.O. Henderson and W.H. Chalconer (Palo Alto: Stanford Univ. Press, 1958). All future references in these footnotes will appear as *CWCE*.
20. David McLellan, *Marx before Marxism*, (London: Macmillan, 1970) p. 157.
21. Marx and Engels, *La Sainte famille*, p. 27.
22. Feuer, p. 42.
23. Arnold Ruge, *Zwei Jahre in Paris* (Leipzig: W. Jurany, 1846) chap. XII. 'Flora Tristan et L'Union ouvrière.'
24. Maximilien Rubel, 'Flora Tristan et Karl Marx', in *La Nef* (Jan 1946) p. 73.
25. Ibid., p. 73.
26. *EPMS*, p. 110.
27. Ibid.
28. Ibid., p. 108.
29. *CWCE*, p. 313.
30. Feuer, p. 43.
31. *TF*, pp. 137–8.
32. Feuer, p. 14.
33. *EPMS*, p. 114.
34. *CWCE*, p. 109.
35. Ibid., p. 93.
36. Ibid., p. 208.
37. Ibid.
38. Ibid., p. 93.
39. Ibid., p. 208.
40. Ibid., p. 312.
41. *EPMS*, p. 114.
42. Feuer, p. 9.
43. *CWCE*, p. 311.
44. Ibid., p. 241.
45. Ibid., p. 109.
46. Ibid., p. 294.
47. Steven Marcus, *Engels, Manchester, and the Working Class* (New York: Random House, 1975) p. 137.
48. *CWCE*, p. 17.
49. Ibid., p. 338.
50. Marcus, *Engels*, p. 71.
51. Ibid., p. 119.
52. Ibid., p. 238.
53. Ibid., p. 157.
54. Ibid., p. 142.
55. Ibid., p. 182.
56. *CWCE*, p. 8.
57. *EPMS*, pp. 75, 89.

58. Michelle Perrot, *Enquêtes sur la condition ouvrière en France au 19è siècle* (Paris: Microéditions Hachette, 1972) p. 24.
59. *CWCE*, p. 270.
60. See introduction to *CWCE* for fuller discussion of this problem.
61. *CWCE*, introduction, p. 116.
62. Perrot, *Enquêtes*, p. 12.
63. *CWCE*, p. 375.
64. Marcus, *Engels*, p. 82.
65. Ibid., pp. 100–1.
66. Régine Pernoud, *Histoire de la bourgeoisie en France, v. 2: Les temps modernes* (Paris: Seuil, 1962) pp. 492–3.
67. See Françoise Basch, *Relative Creatures: Victorian Women in Society and the Novel*, trans. A. Rudolf (New York: Schocken, 1974).
68. Marx and Engels, *La Sainte famille*, p. 27.
69. Ibid., p. 28.
70. Ibid.
71. *CWCE*, p. 160.
72. Ibid.
73. Ibid.
74. Ibid., pp. 160–1.
75. Feuer, p. 25.
76. *CWCE*, p. 162.
77. Ibid., p. 242.
78. Ibid., p. 164.
79. Ibid., p. 165.
80. Feuer, pp. 24–5.
81. *CWCE*, p. 181.
82. Ibid., p. 183.
83. A.J.B. Parent-Duchâtelet, *De la prostitution dans la ville de Paris* (Paris: Ballière, 1837) p. 280.
84. *CWCE*, p. 166.
85. Edward Shorter, 'Capitalism, Culture and Sexuality: Competing Models', *Social Science Quarterly*, LII, no. 2 (Sept 1972) p. 340.
86. *CWCE*, p. 165.
87. Sullerot, *Histoire*, p. 37.
88. Joan W. Scott and Louise A. Tilly, 'Women's Work and the Family in Nineteenth-Century Europe', *Comparative Studies in Society and History* XVII, no. 1 (Jan 1975) p. 40.
89. *CWCE*, p. 166.
90. Engels, *Origin of Family*, p. 221.
91. Honoré de Balzac, 'Avant-Propos', *La Comédie Humaine, Oeuvres complètes*, 1, ed. Marcel Bouteron (Paris: Gallimard, 1959) p. 53.
92. Lorenz von Stein, *Der Socialismus und Kommunismus in das heutigen Frankreich* (1842) quoted in Kaethe Mengelberg's *History of the Social Movement in France 1789–1850* (Totawa, N. J.: Bedminster Press, 1964) p. 257.
93. Ibid., p. 257.
94. *Uo*, p. 68.

95. *Uo*, p. 54.
96. Proudhon, *La Pornocratie ou les femmes dans les temps modernes* (Paris: Alacroix, 1875) p. 262.
97. Marilyn Boxer, 'Foyer or Factory: Working Class Women in Nineteenth Century France'. Paper presented to the Western Society for French History, San Francisco, 22 Nov 1974, p. 3.
98. *Uo*, pp. 79, 49.
99. *Uo*, pp. 55, 69–70.
100. *TF*, p. 265.
101. Pernoud, *Histoire*, pp. 497, 478.
102. Sullerot, *Histoire*, p. 41.
103. Engels, *German Ideology*, p. 52.
104. Feuer, p. 25.
105. Mitchell, *Woman's Estate*, pp. 78, 80.
106. *Uo*, p. 62.
107. *TF*, p. 229.
108. A.L.A. Fée, *Voyage autour de ma bibliothèque* (Paris: Veuver Berger-Levrault, 1885) p. 109.
109. Chazal, *Mémoire*, pp. 4–5.
110. Flora Tristan, 'Pétition pour le rétablissement du divorce à Messieurs les députés' (Paris, 20 Dec 1837) p. 1 (Archives Nationales, pétition no. 133, dossier 71).
111. William Thompson, *Appeal of one Half the Human Race – Women, Against the Pretensions of the Other Half, Men, to Retain Them in Political, and Thence in Civil and Domestic Slavery* (London: Virago, 1983). Cf. E.P. Thompson, *The Making of the English Working Class* (New York: Random House, 1966), p. 453, for the significance of this book.

Chapter 6

1. Puech, *La Vie*, p. 181.
2. Stein, *Der Socialismus*, p. 308.
3. G.D.H. Cole, *Socialist Thought: The Forerunners* (London: Macmillan, 1962) p. 187.
4. Ibid., pp. 187–8.
5. Agricol Perdiguier, *Le livre du compagnonnage I*, p. 14.
6. Puech, *La Vie*, p. 461.
7. Ibid., p. 463.
8. Perdiguier, *Correspondance inédite avec Georges Sand et ses amis*, ed. Jean Briquet (Paris: Klincksieck, 1966), p. 69.
9. Puech, *La Vie*, pp. 322–3, 464.
10. *Uo*, p. xxxii.
11. *TF*, p. 13.
12. Puech, *La Vie*, p. 455.
13. *TF*, p. 13.
14. Puech, *La Vie*, pp. 454, 457–8.

15. Ibid., p. 482.
16. *Uo*, p. 101.
17. Ibid., p. vi.
18. *Promenades,* p. 355.
19. Puech, *La Vie*, pp. 185–6.
20. *Uo*, p. xiv.
21. Puech, *La Vie*, p. 185.
22. Lettre à Considérant, 26 Juillet 1837 (Archives Nationales: 10 AS 42).
23. *TF*, pp. 100–1.
24. *Uo*, p. 116.
25. Ibid., p. 24.
26. *TF*, p. 83.
27. Maurice Agulhon, *Une Ville ouvrière au temps du socialisme utopique: Toulon de 1815 à 1851* (Paris: Mouton, 1971) p. 160.
28. *TF*, p. 21.
29. *Uo*, pp. vii–ix.
30. *TF*, pp. 68, 74, 96.
31. *Promenades* (1842), p. x.
32. *TF*, p. 137.
33. Ibid., p. 58.
34. Karl and Engels, *La Sainte famille*, p. 47.
35. *TF*, p. 160.
36. Puech, p. 446. This is noted as the excuse of the 'workers who refused me', who refused to contribute to *Uo*.
37. *TF*, pp. 50, 119.
38. *Uo*, p. 29.
39. *TF*, p. 49; *Uo*, p. 10.
40. Freud's essay, 'A Special Type of Object-Choice', in *On Creativity and the Unconscious*, p. 170, seems particularly appropriate here.
41. William H. Blanchard, *Rousseau and the Spirit of Revolt* (Ann Arbor: Univ. of Michigan, 1967) p. 254.
42. *Pérégrinations* 1, p. 47.
43. *Uo*, p. xxviii.
44. Ibid., p. ix.
45. *TF*, p. 43.
46. *Uo*, p. xxxii.
47. Ibid. p. 88.
48. *TF*, p. 227.
49. Ibid., p. 67.
50. Ibid., p. 19.
51. George Sand, *Correspondance*, v. 6, p. 219.
52. George Sand, preface to *Le Compagnon du Tour de France 1851* (Lyons: Editions Cosmopolis, 1945) p. 8.
53. George Sand, preface to *Indiana* (Paris: Garnier, 1842) p. 16.
54. *TF*, p. 13.
55. Ibid., p. 137.
56. Feuer, p. 89.

57. *TF*, pp. 52, 125, 176.
58. Constant, *L'Emancipation*, p. 116.
59. Roger Garaudy, *Marxism in the Twentieth Century*, trans. René Hague (New York: Scribner, 1970) p. 171.
60. Ibid.
61. *TF*, p. 139.
62. Ibid., p. 18.
63. *Uo*, p. 37.
64. *TF*, p. 49.
65. Ibid.
66. Ibid., pp. 132, 120, 20.
67. Ibid., pp. 229, 183.
68. Ibid., p. 109.
69. Ibid., pp. 119, 142, 102.
70. Ibid., p. 157.
71. Thibert, *Le Féminisme*, pp. 76–7.
72. Ibid., pp. 76–8.
73. See Herbert Marcuse, 'Socialism and Feminism' in *City Lights*, no. 3 (1974) p. 34.
74. *Uo*, pp. 62, 66–7.
75. Ibid., p. 62.
76. Thibert, *Le Féminisme*, p. 310.
77. Daniel Stern, *Mes Souvenirs*, 3rd. ed. (Paris: Calmann-Lévy, 1880) p. 222.
78. *Uo*, p. 68; *TF*, p. 11.
79. George Sand, *Correspondance*, t. 6, p. 789.
80. *Uo*, pp. 66–7.
81. *TF*, p. 123.
82. G.W.F. Hegel, *Reason in History*, ed. Robert S. Hartmann (New York: Bobbs-Merrill, 1953), p. 83.
83. Jules Janin, *La Sylphide*, p. 5. Notice how Janin's description echoes that image of women depicted in Marequita's song 'La fille de l'Océan.'
84. Sébastien Commissaire, *Mémoires et souvenirs d'un ancien représentant du peuple*, t. 1 (Paris: Garcet et Nisius, 1888) p. 110.
85. Agulhon, *Une ville*, pp. 161, 163–4.
86. *Uo*, p. 50.

Conclusion

1. Hegel, *Reason in History*, p. 17.
2. Ibid., p. 17.
3. Ibid., p. 69.
4. Ibid., p. 71.
5. Ibid., p. 95.
6. Ibid.

Bibliography

Works by Flora Tristan

Books and Articles

'De l'art depuis la Renaissance.' *L'Artiste*, 3e série, 24e livraison, 1838, p. 143. [Later appended to *Méphis*.]

'De l'art et de l'artiste dans l'antiquité et à la Renaissance'. *L'Artiste*, 3e série, 9e livraison, 1838, p. 187. [Later appended to *Méphis*.]

'Episode de la vie de Ribera dit l'Espagnolet'. *L'Artiste*, 13e livraison, 1838, pp. 192–96.

L'Émancipation de la femme, ou le Testament de la paria, ouvrage posthume de Mme Flora Tristan, complété d'après ses notes et publié par A. Constant. Paris: La Vérité, 1846.

Flora Tristan's London Journal, 1840. Trans. Dennis Palmer and Giselle Pincetl. Charlestown, Mass.: Charles River Books, 1980.

'Lettres à un architecte anglais par Mme Flora Tristan'. *Revue de Paris*, no. 37–8, 1837, pp. 280–90.

'Lettres de Bolivar, publiées avec commentaires par Flora Tristan'. *Le Voleur*, 31 July 1838, pp. 90–4.

The London Journal of Flora Tristan 1842, or The Aristocracy and the Working Class of England. Ed. and trans. Jean Hawkes. London: Virago Press, 1982.

Méphis, par Mme Flora Tristan. 2 vols. Paris: Ladvocat, 1838. [The following chapters were published in contemporary journals:

———. ['L'Atelier de Girodet'. *L'Artiste*, 28e livraison, 1838.]

———. ['Les Tribulations d'un riche'. *Le Siècle*, 18 November 1838.]

Nécessité de faire bon accueil aux femmes étrangères, par Mme F. T. Paris: chez Delaunay, 1836.

Pérégrinations d'une paria (1833–1834), par Mme Flora Tristan. 2 vols. Paris: Arthus Bertrand, 1838. [A chapter of this work, 'Les Couvens d'Aréquipa, histoire de Dominga', was published in *Revue de Paris*, November 1836, pp. 225–48.]

Pérégrinations d'une paria 1833–1834. Paris: Maspero, 1979.

Peregrinations of a Pariah: 1833–34. Ed. and introduction by Jean Hawkes. London: Virago Press, 1986.

'Pétition pour l'abolition de la peine de mort à Messieurs les membres de la Chambre des députés'. Paris: Archives Nationales, Section moderne, pétition no. 139, dossier no. 70, 10 December 1838.

'Pétition pour le rétablissement du divorce à Messieurs les députés'. Paris: Archives Nationales, pétition no. 133, dossier no. 71, 20 December 1837.

Promenades dans Londres, par Mme Flora Tristan. Paris: H.-L. Delloye, 1840. Londres: W. Jeffs, 1840. Same work under the title *La Ville Monstre*, 2nd ed. [Very rare, not in Paris libraries. Cited by J. Puech, *La Vie et l'oeuvre de Flora Tristan*, p. 489.]

Promenades dans Londres, ou L'Aristocratie et les Prolétaires Anglais, par Mme Flora Tristan. Edition populaire. Paris: Raymond-Bocquet, 1842. [Contains new Introduction, and a 'Dédicace aux classes ouvrières'. Chapters of *Promenades dans Londres* were published in the following journals:

———. ['Quartier des Irlandais à Londres'. *La Fraternité*, October 1841.]

———. ['Une visite aux chambres de Parlement'. *Le Nouveau Monde*, 21 May 1840.]

Promenades dans Londres, Introductions et notes de François Bedarida. Paris: Maspero, 1978.

Le Tour de France: état actuel de la classe ouvrière sous l'aspect moral, intellectual, matériel. Préface de Michel Collinet. Notes de Jules L. Puech. Paris: Editions Tête de Feuilles, 1973. [Published posthumously.]

Union ouvrière, par Mme Flora Tristan. Edition populaire. Paris: Prévot, 1843.

Union ouvrière. 2nd ed. Paris: Worms & Cie., 1844. [Contains a song, 'La Marseillaise de l'Atelier', and is 26 pp. longer.]

Union ouvrière. 3rd ed. Paris and Lyon [sic]: chez tous les librairies, 1844. [Reproduction of 2nd ed.]

Union ouvrière. [facsimile of 3rd ed.] Paris: Editions d'histoire sociale, 1967. [The first chapters of *Union ouvrière* appeared in *La Phalange*, 29 and 31 March 1843.]

The Workers' Union. Trans. and with an introduction by Beverly Livingston. Urbana, Illinois: University of Illinois Press, 1983.

Correspondence

Letters meant for publication:
'Lettre adressée au Directeur de *La Phalange*, V. Considérant'. Published with his reply in *La Phalange*, 1 September 1836, pp. 180–8.

'Lettre à M. le Rédacteur du Droit'. *Le Droit*, 17 May 1837.

'Lettre à M. le Directeur de *l'Echo lyrique*'. Published with a reply in *L'Echo Lyrique*, 17 September 1843.

'Lettres à Cabet'. Published with a reply by Cabet in his *Populaire de 1841*, 1 October 1843.

'Lettre à A. L. A. Fée [professor in the Faculté de Médecine at Strasbourg, 21 March 1843]', in his *Voyage autour de ma bibliothèque*. Paris: Veuve Berger-Levrault, 1856.

'Lettre à M. le Directeur du *Censeur de Lyon*'. *Censeur de Lyon*, 11 May 1844.

Private correspondence

This area consists mainly of letters Tristan wrote to others without the intention of publication. (Tristan freely published many of the letters she received from Eugène Sue, Blanqui and others regarding *Union ouvrière* in the prefatory introduction to the 3rd edition of that book.)

The major sources for these letters are: the Archives Nationales,[1] Bibliothèque de l'Arsenal,[2] Bibliothèque Marguerite Durand,[3] and Bibliothèque de la ville de Paris. [The most significant letters (to Enfantin, Fourier, Considérant) are reproduced in Jules-L. Puech's *La Vie et l'oeuvre de Flora Tristan*. Puech also reproduces the letters exchanged between Tristan and the various workers' groups in Paris. The latter are not available elsewhere.]

Perhaps the most enlightening letters regarding Tristan's very private personal life are in the collection of A. Breton and C. Bonsel. [It includes: 'Lettres à Traviès'; 'à Olympe'; 'à Mme Maure'. Breton reproduced these letters (1839–1844) in *Le Surréalisme même*, 3, automne 1957, pp. 4–12.]

Other Works Consulted

Aguet, Jean-Pierre. *Les Grèves sous la Monarchie de Juillet, 1830–1847*. Geneva: Droz, 1954.

Agulhon, Maurice. 'Flora Tristan et la grève de l'Arsenal à Toulon'. *Provence historique*, April–June, 1957, pp. 131–54.

———. *Une Ville Ouvrière au temps du socialisme utopique: Toulon de 1815 à 1851*. Paris: Mouton, 1971.

Alem, Jean-Pierre. *Enfantin: le prophète aux sept visages*. Paris: J. J. Pauvert, 1963.

Atkinson, Nora. *Eugène Sue et le roman-Feuilleton*. Paris: Nizet, 1929.

Auger, Hippolyte. *La Femme du monde et la femme artiste*. 2 vols. Paris: Ambroise Dupont, 1837.

Baelen, Jean. 'Une Romantique oubliée', *Bulletin Guillaume Budé*. XXIX, 1970, pp. 504–61.

———. *La Vie de Flora Tristan: Socialisme et Féminisme au XIXe Siècle*. Paris: Seuil, 1972.

Balzac, Honoré de. 'Avant-propos', *La Comédie humaine*. 11 vols. Ed. Marcel Bouteron. Paris: Gallimard, 1949–59.

———. *Eugénie Grandet*. Paris: Garnier-Flammarion, 1964.

1. At the Archives Nationales, the letters can be found in Côte no. 10 AS 42. Also here are the collection of 'Lettres concernant un tombeau pour F.T.', in 10 AS 24–25.
2. At the Bibliothèque de l'Arsenal, Tristan's exchange with Enfantin is in the 'Fonds Enfantin', Carton 7613, nos. 137 and 139.
3. At the Bibliothèque Marguerite Durand, with the exception of her letters to Victor Schoelcher and her publisher, Ladvocat, the letters are to lesser-known individuals, but reveal nonetheless much about her efforts and her concerns for the period 1837–1843. Côte 091/TRI.

————. *La Physiologie du mariage* [1830]. Garnier-Flammarion, 1968.

————. *La Physiologie du mariage pré-originale* [1826]. Ed. Maurice Bardèche. Paris: Droz, 1940.

Balzac, Honoré de, *et al. Les belles femmes de Paris et de la Province accompagnées de lettres aux belles femmes*, 2ᵉ série, 2ᵉ livraison. Paris, 1840.

Banks, J. A. and Olive Banks. *Feminism & Family Planning.* Liverpool: Liverpool University Press, 1964.

Bardèche, Maurice. *Histoire des femmes.* Paris: Stock, 1967.

Basch, Françoise. *Relative Creatures: Victorian Women in Society and the Novel.* Trans. A. Rudolf. New York: Schocken, 1974.

Baschet, Robert. 'Ingres et Delacroix: une esquisse de leur doctrines artistiques'. *Revue des sciences humaines*, XXXIV, no. 136 Oct.–Dec. 1969. pp. 625–43.

Beaulieu, Paul-Leroy. *Le Travail des femmes au XIXᵉ siècle.* Paris: Charpentier et cie., 1873.

Blanc, Eléonore. *Biographie de Flora Tristan.* Lyons: chez l'auteur, rue Luzerne, 1845.

Blanc, Louis. *Histoire de dix ans, 1830–40.* Paris: F.-H. Jeanmaire, 1882.

————. *History of Ten Years 1830–1840* [1845]. 2 vols. New York: Augustus M. Kelley, 1969.

Blanchard, William H. *Rousseau and the Spirit of Revolt.* Ann Arbor: University of Michigan, 1967.

Boas, George. *French Philosophies of the Romantic Period.* New York: Russell and Russell, 1964.

Bolster, Richard. *Stendhal, Balzac et le féminisme romantique*, Paris: Lettres modernes, 1970.

Booth, Wayne. *The Rhetoric of Fiction.* Chicago: University of Chicago Press, 1961.

Bory, Jean-Louis. *Eugène Sue, la roi du roman populaire.* Paris: Hachette, 1962.

Bouglé, Célestin. *Chez les prophètes socialistes.* Paris: Librairie Félix Alcan, 1918.

————. *Socialismes Français.* Paris: Armand Colin, 1933.

Bourgin, Hubert. *Fourier: Contribution à l'étude du socialisme français.* Paris: Société nouvelle de librairie et d'édition, 1905.

Boxer, Marilyn J. 'Foyer or Factory: Working Class Women in Nineteenth Century France'. Paper presented to the Western Society for French History, San Francisco, 22 November 1974.

Bravo, Gian Mario. *Les Socialistes avant Marx.* 3 vols. Paris: F. Maspero, 1970.

Brée, Germaine. *Women Writers in France.* New Brunswick, New Jersey: Rutgers University Press, 1973.

Breton, André. '7 Lettres' [présentées par André Breton]. *Le Surréalisme même*, 3, automne 1957, pp. 4–12.

Brinton, Crane. *French Revolutionary Legislation on Illegitimacy, 1789–1804.* Cambridge, Mass.: Harvard University Press, 1936.

Brown, Norman O. *Life Against Death: The Psychoanalytical Meaning of History.* Middletown, Conn.: Wesleyan University Press, 1959.

Cantagrel. *Le Fou du Palais royal.* Paris: Librairie phalanstérienne, 1841.

Cassagnac, Granier de. 'La Femme libre'. *Le Siècle*, 28 January 1838.

Chacornac, Paul. *Eliphas Lévi: Renovateur de l'occultisme en France*. Paris: Chacornac Frères, 1926.

Champfleury, Jules. *Vignettes romantiques (1825–40)*. Paris: Dentu, 1883.

Charléty, Sébastien. *Histoire du Saint-Simonisme (1825–64)*. (Coll: Bibliothèque Méditations.) Paris: Editions Gonthier, 1931.

———. *La Monarchie de Juillet, 1830–1848. Histoire de la France contemporaine depuis la Révolution jusqu'à la Paix de 1919*, vol. 5. In 10 vols. Ed. Ernst Lavisse. Paris: Hachette, 1920–22.

Chazal, André. *Mémoire à consulter pour M Chazal contre madame Chazal avec pièces justificatives*. Paris: Tribunal civil de 1re instance de la Seine, 3e chambre, 7 February 1838. ['Receuil des Factums de la Bibliothèque Nationale', 40 F3, Pièce 6.318.]

Chevalier, Louis. *Classes laborieuses et classes dangereuses à Paris pendant la première moitié du XIXe siècle*. Paris: Plon, 1958.

Clark, T.J. *The Absolute Bourgeois: Artists and Politics in France, 1848–1851*. Greenwich, Conn.: New York Graphics Society, 1973.

———. *Image of People: Gustave Courbet and the Second French Republic*. Greenwich, Conn.: New York Graphics Society, 1973.

Cole, G. D. H. *Socialist Thought: The Forerunners 1789–1850*. London: Macmillan, 1955.

Commissaire, Sébastien. *Mémoires et souvenirs d'un ancien réprésentant du peuple*. 2 vols. Paris: Garcet et Nisius, 1888.

Considérant, Victor. *Destinées sociales*. 3 vols. Paris: Phalanstère, 1851.

———. *Le Socialisme devant le vieux monde ou le vivant devant les morts*. Paris: Librairie phalanstérienne, 1849.

Constant, Benjamin. 'De Madame de Staël et ses ouvrages', in *Adolphe*. Paris: Garnier, 1963.

Cruikshank, John. *French Literature and its Background*. 6 vols. London: Oxford University Press, 1968–70.

Cuvillier, A. *Un journal d'ouvriers: L'Atelier 1840–50*. Paris: Félix Alcan, 1914.

Dansette, Adrien. *Religious History of Modern France*. 2 vols. London: Herder and Herder, 1971.

Darnton, Robert. *Mesmerism and the End of the Enlightenment in France*. New York: Schocken, 1970.

Daumard, Adeline. *Les Bourgeois de Paris au XIXe siècle*. Paris: Flammarion, 1970.

Debout, Simone. 'La Geste de Flora Tristan'. *Critique*, no. 308, January 1973, pp. 81–92.

Decreus-Van Liefland, Juliette. *Sainte-Beuve et la critique des auteurs féminins*. Paris: Boivin, 1949.

Delescluze, Etienne-Jean. *Souvenirs de soixante années*. Paris: Michel Lévy, 1862.

Deniel, Raymond. *Une Image de la famille et de la société sous la Restauration: étude de la presse catholique*. Paris: Editions ouvrières, 1965.

Desanti, Dominique. *Flora Tristan: la femme révoltée*. Paris: Hachette, 1972.

———. *Flora Tristan: Vie et oeuvres melées*. Paris: u.g.e. 10/18/, 1973.

————. *A Woman in Revolt. A Biography of Flora Tristan.* Trans. Elizabeth Zelvin. New York: Crown, 1976.

Desbordes-Valmore, Marceline. *L'Atelier d'un peintre: scènes de la vie privée.* 2 vols. Paris: Charpentier, 1833.

Dolléans, Edouard. *Le Chartisme, 1830–1848.* 2 vols. Paris: A. Floury, 1912.

————. *Féminisme et le mouvement ouvrier: George Sand.* Paris: Editions ouvrières, 1951.

————. *Histoire du mouvement ouvrier, 1830–1871.* 2 vols. Paris: Armand Colin, 1957.

Duby, Georges and Robert Mandrou. *Histoire de la civilisation française, XVIIe–XXe siècle.* Paris: Armand Colin, 1958.

Duhet, Paule-Marie. *Les Femmes et la Révolution, 1789–1794.* Paris: Juilliard, 1971.

Egbert, Donald Drew. *Social Radicalism and the Arts in Western Europe.* New York: Knopf, 1970.

Ehrenzwieg, Anton. *Hidden Order of Art: A Study in the Psychology of Artistic Imagination.* London: Weidenfeld and Nicolson, 1967.

Engels, Friedrich. *Condition of the Working Class in England.* Ed. and trans. W. O. Henderson and W. H. Chaloner. Palo Alto, California: Stanford University Press, 1958.

————. *The Origin of the Family, Private Property and the State* [1884]. Ed. Eleanor B. Leacock. New York: International Publishers, 1972.

Erdan, Alexandre [pseud. for Alexandre-André Jacob]. *La France mystique, ou le tableau des excentricités religieuses de ce temps.* 2 vols. Amsterdam: R. C. Meyer, 1858.

Evans, David Owen. *Le Roman social sous la Monarchie de Juillet.* Paris: Presses universitaires de France, 1934.

Fée, A. L. A. *Voyage au tour de ma bibliothèque.* Paris: Veuve Berger-Levrault, 1856.

Les Français peints par eux-mêmes: Encyclopédie morale du XIXe siècle. 4 vols. Paris: L. Curmer, 1840–42.

Francastel, Pierre. *Histoire de la peinture française de David à Picasso.* 2 vols. Paris: Editions Meddens S. A., 1955.

Friedlander, Walter. *David to Delacroix.* Trans. Robert Goldwater. New York: Schocken, 1969.

Freud, Sigmund. *The Interpretation of Dreams.* Trans. James Strachey. New York: Avon, 1968.

————. *On Creativity and the Unconscious.* Ed. Benjamin Nelson. New York: Harper & Row, 1965.

————. *The Psychopathology of Everyday Life.* Ed. James Strachey. Trans. Alan Tyson. New York: Norton, 1965.

————. *Studies in Parapsychology.* Trans. A. A. Brill. New York: Macmillan, 1963.

————. *Totem and Taboo.* Trans. James Strachey. New York: Norton, 1952.

Garaudy, Roger. *Marxism in the Twentieth Century.* Trans. René Hague. New York: Scribner, 1970.

Garden, Maurice. *Lyon et les Lyonnais au XVIIIe siècle*. Paris: Les Belles Lettres, 1970.

Gardner, Helen. *Art Through the Ages*. 5th ed. Revised by H. de la Croix and R. G. Tansey. New York: Harcourt, Brace and World, 1970.

Gautier, Théophile. *Mademoiselle de Maupin*. Ed. A. Boschot. Paris: Garnier, 1955.

Génin, Francois. *Les Jésuites et l'université*. 2nd ed. Paris: Paulin, 1844.

George, A. J. *French Romanticism*. Syracuse, N.Y.: Syracuse University Press, 1955.

Girard, René. *Mensonge romantique et vérité romanesque*. Paris: Bernard Grasset, 1961.

Godechot, Jacques, *et al. Histoire générale de la presse française (1815–1871)*. Paris: Presses universitaires françaises, 1969.

Goldmann, Lucien. *Pour une sociologie du roman*. (Coll: Collection idées.) Paris: Gallimard, 1965.

Goldsmith, Margaret L. *Seven Women Against the World*. London: Methuen, 1935.

Goncourt, Edmond and Jules Goncourt. *La Femme au dix-huitième siècle*. Paris: Charpentier, 1887.

Guizot, Pierre. *Mémoires: To Illustrate the History of My Time*. 8 vols. London: Richard Bentley, 1858–67.

Hanson, Anne Coffin. *Manet: 1832–1883*. Philadelphia: Philadelphia Museum of Art, November–December, 1966. [Exhibition catalog.]

Haskell, Francis. *Patrons and Painters: A Study in the Relations Between Italian Art and Society in the Age of the Baroque*. New York: Harper and Row, 1971.

Hauser, Arnold. *The Social History of Art*. 4 vols. Trans. Stanley Godman. New York: Random House, 1958.

Hegel, G. W. F. *Reason in History*. Ed. Robert S. Hartmann. New York: Bobbs-Merrill, 1953.

Hennequin, Victor. *Les Amours au Phalanstère*. Paris: Librairie phalanstérienne, 1849.

Herbert, Eugenia. *The Artist and Social Reform: France and Belgium, 1885–1898*. Freeport, N. Y.: Books for Libraries Press, 1971.

Holt, Elizabeth. *From the Classicists to the Impressionists: A Documentary History of Art and Architecture*. Garden City, N. Y.: Anchor/Doubleday, 1966.

Hodgson, Geraldine. *Studies in French Education from Rabelais to Rousseau*. Cambridge: Cambridge University Press, 1908.

L'Homme, Jean. *Economie et Histoire*. Geneva: Droz, 1967.

————. *La Grande Bourgeoisie au pouvoir (1830–1880): essai sur l'histoire sociale de la France*. Paris: Presses universitaires de France, 1960.

Hudson, Nora E. *Ultra-Royalism and the French Restoration*. Cambridge: Cambridge University Press, 1936.

Hunt, Herbert J. *Le Socialisme et le romantisme en France: étude de la presse socialiste de 1830 à 1848*. Oxford: Clarendon Press, 1935.

Iknayan, Marguerite. *The Idea of the Novel in France: The Critical Reaction, 1815–1848*. Geneva: Droz, 1961.

Ivray, Jehan d'. *L'Aventure saint-simonienne et les femmes*. Paris: Félix Alcan, 1928.

Jakobson, Roman. *Essais de linguistique générale*. Paris: Editions de Minuit, 1966.

Janin, Jules. 'Madame Flora Tristan'. *La Sylphide*, I, 1re livraison, 5 January 1845, pp. 3–8.

———. 'Madame Flora Tristan'. *La Sylphide*, II, 2e livraison, 12 January 1845, pp. 2–20.

Jullian, Philippe. *Delacroix*. Paris: Albin-Michel, 1963.

Kipeczi, Béla. 'A Marxist View of Form in Literature'. *New Literary History*, III, no. 2. Winter 1972, pp. 355–72.

Lacassagne, Jean-Pierre, ed. *Pierre Leroux et George Sand: Histoire D'une amitié: d'après une correspondance inédite, 1836–1866*. Paris: Klinckseck, 1973.

Laclos, Choderlos de. *Oeuvres complètes*. Ed. Maurice Allem. Paris: Gallimard, 1951.

Langer, Suzanne. *Philosophy in a New Key*. 1st ed. Cambridge, Mass.: Harvard University Press, 1951.

Laporte, Roger. 'La Déesse blanche'. *Critique*, XXXI, no. 333, February 1975, pp. 217–31.

Launay, Vicomte de [pseud. for Delphine de Girardin]. *Lettres parisiennes*. 4 vols. Paris: Michel Lévy, 1857.

Legouvé, Ernest. *Histoire morale des femmes* [1848]. 7th ed. Paris: Didier, 1882.

Lepointe, Gabriel. 'La Femme au XIXe siècle en France'. *Société Jean Bodin*, XII, 1962, pp. 419–513.

Lichtheim, George. *Marxism*. New York: Praeger, 1961.

Lockwood, Helen Drusilla. *Tools and the Man, A Comparative Study of the French Workingman. English Chartists in Literature of 1830–1848* [1927]. New York: AMS Press, 1966.

Luppé, Albert-Marie-Pierre, comte de. *Les Jeunes Filles à la fin du 18e siècle*. Paris: Librairie ancienne Edouard Champion, 1925.

Machérey, Pierre. *Pour une théorie de la production littéraire*. (Coll: Théorie no. 4.) Paris: F. Maspero, 1970.

McClellan, David. *Marx before Marxism*. London: Macmillan, 1970.

McLaren, Angus. 'Doctor in the House: Medicine and Private Morality in France, 1800–1850'. *Feminist Studies*, II, no. 2–3, 1975, pp. 39–51.

Maigron, Louis. *Le Romantisme et les moeurs. Essai d'étude historique et sociale*. Paris: Honoré Champion, 1910.

Mannheim, Karl. *Ideology and Utopia. An Introduction to the Sociology of Knowledge*. London: Routledge and Kegan Paul, 1954.

Marcus, Steven. *Engels, Manchester, and the Working Class*. New York: Random House, 1974.

Marcuse, Herbert. *Eros and Civilization: A Philosophical Inquiry into Freud*. Boston: Beacon Press, 1974.

———. *Reason and Revolution: Hegel and the Rise of Social Theory*. Boston: Beacon Press, 1960.

———. 'Socialism and Feminism'. *City Lights*, December 1974.

———. *Studies in Critical Philosophy*. Trans. Joris de Bres. Boston: Beacon Press, 1972.

Marx, Karl. *A Contribution to the Critique of Political Economy.* Ed. Maurice Dobb. Trans. S.W. Ryazanskaya. New York: International Publishers, 1970.

Marx, Karl and Frederick Engels. *Basic Writings on Politics and Philosophy.* Ed. Lewis S. Feuer. Garden City, N.Y.: Anchor/Doubleday, 1959.

———. *Collected Works.* 21 vols. New York: International Publishers, 1975.

Mauchamps, Herbinot de. 'Pérégrination [sic] d'une Paria (1833–1834), par Mme Flora Tristan'. *Gazette des Femmes,* 1 January 1838, pp. 10–11.

Mauron, Charles. *Des métaphores obsédantes aux mythes personnels: introduction à la psychocritique.* Paris: Corti, 1964.

May, Gita. *De Jean-Jacques Rousseau à Madame Roland.* Geneva: Droz, 1964.

———. 'Mme Roland devant la génération romantique'. *French Review,* XXXVI, no. 4, February 1963, pp. 459–68.

Méritens, Hortense Allart de [pseud. Mme. P. Saman]. *Les Enchantements de Prudence.* Paris: Calmann-Lévy, 1877.

———. *La Femme et la démocratie de nos temps.* Paris: Chez Delaunay, 1836.

Michelet, Jules. *L'Amour.* Paris: Charpentier, 1889.

Mitchell, Juliet. *Woman's Estate.* New York: Pantheon, 1971.

Morazé, Charles. *Triumph of the Middle Class.* Garden City, N.Y.: Anchor/Doubleday, 1968.

Muiron, Just. *Etudes sociales.* Paris: Hermann, 1841.

Offen, Karen. *The Woman Question as a Social Issue in Republican France before 1914.* [Unpublished ms.] 1973.

Ourliac, Paul et J. de Malafosse. *Histoire du droit privé, v. 3: le droit familial.* Paris: Presses universitaires de France, 1968.

Pankhurst, Richard K. 'Anna Wheeler – pioneer feminist'. *Political Quarterly,* XXV, no. 2, April–June 1975, p. 132–42.

Parent-Duchâtelet, A. J.-B. *De la prostitution dans la ville de Paris.* 2nd ed. 2 vols. Paris: Baillière, 1837.

Paris ou le livre des cent et un. Paris: Ladvocat, 1833.

Patouillet, Louise. *L'Emancipation des femmes et la presse en France jusqu'en 1870.* Paris: Presse française, 1938.

Perdiguier, Agricol. *Correspondance inédite avec George Sand et ses amis.* Ed. Jean Briquet. Paris: Klincksieck, 1966.

———. *Le Livre du compagnonnage.* 2 vols. Paris: Pagnerre, 1841.

Pernoud, Régine. *Histoire de la bourgeoisie en France.* 2 vols. Paris: Seuil, 1962.

Perrot, Michelle. *Enquêtes sur la condition ouvrière en France au 19ᵉ siècle.* Paris: Microéditions Hachette, 1972.

Peterson, M. Jeanne. 'The Victorian Governess: Status Incongruence in Family and Society', in *Suffer and Be Still, Women in the Victorian Age.* Ed. Martha Vicinus. Bloomington: Indiana University Press, 1973.

Pinkney, David H. *The French Revolution of 1830.* Princeton: Princeton University Press, 1972.

Plekhanov, G. V. *Fundamental Problems of Marxism.* Trans. Julius Katzer. New York: International Publishers, 1971.

Proudhon, P. J. *La Pornocratie ou les femmes dans les temps modernes.* Paris: Alacroix, 1875.

Puech, J.-L. *La Tradition socialiste en France.* Paris: Garnier, 1921.

———. *La Vie et l'oeuvre de Flora Tristan.* Paris: Marcel Rivière, 1925.

Puech, Marie-Louise. 'Le Mystère de la *Gazette des Femmes*: la presse féministe sous Louis-Philippe'. *La Grande Revue*, March, 1935. [Bibliothèque Marguerite Durand.]

Quérard, J. N. *Les Supercheries littéraires dévoilées.* 3 vols. Paris: [publisher unknown] 1869–70.

Rank, Otto. *The Double, A Psychoanalytic Study.* Trans. Harry Tucker, Jr. Chapel Hill: University of North Carolina, 1971.

Reich, Wilhelm. *Sex-Pol: Essays 1929–34.* Ed. Lee Baxandall. New York: Random House, 1972.

Reybaud, Louis. *Études sur les réformateurs contemporains.* 2nd ed. 2 vols. Paris: Guillamin, 1843.

———. *Jérôme Paturot à la recherche d'une position sociale*, 3rd ed. Paris: Calmann-Lévy, 1879.

Roger, Jacques. 'Lectures des textes et histoire des idées' in *Chemins actuels de la Critique.* Ed. Georges Poulet. Paris: Union générale d'editions, 1968.

Rosenthal, J. 'Les Conditions sociales de la peinture sous la Monarchie de Juillet'. *Gazette des Beaux Arts*, III. February 1910, pp. 93–114; March 1910, pp. 217–41; April 1910, pp. 332–51.

Rousseau, Jean-Jacques. *Oeuvres complètes.* Ed. Bernard Gagnebin and Marcel Raymond. 4 vols. Paris: Gallimard, 1959–1967.

Rubel, Maximilien. 'Flora Tristan et Karl Marx'. *La Nef*, January 1946, pp. 68–76.

Ruge, Arnold. *Arnold Ruges briefwechsel und tagebuchblätter aus den jahren 1825–1880.* Berlin: Weidmann, 1886.

———. *Zwei Jahre in Paris.* Leipzig: W. Turann, 1846.

Sand, George. *Le Compagnon du Tour de France* [1840]. Lyons: Editions Cosmopolis, 1947.

———. *Correspondance.* 10 vols. Ed. Georges Lubin. Paris: Garnier, 1964–75.

———. *Indiana.* Paris: Garnier, 1962.

———. *Lélia* [présenté par Pierre Reboul]. Paris: Garnier, 1960.

Sartre, Jean-Paul. *Being and Nothingness.* Trans. Hazel F. Barnes. New York: New York Philosophical Library, 1956.

Schnapper, Antoine. 'Painting During the Revolution, 1789–99', in *The Age of Revolution.* Ed. Robert Rosenblum. New York: Metropolitan Museum, 1975. [Exhibition catalogue]

Scott, Joan W. and Louise A. Tilly. 'Women's Work and the Family in Nineteenth-Century Europe'. *Comparative Studies in Society and History.* XVII, no. 1, January 1975, pp. 36–64.

Shorter, Edward. 'Capitalism, Culture and Sexuality: Competing Models'. *Social Science Quarterly*, LIII, no. 2, September 1972, pp. 338–56.

———. 'Illegitimacy, Sexual Revolution and Social Change in Modern Europe'. *Journal of Interdisciplinary History*, II, no. 2, autumn 1971, pp. 237–64.

————. *The Making of the Modern Family*. New York: Basic Books, 1975.

Silver, Catherine Boudard. 'Salon, Foyer, Bureau: Women and the Professions in France', in *Clio's Consciousness Raised*. Ed. Mary Hartmann and Lois W. Banner. New York: Harper & Row, 1974.

Souvestre, Émile. 'Le Riche et le pauvre', in *Magasin theatral*, vol. 15. Paris, 1937.

Staël, Germaine Necker, baronne de. *De la littérature considérée dans ses rapports avec les institutions sociales*. 2 vols. Ed. Paul Van Tieghem. Geneva: Droz, 1959.

Stein, Lorenz von. *History of the Social Movement in France, 1789–1850*. Trans. Kaethe Mengelberg. Totawa, New Jersey: Bedminster Press, 1964.

Stern, Daniel [pseud. for Marie d' Agoult]. *Histoire de la Révolution de 1848*. *Paris*: Armand Colin, 1966.

————. *Mes Souvenirs*. 3rd ed. Paris: Calmann-Lévy, 1880.

Sullerot, Evelyne. *Histoire de la presse féminine en France, des origines à 1848*. Paris: Armand Colin, 1966.

————. *Histoire et sociologie du travail féminin*. Paris: Gonthier, 1969.

Swingewood, Alan and Diana Laurenson. *The Sociology of Literature*. London: MacGibbon and Kee, 1972.

Talmon, J. L. *Political Messianism: The Romantic Phase*. New York: Praeger, 1960.

————. *Origins of Totalitarian Democracy*. New York: Praeger, 1968.

Thévoz, Michel. 'Peinture et idéologie'. *Les Temps Modernes*, no. 330, January 1974, pp. 1281–1303.

Thibert, Marguerite. *Le Féminisme dans le socialisme français de 1830 à 1850*. Paris: Marcel Giard, 1926.

————. 'Féminisme et socialisme d'après Flora Tristan'. *Revue d'Histoire économique et sociale*, 1921, pp. 115–36.

————. *Le Rôle social de l'art d'après les Saint-Simoniens*. Paris: Marcel Rivière, 1927.

Thomas, Édith. *Pauline Roland, socialisme et féminisme au XIXᵉ siècle*. Paris: M. Rivière, 1956.

Thompson, E. P. *The Making of the English Working Class*. New York: Random House, 1966.

Thompson, William. *Appeal of one Half the Human Race, Women, Against the Pretensions of the Other Half, Men, To Retain Them in Political, and Thence in Civil And Domestic Slavery*. London: Virago, 1983.

Vier, Jacques. *La Comtesse d'Agoult et son temps*. 6 vols. Paris: A Colin, 1955–63.

Villiers, Baron Marc de. *Histoire des clubs des femmes et des légions d'Amazones, 1793–1848–1871*. Paris: Plon, 1910.

[Voilquin], Suzanne V. *Souvenirs d'une fille du peuple, ou la Saint-Simonienne en Egypte 1834–36*. Paris: Souzet, 1866.

Watt, Ian. *Rise of the Novel*. Berkeley: University of California Press, 1959.

Wattell, H.M.J., ed. *Code Napoléon*. Leiden: Blankenburg, 1888.

White, Harrison and Cynthia. *Canvases and Careers: Institutional Change in the French Painting World*. New York: Wiley, 1965.

Wollstonecraft, Mary. *Vindication of Rights of Women*. Ed. Charles W. Hagelman, Jr. New York: Norton, 1967.

Yedicka, Joseph W. 'Speculation in the 2nd Empire: "La Question d'Argent" of Dumas fils.' *French Review* XXXIV, no. 6, May 1963, pp. 606–16.

Most Notable Recent Works

Michaud, Stéphane, ed. 'Flora Tristan: Trente-Cinq Lettres'. *International Review of Social History* XXIV, 1979.

Michaud, Stéphane, ed. 'Un Fabuleux destin: Flora Tristan'. Actes du Premier Colloque International, 3–4 May 1984. Dijon: Université de Dijon Presse, 1984.

Michaud, Stéphane, ed. *Flora Tristan: Lettres, reunies, presentées et annotées.* Paris: Editions du Seuil, 1980.

Moon, Joan S. 'Feminism and Socialism: The Utopian Synthesis of Flora Tristan', in *Socialist Women: European Feminism in the 19th and 20th Centuries*. Ed. Marilyn Boxer and Jean Quataert. New York: Elseviers, 1978.

Moses, Claire Goldberg. French Feminism in the 19th Century. Albany: SUNY Press, 1984.

Rabine, Leslie Ruth. 'The Other Side of the Ideal: Women Writers of Mid-Nineteenth Century France'. Ann Arbor, Michigan: Xerox University microfilms, 1974.

Strumingher, Laura. *Women and the Making of the Working Class*, Lyon, 1830–70. St Albans, Vermont: Eden Press, 1979.

Strumingher, Laura. *The Odyssey of Flora Tristan*. New York: P. Lang, 1988.

APPENDIX A

1. Indispensable to a study of Flora Tristan and of the connection between developments in the areas of literature, feminism and socialism during the July Monarchy is a study of the press. The efforts of Godechot and others (*Histoire générale de la presse française*) and of Sullerot (*Histoire de la presse féminine*) as well as the extensive bibliography provided by Puech (*La Vie et l'oeuvre ...*) and Thibert (*La féminisme dans le socialisme français ...*), offer invaluable data in this regard. [These works are cited above.] Here follows a list of the major feminist and feminine journalistic endeavours of the 1830s. Many of these periodicals can be studied at the Bibliothèque Nationale.

La Femme Libre, ou *Femme Nouvelle*, ou *Tribune des Femmes*, August 1832–February 1834. Jeanne Désirée [Veret], fondatrice; Marie-Reine Guindorff, directrice.

Le Journal des femmes, gymnase littéraire, May 1832–January 1837. Rédactrice: Fanny Richomme.

Le Conseiller des Femmes, journal Hebdomadaire, November 1833. Rédactrice: Eugénie Niboyet.

La Mère de famille, 1833–1836. Fondée par Madeleine Sirey.

Mosaique Lyonnaise, journal Littéraire, 1834. Rédactrice: Eugénie Niboyet.

Le Citateur Féminin, receuil de la littérature féminine, ancien et moderne, January–July 1835.

Gazette des femmes, journal de législation et de jurisprudence ... (1836–1838). Rédigée par une société de femmes et hommes de lettres, Mme. Pourtet and M. Herbinot de Mauchamps.

2. The satire against feminism during this period can be followed in such journals as:

L'Atelier, 31 May; 31 August 1843. Redigé par des ouvrièrs.

Le Charivari, 1844, 1848–9 [and elsewhere].

Le Droit, 6 and 11 June 1848.

Le Figaro, 15 January 1826.

Le Populaire de 1841, 10 June 1843; 5 June; 12 July; 22 August 1844; 28 November 1847. Rédigé par É. Cabet.

La Revue des deux mondes, 14 November 1832.

La Revue du Progrés, 1 October 1840. Dirigée par Louis Blanc.

La Ruche populaire, August 1840. Rédigéé par des ouvriers.

Le Siècle, 28 January 1838.

L'Union, December 1844; November–December 1845. Fondé par l'ancien comité de la *Ruche populaire*.

3. Tristan's efforts were reviewed in the contemporary reformist and socialist press.

La Democratie pacifique, 16 June 1844.

Le Nouveau monde, 11, 21 May; 11 June; 11 July 1840. Dirigé par Jean Czynski. [Fourierist.]

La Phalange, 1 September 1836; November 1837; January–July 1843. Dirigée par Victor Considérant. [Fourierist.]

APPENDIX B

A large number of brochures and pamphlets relating to 'l'Affranchissement des femmes' and recording the evolution of Saint-Simonian feminism can be seen at the bibliothèque de l'Arsenal, Fonds Enfantin. At the Bibliothèque Nationale, these papers are collected in the large catalog *Histoire de France*, v. 5 (histoire des religions) under the title: *Publications Saint Simoniennes* (1830–1836). [Côte: LD 190.] This collection is indispensable; it includes such titles as:

'Appel d'une Femme au peuple sur l'affranchissement de la femme, par Claire Demar.' [1833]

'1833 ou L'année de la Mère: Mission du Midi, Lyon, Chez Mme Durval.'

'La Femme dans la crise actuelle, par Palmyre Bazard.' [1832]

'Liberté, femmes!! par Pol Justus.' [1833]

'Ma loi d'avenir, par Claire Demar.' [published posthumously, 1834]

'Parole de femme, signée E. Soudet.' [1838]

Index

Note: FT = Flora Tristan